RECLAIMING THE AMERICAN DREAM

Proven Solutions
for Creating
Economic Opportunity
for All

RECLAIMING
the
AMERICAN DREAM

BEN HECHT

BROOKINGS INSTITUTION PRESS
Washington, D.C.

Library of Congress Cataloging-in-Publication Data

Names: Hecht, Bennett L., 1959– author.
Title: Reclaiming the American dream : proven solutions for creating economic
    opportunity for all / Ben Hecht.
Description: Washington, D.C. : Brookings Institution Press, [2018] |
    Includes bibliographical references and index.
Identifiers: LCCN 2018012375 (print) | LCCN 2018013518 (ebook) | ISBN
    9780815734895 (ebook) | ISBN 9780815734888 (pbk. : alk. paper)
Subjects: LCSH: United States—Economic conditions—2009– | United
    States—Economic policy—2009– | United States—Social policy—1993– |
    Equality—United States.
Classification: LCC HC106.84 (ebook) | LCC HC106.84 .H43 2018 (print) | DDC
    330.973—dc23
LC record available at https://lccn.loc.gov/2018012375

ISBN 978-0-8157-3488-8 (pbk. : alkaline paper)
ISBN 978-0-8157-3489-5 (ebook)

Typeset in Electra
Composition by Westchester Publishing Services

For Joseph C. & Phyllis Hecht

The American Dream is that dream of a land in which life should be better and richer and fuller for everyone, with opportunity for each according to ability or achievement. A dream of social order in which each man and each woman shall be able to attain to the fullest stature of which they are innately capable, and be recognized by others for what they are, regardless of the fortuitous circumstances of birth or position.

James Truslow Adams, *The Epic of America*

What is key to America's understanding of class is the persistent belief—despite all evidence to the contrary—that anyone, with the proper discipline and drive, can move from a lower class to a higher class.

Michelle Alexander, *The New Jim Crow:*
Mass Incarceration in the Age of Colorblindness

They took our coal out of here and everybody got rich on it. And what did we get? We got black lung. We don't have good water to drink, we don't have roads, we don't have anything except a bunch of broken down old coal miners that's forgotten.

Jerry Blackburn, retired Virginia coal miner

O, yes, I say it plain, America never was America to me,
And yet I swear this oath—America will be!
Langston Hughes,
"Let America Be America Again"

CONTENTS

ACKNOWLEDGMENTS

I want to thank and acknowledge all the people who helped to make this book a reality. I am especially indebted to the Rockefeller Foundation's Bellagio Center Residency Program for providing me with a month-long fellowship in June 2016. This book would not have been completed but for my time there, the supportive environment, incredible workspace, and inspiration and mentoring by the other Bellagio fellows. Never having had a month just to work on one project before, I want to give special thanks to Professor Barbara Prainsack, who began her fellowship on the same day that I did, and who helped me to develop an approach and discipline for using my time there to its fullest.

Oscar Perry Abelo, Alyssa Campbell, Lexie Frosh, Claire Huttenlocher, Joseph Lee, Alex Leibovitz, Megan McGlinchey, Hila Mehr, Annie Pope, and Mary Schletzbaum—all provided me with the research that I used in Bellagio and after. I am incredibly grateful especially for the efforts of Megan McGlinchey, who began working in 2016 as a summer intern at Living Cities in Washington, D.C., while I was in Italy. Taking advantage of the time difference between Italy and the United States, I would send Megan research requests before I would go to sleep, and her answers or proposed text would magically appear sometime the next day. When she became a full-time employee that fall, Megan helped me turn the promising product of my fellowship into this final book. It wouldn't have been possible without her tireless help, constant good nature, and overall guidance.

Special thanks to all of the people who opened their doors to me and spent time explaining and detailing their work including, in alphabetical order:

Mayor Steve Adler, Tony Aguilar, Julian Alssid, Matthew Baer, Ross Baird, Ben Berkowitz, Clara Brenner, Jordan Brown, Kesha Cash, Charlie Catlett, Nikia Clarke, Susan Crawford, Harold DePriest, Mike Dinkin, Derek Douglas, Jeanine Duncliffe, Jackie Dyess, Martin Eakes, Dave Edinger, Jeff Edmondson, Tom Esselman, Sharon Feigon, Mayor Greg Fischer, Julia Fischer, Kelly Fitzsimmons, Danny Gardner, Brett Goldstein, Marek Gootman, Joanna Harries, Glenn Harris, Fred Hurtz, Letetia Jackson, Nigel Jacob, Daniel King, Patrick Kirwan, Kelly Kline, Sheryl Lane, Julie Lenzer Kirk, Jon Li, Greg Lindsey, Amy Liu, Lula Luu, Sabrina Manville, David Martinez, Mayor Ben McAdams, Noelle Melton, Brad Miller, Kay Mooney, Jay Nath, JaNay Queen Nazaire, Julie Nelson, Orlando Ochoa, Jennifer Ong, Jen Pahlka, Mike Papineau, Karina Quintana, Rip Rapson, Ben Rattray, Timothy Renick, Theresa Reno-Weber, David Rose, Eric Rosengren, Hollie Russon Gilman, Mary Jane Ryan, Zoe Schlag, Marlene Seltzer, Susan Shaheen, Alexander Shermansong, Luis Silos, Ben Sio, Libby Smiley, Ted Smith, Jake Solomon, Jamez Staples, Robin Steffen, Martin Sundquist, Greg Tehven, Terri Thao, Harriet Tregoning, Joel Vargas, James Weinberg, Joseph Weisbord, Charles West, Todd Williams, Detra Wright, Ellen Wu, Nancy Zimpher, and Ashley Zuelke.

Many, many people at Living Cities have helped to make this book a reality. Nadia Owusu encouraged me early on to turn my rantings and observations into a book that others could benefit from. Elodie Baquerot, Ellen Ward, and Jessica Fontaine all have helped me in ways too numerous to mention. The Living Cities board wholeheartedly supported my thirty-day fellowship and is helping to promote the book. Thank you.

I also want to acknowledge and thank my wife, Lynn Leibovitz, and my children, Eliza and Sam, for their love, patience, and support. Their "reality checks" on my work have always made it and me better.

RECLAIMING THE AMERICAN DREAM

INTRODUCTION

My grandparents came to this country at the turn of the twentieth century with absolutely nothing. My parents grew up poor with them. Drafted by the Army at nineteen, my father left his home in Brooklyn to fight in World War II. When he returned, the GI bill enabled him to become the first in his family to graduate college. In 1962, when I was three years old, he got his doctorate from New York University, a professorship at a small, New Jersey public college, and a $22,000 house with a backyard in the suburbs. My family was living the American Dream.

This ideal, first articulated by James Truslow Adams in 1931, of an upwardly mobile "land in which life should be better, richer and fuller for everyone, with opportunity for each according to ability"[1] certainly has had incredible staying power in the history of our nation and in the hearts and minds of the American people. In fact, by the 1970s, this dream had largely come true for millions of Americans, like my parents and me. Gaps between whites and blacks, and low-, middle- and upper-income Americans, were narrower than they had ever been in terms of income, wealth, and college attainment.

But in retrospect, even as a kid, I knew that the American Dream had its limitations. In July 1967 a week of rioting had set Newark, New Jersey, ablaze. Fresh out of elementary school for summer vacation, my friends and I would go outside every morning to play in the street. The black smoke billowing down Bloomfield Avenue from Newark to my hometown was an impossible sight to ignore. It's a picture that remains seared in my memory today. Nine months later, in April 1968, Martin Luther King Jr. was dead, and similarly jarring images filled the nightly news for weeks. These experiences drive my work still.

From that time until now, the economic gaps between Americans have widened to levels not seen since the Roaring Twenties. We have all heard the statistics. The vast majority of income now goes to the top one-tenth of 1 percent of the population. Higher-income students are graduating from college at rates six times that of lower-income students. Progress made in closing the economic chasm between white, black, and brown Americans has not only stalled but has been reversed. Blacks now earn 59 cents and Latinos 72 cents for every dollar earned by a white household. The median wealth of white households is twenty times that of black households and eighteen times that of Latino households. Most of America hasn't had a meaningful raise in forty years.

Exasperation with the status quo could not have been more evident in the last presidential election cycle, when decades of economic anxiety and frustration finally seemed to come to a head. The belief that the system is "rigged" against everyday people was undeniably front and center in the minds of many Donald Trump and Bernie Sanders voters. In the wake of the election, we've witnessed that frustration over lack of economic mobility buffet our most basic political norms and institutions in ways that we had not seen in decades. Much of the focus during and after the election has been on the disaffected, white "Trump voter," that is, the millions of Americans with only high school degrees who have faced lifelong struggles in the job market. For them, the promise of the American Dream was deeply internalized; they never expected that they might end up worse off economically than their parents.[2]

To some extent, it's surprising that this demographic hadn't been more vocal before then. In a widely cited 2015 study, Princeton University professors Anne Case and Angus Deaton found that the mortality rate for white, middle-aged Americans with low educational attainment had risen steadily since 1999.[3] The researchers believe that the spike in these deaths, attributed to drugs, alcohol, suicide, heart disease, and cancer, tells the "story of the collapse of the white, high-school–educated working class after its heyday in the early 1970s and the pathologies that accompany that decline." These Americans, they argued, live in a "sea of despair."[4]

But the plight of Americans of color, many of whom never had expectations that the American Dream was meant for them, also was impossible to ignore. The deaths of unarmed black men at the hands of police officers sparked the Black Lives Matter movement and competed for news headlines with the presidential campaign. The rapid spread of this activist platform brought conversations about our deep-rooted racial inequities to the fore.

In this regard, our American Dream has always failed to live up to its idealized promise. As a country with racism in our groundwater—founded upon the destruction of one people and the enslavement of another—racial opportunity gaps have been created and perpetuated by parties, public and private, throughout our history.

The consequences of this history are hard to erase and glaringly evident in today's racial disparities. Those disparities exist across almost all indicators of economic health and well-being. One of the most obvious examples of this reality is in the enduring legacy of redlining. Redlining—or refusing to make loans to people of color because they lived in certain neighborhoods or restricting their ability to move into majority white neighborhoods—was actually codified in 1936 in the U.S. Federal Housing Administration (FHA)'s official underwriting manual. It was practiced by mortgage lenders all over the country for decades until the passage of the Fair Housing Act in 1968.[5] By refusing to back loans to people of color, the FHA kept them locked out of the opportunity to build wealth through homeownership, and set a course for the patterns of racial segregation, concentrated poverty and chronic disinvestment that still characterize many U.S. communities today.

Even explicitly race-neutral policies, such as the GI bill, which helped millions of returning veterans, like my father, buy homes and attend college were largely administered at the states' discretion. As a result, black veterans were overwhelmingly pushed toward vocational and trade schools instead of academic institutions. While 28 percent of white veterans went to college on the G.I. bill, only 12 percent of black veterans did so.[6] Too many of today's structures and systems continue to replicate insidious patterns of exclusion.

This disconnect between our nation's stated values—of equality and opportunity for all—and the reality of deep-rooted racial inequities has always represented an immense moral dilemma for our country—one that we've never fully grappled with. But today, because of our rapidly transforming demographics, it poses an economic imperative as well.

From our earliest days, the United States has been a nation of immigrants, the vast majority of whom only came to be considered "white" over time.[7] As recently as 1970, whites constituted 80 percent of the population (175 million people) with the remaining 20 percent (27 million people) made up of people from different racial groups.

However, the nation's racial composition has been in flux ever since. In fact, by 2050 the United States will no longer have a racial majority at all.[8] Four states, including California and Texas, as well as Washington, D.C., already have populations with majorities of people of color. In 2010 ten more had majority child populations of color, and more than 35 of the largest 100 metropolitan areas did as well.[9] The changing racial composition of our population has been acknowledged and discussed for years, but the economic implications of this shift are neither well understood nor broadly acknowledged by the public. According to the Brookings demographer William Frey, increased Hispanic and Asian immigration, combined with a rapidly growing multiracial population, has enabled the U.S. population to continue to grow despite a shrinking white population.[10] Figure I-1 illustrates those changes and projections of population growth. In fact, some cities, such as Scranton, Pennsylvania, and Pittsfield, Massachusetts, would have had a declining population in recent years had it not been for a rapid increase in the number of Hispanic residents.[11]

This "diversity explosion," as Frey calls it, is what has enabled us so far to avoid the plight of many other developed countries in Europe and Asia.[12] These countries, marked by low birthrates and little immigration, have been struggling with how to address the economic implications of an aging workforce, an insufficient number of young adults to replace workers when they retire, and a gross domestic product (GDP) that, like most Western economies, is heavily reliant on consumer spending.[13]

FIGURE I-1. U.S. Population, White and Minority, 1970–2050

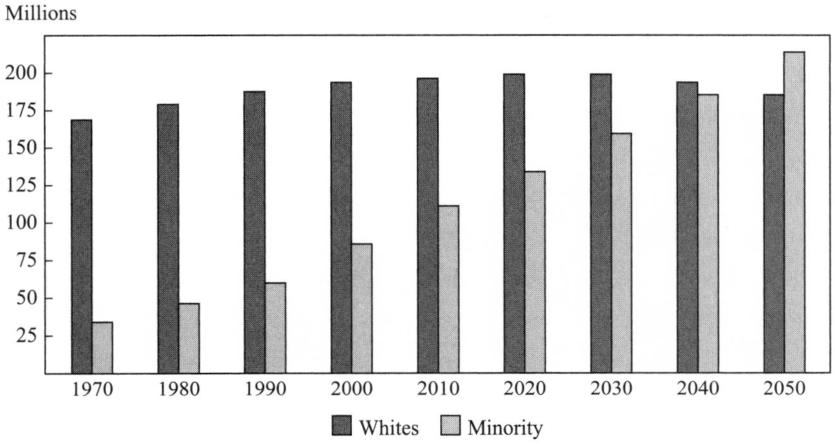

Millions

Source: U.S. censuses and Census Bureau, various years.

That the U.S. population is still growing gives us a chance to avoid the economic stagnation that other countries face; but that result is by no means guaranteed. Over the past forty years, consumer spending as a percentage of our GDP has actually risen, from 64 percent in the 1970s to 73 percent today.[14] Our economic future, in large part, rests on an ever-increasing number of the fastest-growing segment of our population, people of color, having the economic mobility and financial wherewithal sufficient to sustain such a consumption-based economy by 2050 if not sooner.

A common adage aptly describes our current predicament: Insanity is doing the same thing, over and over again, but expecting different results. If history is to be our guide, then we are truly insane if we think that we can achieve greater economic mobility by staying the course. Our current ways of working have created greater disparities over the past forty years, not reduced them. People of color have fared much worse than whites across substantially every measure, from income and wealth to college completion and debt.

This is not the America any of us want. And it is not one that we must accept. Believe it or not, many of the solutions that we need to revive America as the land of opportunity to reclaim the American Dream for all—already exist. I have seen them myself over the past ten years in my job as president and CEO of Living Cities, a collaboration of the nation's leading foundations, such as the Bill and Melinda Gates, Ford, and Rockefeller Foundations, and financial institutions, such as Bank of America, Prudential, and Morgan Stanley.

We work with, and have helped channel more than $20 billion alongside, remarkable public, private, and philanthropic leaders in more than 100 communities across the country. Frustrated with dysfunction and inertia in Washington, D.C., these innovators have been quietly but doggedly developing solutions to our most vexing challenges to upward mobility for low-income Americans, especially people of color—addressing education, jobs, wealth creation, and more. Technology, social networks, and philanthropy have enabled these ideas to spread virally around the country in ways that were impossible even five years ago.

Although much of the nation is wringing its hands in despair over our economic future, and the recent presidential candidates offered few concrete ways to directly address the problems of poor and working-class voters, those answers exist. They have been hiding in plain sight, right in front of our eyes. I know we can restore the American Dream for all Americans because we already are—in places big and small, all over the country.

These are not academic theories relevant only to policy wonks or unique one-offs only possible in wealthy, coastal cities. Each of the examples in the following chapters has been proved time and time again across the country—many, in fact, in hundreds of places, both urban and rural. One such example, early-college high school, has already resulted in tens of thousands of young people in twenty-eight states receiving both a high school diploma and a college degree entirely for free upon high school graduation.

When I talk about these examples—whether at conferences, to corporations, or just to friends in passing—people are incredulous. Inevitably, they ask me the following two questions: "Why isn't that happening all over the country?" and "What else do we know works that we aren't doing everywhere?" Now you see why I had to write this book, and why you have to not only read it but act on it.

When implemented together, this set of distinct but interrelated examples provide us with a blueprint for how to overcome the biggest barriers to restoring and reinvigorating the American Dream for all: better education, more income, increased wealth, greater access to opportunity, and the restoration of a civic commitment to a greater good.

BETTER EDUCATION

Education, long considered the cornerstone of opportunity and upward mobility in America, hasn't been leveling the playing field the way that it used to. In my grandparents' and parents' generations, for example, a free public school education and high school diploma often were all you needed to get a good manufacturing job at a wage that could support your family. In fact, in the 1970s, only 28 percent of jobs required more than a high school education. But tectonic economic changes have resulted in 7 million fewer low-skilled, high-paying manufacturing jobs than existed in the 1970s.[15] These trends show no indication of slowing. By 2020, 65 percent of jobs will require education beyond high school.[16]

As our nation's labor market continues to transform, it's more critical than ever that everyone have access to an education that equips them to thrive in our twenty-first-century economy and beyond. Which is why the four education-related solutions presented in chapters 1 through 4 are so promising. We are already enabling hundreds of thousands of Americans to successfully and cost-effectively earn college credits and degrees from wherever they are sitting right now—whether still in high school, enrolled in college, or on the job. These are not people who have dropped out of the system and are very difficult to nudge back in, but instead low-hanging fruit—students who simply need the support from these innovations to succeed. At the same time, we are seeing dozens of places, from Birmingham, Alabama, to Boise, Idaho, that are fixing the entire education system wherever it is broken, so that every citizen, regardless of race, income, or geography, can actually benefit from our nation's great equalizer.

MORE INCOME

Our post–World War II economy was so robust that companies were able to create jobs that paid relatively well, at every skill level. This is something that absolutely amazes me every time that I hear it: from the late 1940s to the early 1970s, incomes grew rapidly and at roughly the same rate up and down the income ladder, actually doubling for everyone in inflation-adjusted terms. It's hard to fathom that when you look at today's realities. Since that time, the top 0.1 percent of the population has seen their incomes rise by 200 percent while incomes for those in the middle tier saw theirs rise by only 6 percent.

Part of the reason for this disparity is the loss of those 7 million well-paying manufacturing jobs. But it also has a lot to do with the fact that we stopped creating as many start-up companies as we used to. Young companies have historically generated the vast number of new, good-paying jobs—often resulting in 2 million to 3 million jobs a year. Fewer start-ups means fewer available jobs.

Chapters 5 and 6 highlight solutions that address people's pocketbooks, revealing how we have already started reversing that downward trajectory in dozens of places. We have figured out how to get money into the hands of capital-starved start-ups, especially to the fastest-growing group of entrepreneurs, people of color, who have begun creating new and better jobs, whether they live in Des Moines, Iowa, or Salt Lake City, Utah. We have learned how to help young companies exponentially grow their revenues and hire more employees even faster by harnessing local assets, like universities and hospital supply chains, and finding new ways of working together to stimulate economic development, such as innovation districts.

INCREASED WEALTH

Homeownership has a long held a special place in American culture—often considered the paragon of the American Dream come true—in large part because it has been the primary driver of economic mobility for millions of Americans. A recent survey by the Federal Reserve Bank found that a homeowner's net worth today is a whopping thirty-six times that of a renter.[17] That wealth can be tapped for emergencies, like car repairs or to smooth dips in income due to a temporary layoff, but it is also often invested so earnings can be used to help pay for a child's college tuition or retirement. Wealth means financial security—a gift that can be passed down and be reproduced generation after generation. It's really that simple.

But extending the benefits of homeownership to those Americans historically excluded from them has been much less simple. Throughout our history, redlining, unduly restrictive mortgage financing standards, and predatory lending practices have kept lower-income Americans, especially people of color, from building wealth through homeownership. Today, whites have almost twenty times the wealth of families of color—in large part because of these discriminatory practices. The wealth gap between races would shrink by 30 percent if families of color were as likely as white households to own their homes.

The wealth-building example in chapter 7 shows how we can close this gap using proven approaches that have been working for more than twenty years. In fact, before the Great Recession of 2007, one lender alone, Self-Help Credit Union, helped more than 50,000 lower-income individuals and borrowers of color to become homeowners in forty-eight states. We can and must revive these proven practices, and do so at a scale we have never achieved before, so millions more Americans can build wealth through ownership of their homes.

GREATER ACCESS TO OPPORTUNITY

In many ways, life in post–World War II America was a lot less complicated. For so many Americans—from coal miners to auto workers—lower-skilled jobs were plentiful, nearby, and paid well, and they employed you for life. Opportunity was local, so access was easy.

That way of life has been disappearing now for almost forty years. Simply finding a job and getting back and forth to work has gotten a lot harder. Where you used to be able to open the newspaper to find a job, now you have to both find a job and apply to it online. The job search is becoming increasingly digital at every turn; a recent survey found that 92 percent of employers now rely on social networks, like LinkedIn, for recruiting.[18] The spatial mismatch between where the jobs now are and where workers live has also grown. Today, 11 million Americans travel more than an hour each way to work, often spending more than 40 percent of their income just to get there and back.[19]

And the changing nature of the labor market means that most Americans will have a good chance of facing these challenges time and time again throughout their lives.[20] Whereas my father worked at the college in New Jersey for forty years, the average American today stays in a job for just a little over four years.[21] Whether by choice or by necessity, the reality is that many workers are perpetually looking for the next job, equipped with only the skills they use in their current one. Without Internet access, both finding that next position and learning the skills needed to fill it pose a daunting challenge.

While the American worker has been struggling to adapt to these changes for decades, two new tools in the arsenal—smartphones and high-speed broadband at home—both powered by technology that didn't exist even a decade ago, are empowering people across the country to participate in a labor market that has increasingly transferred to the digital realm. These tools are expanding the "geography of opportunity" available to lower-income workers as never before. Chapter 8 highlights shared-use mobility strategies, often technology enabled, that are bringing new and affordable options for workers to get from point A to B. And as more and more communities across the country, as detailed in chapter 9, expand the reach of broadband Internet access, we are already seeing Americans at every income level use this tool to search, network, and land jobs, as well as to stay current on the skills they will need to advance.

RESTORING AND SUSTAINING A COMMITMENT
TO THE GREATER GOOD

As I see it, the idea of America as the land of opportunity was the result of actions we have taken collectively as a society, over 200 years, to ensure that everyone could achieve to the fullest extent of his or her own abilities. At times during our history that has meant affirmatively taking steps such as providing free public schooling and advocating for the GI bill, a program that made all the difference to the millions of veterans like my father. At other times, it meant taking steps to level a playing field that had become too uneven, like trust-busting companies that were preventing competition, or passing the Civil Rights Act of 1964 that outlawed discrimination based on race, color, religion, sex, and national origin.

Chapters 10, 11, and 12 explain how an ongoing civic commitment to taking the long-term actions necessary for every American to have a chance to succeed is taking hold in place after place. Elected officials at the local level are putting the term "public servant" into action, using their positions to not only rally citizens around a commitment to the greater good but also make government a more effective contribution to it. Extraordinary new efforts, often enabled by technology, are making it easier than ever before for citizens to further strengthen the social fabric by engaging deeply with their government and in their communities. And new tables of cross-sector leaders, many from the business community, are coming together to provide the continuity required for large-scale change and help the community to weather inevitable challenges over time. The virtuous interaction of government, deeply engaged citizens, and a civic infrastructure of diverse leaders is enabling communities to get consistently better outcomes around the things that truly matter to citizens: education, income, wealth, and access to opportunity for all.

The solutions for reclaiming the American Dream are already known—and just waiting to be even more broadly adopted. But it will require that each of us lead from wherever we sit, whether that is as an elected leader, engaged resident, corporate CEO, philanthropist, or investor. Each of us has to exercise whatever authority we have, real or apparent, to establish these solutions in more places. What we're in desperate need of now is not just any one program or initiative but rather a "new normal," or new ways of working, everywhere. From education and transit to homeownership and civic participation, this means fundamentally altering the systems that have been failing us abysmally for decades. No laws or regulations have to be changed to create this new normal. The barriers to implementation are simply resistance on the part of individuals to change their own behaviors. Each of us must act now to take the future into our own hands and help to bring every American along with us.

Part I

ENABLING OPPORTUNITY THROUGH EDUCATION

Education has long been the greatest enabler of opportunity and economic mobility in America. We know that every year of education beyond high school adds $250,000 to an individual's lifetime earnings.[1] Every year. So one would think that we would be doing everything imaginable to make sure that all Americans had at least one year of postsecondary credits, an associate's degree (roughly the equivalent of two years of higher education), or even a bachelor's degree. Well, the stark reality is that we haven't been. And we can't claim to be until the examples described in this section are adopted everywhere.

A little history is in order. For more than a hundred years, no one did education better than the United States. We democratized education early with the first public school in 1635 and universalized it by 1918—the year every state in the Union had passed laws requiring compulsory attendance through elementary school.[2] By 1920, 30 percent of all Americans between the ages of fourteen and seventeen had already attended some form of high school.

College soon followed. As the Industrial Revolution took hold, employers' demand for a more formally educated workforce made college a top priority for business and government. In 1862 Congress created land grant colleges for every state. In 1890 it funded what would become historically black colleges.

With this early start and broad public support for public education, it should come as no surprise that for most of the twentieth century, we consistently produced more high school and college graduates than any country in the world. The benefits of a well-educated workforce were manifest in our economy and standard of living, which were the envy of the world. But today, we trail fourteen other countries around the globe in college attainment. The share of Americans with a college degree, about 40 percent, has barely budged over the past thirty years.

During the same time period, a number of factors have made the situation even worse. While more Americans are enrolled in college than ever before, more than 40 percent fail to get a degree in six years; one-third drop out after just their first year. Even worse, these students are dropping out with enormous debt and without the skills to advance in our economy. Without a sufficiently skilled workforce, U.S. employers now import an extraordinary number of workers, from secretarial to advanced manufacturing fields, for their middle- and higher-wage jobs.[3] This reality further contributes to the steady widening of the income gap between the well educated and the less educated.[4]

The four examples that follow are solving these problems, not just in one place but in many. They are helping Americans get the post–high school degrees and attain the skills that they need to get better jobs, make more money, and do it all while accumulating the least amount of debt. Together, they show us the path we must take to restore our education system to its former status, as an engine of lasting American economic mobility.

I

ENABLE HIGH SCHOOL STUDENTS TO EARN FREE COLLEGE DEGREES

Luis Silos has clocked hundreds of clinical hours over the past two years on the path to earning his associate's degree in nursing. This semester, in addition to his classes, he spends his days from 6:30 a.m. to 3:00 p.m. in rotation on the hospital floor, experiencing what the work is like in different roles and departments as he completes the requirements to graduate this coming May. For Luis, becoming a registered nurse practitioner is just the first step toward a career in the medical field. He has his sights set on becoming a surgeon. And he's got plenty of time, because Luis is a just a senior in high school. This year, he's preparing to graduate from Pharr–San Juan–Alamo North with both his high school diploma and an associate's degree that he's earned completely free of charge.

Luis attends an early-college high school, a model made possible through collaboration between high schools and local college and university partners. The high schools, located on or near college campuses, provide high school students with exposure to real college coursework at no cost. In Luis's school district in southwestern Texas, where almost 90 percent of students are considered economically disadvantaged, the opportunity to earn those credits without the burden of the price tag is invaluable.[1] "They take care of the transportation, meals, books—everything is provided by the district," explains Luis. "All you have to worry about is getting the grade."[2]

Early-college high schools like Luis's offer an environment that not only motivates and pushes students but also equips them with habits—like time management and study skills—needed for future academic success. Most fundamental, it provides students with the opportunity to earn an associate's degree or college credits that will pave the way for a dramatically better financial future.

For Luis, that means medical school. For Orlando Ochoa, a student at nearby Memorial High School, the vision includes Yale Law School and a career in public-interest law, advancing his passion for social justice. Orlando is preparing to graduate with eighty-six college credits and an associate's degree in sociology. "The idea of college always seemed at arm's length—not quite within reach, but in sight," he says. "This program left me with a new confidence in myself and in my future educational and career goals."[3]

Luis and Orlando share that assured outlook, about both the experiences they've gained in high school and what the future may hold. "By the time we get to college," explains Luis, "we already have the experience of what that life is like. We know how rigorous the programs are, so we're more prepared—we're not really even freshmen."[4]

If not for the opportunities provided by the early-college high school model, their stories might have gone differently. The odds for successfully getting a college credential are alarmingly stacked against young people like Luis and Orlando. Since 2008, the rates of college enrollment among low-income students, white, black, and brown, have declined more steeply than any other group, down to just 45 percent.[5] This problem is exacerbated by the fact that postsecondary education is becoming a requirement for more and more of today's stable, well-paying jobs—particularly in fast-growing fields like STEM (science, technology, engineering, and mathematics), information technology, and health care.

Each year of education past high school adds approximately $250,000 to an individual's overall lifetime earnings.[6] The impact of this is visible in the labor market statistics, as well. The unemployment rate stands at 5.2 percent for people with only a high school diploma, compared with

3.6 percent and just 2.7 percent for those with an associate's or bachelor's degree, respectively.[7]

By 2020 it's estimated that a full 65 percent of jobs will require some form of postsecondary degree.[8] There are two sides to that coin. That statistic tells us that we must double-down on efforts to prepare young people with twenty-first-century skills and credentials. But it also means that if we don't, we'll be facing a worsening skills gap, which will threaten our overall economic growth and prosperity.[9] That's why early-college high schools are so extraordinary. They equip students early on with the credentials and skills that they and our economy desperately need, and they build pathways to bridge the gap between high school and college.

The story began in 2002, when a group of philanthropic institutions led by the Bill and Melinda Gates Foundation collaborated with Jobs for the Future, a nonprofit working at the intersection of education and economic opportunity, to launch the Early College High School Initiative. With $100 million in funding from these foundations, 280 high schools across the country—from California to North Carolina—were either established or redesigned to implement this new, blended model.[10]

The design specifications for an early-college high school vary from district to district and school to school, but there are a few unifying elements. The first key feature is partnership. Early colleges hinge on a close relationship with local universities, community colleges, or other community partners so that institutions have a shared sense of responsibility for student success. Second, early colleges provide students with opportunities to earn from one semester up to two years of transferable college credit at no cost—whether that takes place on a college campus, with an accredited professor in the high school classroom, or online. Finally, these schools foster a college-oriented culture, building in the necessary personal and academic support systems to ensure that students are managing the more challenging coursework and to prepare them for the rigors of college.

The goals of the initiative have always been centered on the success of low-income youth, English-language learners, first-generation college attenders, and students of color. Overwhelmingly, these are the students whom the education system is systematically failing; they are overrepresented among high school dropouts and underrepresented among the ranks of college graduates.[11] The early-college model is based on the conviction that such students—young people like Luis and his classmates—are capable of not only meeting but exceeding traditional college-ready standards. What they lack more than anything is opportunity.

That's one thing that distinguish this model from advanced-placement classes, the International Baccalaureate, or other more widespread programs geared toward already high-performing students. "These are kids in high school who, in many cases, were hanging on by a thread," explains Marlene Seltzer, the former president and CEO of Jobs for the Future. "We wanted to show that a degree was not only possible, but probable for these students."[12]

From the start, the Gates Foundation and its fellow funders committed to tracking data over time to understand whether they were getting desired results and to determine how to change course if they were not. When the initiative launched, the partners commissioned a ten-year project to collect, store, analyze, and report out on data that would help them in that process. The Early College High School Student Information System, supported by Jobs for the Future, maintains this information, including evidence and documentation of student progress in schools across the country.[13] It also captures demographic data to help identify whether students benefit in equal measure.

The partners used this information to conduct a study over time aimed at answering a pretty basic question: Are students getting better outcomes, and if so, is the impact felt equally by all types of students? What they found was that the model was changing the trajectory of overall academic performance in the schools. Ninety percent of students enrolled in early-college high schools were graduating successfully, significantly greater than the national rate of 78 percent.[14]

On top of that, the average early-college student was earning thirty-eight college credits by graduation day; for context, that has the potential to shave off about one-third of the cost of a bachelor's degree.[15] Finally, the study found that 30 percent of graduates from early-college high schools had earned an associate's degree or a college certificate along with their diploma.[16]

When I spoke with Seltzer about this model, she remarked how audacious their goals have become, now that they've seen what's possible. "Along the way, you start to hear people looking at the stats and saying, 'Well, only 30 percent of the kids get an associate's degree,' and you have to encourage them to take a step back and recognize how crazy that is, in and of itself. That 30 percent is kids who may not have even finished high school, much less earned a degree!"[17]

The Pharr–San Juan–Alamo Independent School District (PSJA-ISD), where Luis and Orlando will receive their diplomas, is one outstanding example of an entire district implementing this approach. Situated about ten miles north of the Rio Grande near the border between Texas and Mexico, the PSJA-ISD serves 32,000 students across three cities.[18] Ninety-nine percent of students in the district are Hispanic, 90 percent are considered economically disadvantaged, and the vast majority of their parents did not attend college.[19]

In 2007 the district's dropout rate was twice the average of the rest of the state.[20] That year, the district committed to radically altering those statistics and testing out new interventions that would ensure that all students could graduate ready for college. Driving these efforts was a new superintendent, Daniel King.

King came from the neighboring Hidalgo Independent School District, a substantially smaller district representing just 3,300 students.[21] Under King's leadership, it had transformed from one of the lowest-performing districts in the state into a vanguard of the early-college model. In PSJA-ISD, the challenge was going to be determining whether that success could be scaled. Fortunately, he had a sympathetic ally and natural partner in Shirley Reed, the founding president of nearby South Texas College, who had long been deeply committed to the success of students across the region. That relationship made it possible to hit the ground running with dual enrollment opportunities.

King's initial approach probably baffled some of his colleagues. In partnership with South Texas College, his first step was to launch a new district academy, the College, Career, and Technology Academy, specifically for former dropouts. The academy offered a tailored curriculum that allowed students to simultaneously complete requirements for high school graduation and begin taking college coursework. By starting with a program that targeted high school dropouts, King was able to take advantage of already available state funding meant to encourage districts to reach out and reengage this demographic.

The recovery campaign was high-touch, designed to increase the chances that students would see the message everywhere and remember it. Billboards and brochures were placed around town advertising the new academy. Superintendent King himself joined other members of the district in going door to door to potential participants to spread an attention-grabbing message: You dropped out of high school? Come take college courses today, for free.

By piloting the program at a small scale with existing designated funding, King cleared an easier path to implementing the early-college model more broadly. When his gamble worked—when nearly 900 former dropouts ended up graduating—all he had to do was point to the data to rally the political will necessary for scaling up.[22] If those disengaged students were able to achieve such high rates of success, argued King, how can we refuse the same opportunity to the rest of our students?

Today, all four high schools in the district offer an early-college program. In three years, the graduation rate rose from 62 percent to 87 percent, and it has remained around 90 percent in the years since.[23] The curriculum is not always easy, as the students will be the first to attest. Karina Quintana, a senior at PSJA-ISD who will soon graduate with associate's degrees in interdisciplinary studies and mathematics, is quick to remind that they're still high school students, "so in addition to having essentially the full workload of college students, we also have other classes as part of the high school curriculum. Time management is incredibly important, especially with extracurriculars."[24] It is a sentiment echoed by Luis and Orlando, both of whom credit the high level of personalized support they received from counselors and administrators with keeping them balanced and on track.

In addition, what King and other administrators have learned about this model is that the most successful instances offer multiple pathways to success. Some students may benefit most from sampling only a few college-level courses during their time, to gain exposure to the demands of college slowly without diving into an entire course load. Others are ready and willing to take steps to complete the degree. Some students may thrive in schools that focus on a STEM-intensive curriculum, designed to prepare students to pursue high-skilled, in-demand jobs in health, information technology, and advanced manufacturing. "Part of the potential power of the strategy," says Joel Vargas of Jobs for the Future, "is that you can create multiple routes to postsecondary attainment, that aren't unidirectional and that meet the needs and interests of all young people and lead them to a destination of value."[25]

This model has been implemented successfully all over the country, from southwestern Texas to rural Georgia to postindustrial Rust Belt cities in Ohio. Jordan Brown, a second-year medical student working toward his doctorate in osteopathy, earned his associate's degree while at Lorain County Early College High School. There, he was exposed to an array of college-level courses that allowed him to explore and hone his interests. Jordan had always known that he wanted to go into the medical field, so while in high school he took advantage of opportunities to receive certifications in emergency response and as a state-trained nurse aide.

But rather than the certifications and the degree, Jordan cites his increased confidence as the most valuable offering of the school. Being able to start small and ramp up, taking a few college-level courses at a time and developing good study habits along the way gave him leeway to learn through trial and error about how to be successful. The risk was low; counselors and school administrators provided a supportive environment, and he wasn't shouldering any of the cost—or debt—associated with the courses. "I remember being told that there would be more obstacles in college, especially if you didn't develop a system around to support you," explained Jordan. "But I still felt that I was at an advantage, because through this program I had developed the confidence to move forward through those challenges, instead of just getting paralyzed with stress and staying stagnant."[26]

Nine early-college high schools across the state of Ohio are part of a network supported by the education enterprise KnowledgeWorks.[27] Across those campuses, 79 percent of students earn at least one year's worth of college credits, and 95 percent continue on to higher education after graduating.[28] In Youngstown, often the poster child of a city grappling with postindustrial decline, the early-college high school is at the top of rankings, both statewide and nationally, with a 100 percent graduation rate.[29]

Across the country, students like Jordan, Orlando, Karina, and Luis are proving the extent of what's possible when students are given the resources and chances to succeed. "I know that sometimes people think we're not prepared for it. People didn't believe that it's possible," says Luis. "But I believe that we are prepared. Most of the students are mature enough to know what we want, and know how to do the work. Most students are ready and willing to take advantage of the opportunity."[30]

With college attainment among all Americans still hovering around 40 percent and incomes staying stagnant, early colleges provide us with a proven path that can help those Americans who need it the most.[31] Yet of the 26,000 public high schools across the country, only 280 offer an early-college program, which means there is huge untapped potential to reach hundreds of thousands more students across the country. By 1918, every state in the union had made free public education the law. By 2018, every state should be well on its way to making early-college high school a reality.

A NEW NORMAL: GETTING A COLLEGE DEGREE
AND A HIGH SCHOOL DIPLOMA, TOGETHER

With attention to a few key components, high schools could make getting a college degree along with a high school diploma the new normal in America. The first component, having postsecondary institutions in close proximity to high schools, can already be found in every part of the country—rural and urban. That means communities need to focus on the following three elements to make this approach a success.

Coordination across Institutions

Put simply, this model is about partnership. Although high schools, community colleges, and universities each play a role in ensuring students' success, these institutions rarely operate as an integrated system. The early-college model requires collaboration among actors that are accustomed to working in isolation. For one thing, that can mean aligning curriculum. When San Diego Community College launched a new partnership with the local school district, it established an Early College Curriculum Committee with faculty from the high school and college to map out optimized course pathways to help bridge gaps between the school systems.[32] It also may involve sharing human resources—like in PSJA-ISD, where the district has made a number of guidance counselors available to high school students on college campuses—or taking measures to ensure that college credit hours earned in high school will transfer seamlessly to local universities.

Rigid funding structures also pose a barrier to coordination and help to create the sense of a zero-sum game. School districts are generally funded from sources different than higher education and vice versa. In fact, in many states that want to restrict double-dipping, school districts actually lose funding when students enroll in college-level courses.[33] Implementing the early-college model requires blurring lines between systems that often disincentivize cooperation. Marlene Seltzer of Jobs for the Future describes the challenge best: "Somebody's got to pay for it. And everybody looks at the price tag and says, we don't have that in our budget."[34] But the case of PSJA-ISD demonstrates that it doesn't necessarily require a lot of new money. What it does require is a willingness to view resources in any given region as more fluid, whether that means pooling and redistributing funding streams, campus space, faculty, or student data to make cooperation possible.

Leadership is a powerful ingredient in this process. In PSJA-ISD, King was able to galvanize the entire district around a commitment to preventing dropouts and encouraging college readiness. Together with Shirley Reed, founding president of South Texas College, these two leaders were willing to use some political capital, and were able to steer their institutions to look toward the big picture, into partnerships that would maximize each of their roles in promoting a college-going culture. In each case, those institutions realized that they could modestly change the way that they did their work yet contribute to getting rapid and transformative outcomes for local students.

One of the most powerful things about the early-college model is that it provides a tangible way for all the actors in the local education system, K–12, community colleges, and universities, to hold a mirror up to their own institutions and ask how they need to change to achieve student success, not just to meet enrollment goals. Local leaders can lead the charge, and those who aren't willing to work together for the best interest of students need to be held accountable.

Willingness to Pilot and Experiment

Established institutions aren't always comfortable or adept at experimentation. But often, that's the best way to build a successful early-college high school program in a new place. That's because the model won't look the same everywhere. Rather, it can and should be built in a way that takes advantage of unique local conditions and makes the approach more likely to gain acceptance in that environment. In Minnesota, for example, the state has a requirement that 2 percent of school revenue be set aside for staff development.[35] Districts creatively have allowed teachers to put this money toward classes that will certify them to teach college-level courses in high school classrooms.[36] In North Carolina, early-college high schools are mandated to be located on a college campus so that students get an immersive experience; whereas in Missouri, dual-credit instructors can teach in high school classrooms as long as they are subject to the same supervision and evaluation process as typical college instructors.[37]

The flexibility of this model also allows for easy adaptation for different environments and local needs. It's provided the blueprint for a number of STEM-intensive schools. One such example, Pathways in Technology Early College High School (P-TECH) in New York, actually involved a partnership between the City University of New York, the New York City Department of Education and IBM to design a curriculum that would prepare students for high-tech industries.[38] Chicago is now exploring a similar partnership with some of their major employers.

Pilot efforts can also serve as proofs of concept, as they did in the case of King's dropout academy. By demonstrating measurable results at a manageable scale, pilots can build confidence that change is possible, surface unforeseen barriers, show how resources will have to be shifted among institutions, and lay the groundwork for permanent change. Sometimes that means piloting in one school as a way of transforming an entire district. In Dayton, Ohio, Dunbar Early College High School recently welcomed its first class of 500 students.[39] As the first early-college high school in the Dayton public school district, they hope to use it as a model for pursuing other partnerships and redesigning the rest of the local high schools.[40]

Like so many of the examples in this book, this experimentation was often made possible by local or national philanthropy. Time and time again, I have found that a very modest amount of philanthropic dollars can help actors try something new to see if it works. They are often willing to disrupt old ways of working (and the resources dedicated to those approaches) once a new way is proved—but not before then. Funding pilots like these often become highly leveraged investments on the part of philanthropy.

More Conducive Policies

Local institutions must work together differently, but certain changes to state and federal policies would help make scaling this work even easier. States like California, North Carolina, Ohio, Texas, and Colorado have helped pave the way by reducing policy barriers that restrict dual enrollment, cap the number of credits students can earn in high school, or stymy the transfer of credits between institutions.[41]

Beyond just reducing road blocks, states can also enact policies to incentivize innovation. Simply offering policy language that defines the model, as has been done in North Carolina, Ohio, and Texas, helps set the stage for its spread and maintains high-quality implementation from district to district. In North Carolina, the state's openness to experimentation has spawned partnerships between the North Carolina Community College System and the State Board of Education, which have resulted in the growth of seventy-five early-college high schools serving 15,000 students.[42]

Less common but no less interesting is the growth of performance-based funding, which allocates money for education systems based on outcomes or improvement toward goals as opposed to enrollment numbers. In states like Indiana and Texas where this is being experimented with, advocates hope that the funding model will incentivize collaboration between institutions rather than competition.[43] With all of the unmet demand for early-college programs, these are steps that should be on every legislative agenda in the coming session.

At the federal level, one of the biggest barriers to scale is that Pell Grants—the most prominent source of federal financial aid—can't be used by students in high school. The Department of Education is now exploring alternatives through the Experimental Sites initiative, which is granting forty-four pilot colleges across twenty-three states the ability to offer Pell Grants to high school students taking dual-enrollment classes.[44] This moderate policy shift could go a long way toward helping the model scale by opening up another significant funding stream to cover the costs of early-college course work.

2

GRADUATE ALL ENROLLED
COLLEGE STUDENTS

Just over a decade ago, Timothy Renick was confronting a serious problem. As vice provost at Georgia State University (GSU), he was deeply troubled by patterns in the university's dropout rates. Only 25 percent of black students and 22 percent of Hispanic students were making it to graduation day. Students of color and low-income students were foundering.[1] At a school like GSU, where 60 percent of students are from low-income families, that was translating into thousands of students. Year after year, those abysmal statistics had been allowed to persist without much resistance on the part of the administration. There is a fatalistic mindset, Renick explains, that is all too common within our higher education institutions: that demographics are destiny and that there is very little that a university can do to change the fates of these low-income students who were overwhelmingly falling out of the system.[2]

"There's often this view that there are factors outside of their control that make success possible," Renick observes. "So it's not that they don't care; it's that they don't think they can make a difference." Faculty members, despite all the best intentions, were often getting hung up on the "if only"s, he goes on to say: "if only K–12 education could improve, if only access to resources for high schoolers would increase, if only state funding would increase, all of which are obstacles to increasing retention and de-creasing the achievement gap at the college level."[3] But wishful thinking was not driving students toward better results.

It was time for a radically different approach. The first step was for lead-ership to begin shifting focus onto the factors that were within their con-trol. "What GSU has done is put the mirror on ourselves and asked, 'In what ways are *we* the obstacle?'" explains Renick.[4] What they found was that there were plenty of ways that status quo operations at the university were posing challenges for the students most in need of support. For example, freshmen were confronted with over 150 different majors from which to choose but were receiving little meaningful guidance on select-ing a program or understanding the requirements to stay on track. So the university began piloting an optional program that grouped new students with similar interests (what they called "meta-majors," such as business, arts, behavioral sciences, and so on) into twenty-five-person learning communities. Each group was then assigned an adviser specific to that field. This person would work with the students to help them select an aca-demic track, keep them on schedule to fulfill requirements, and under-stand various career paths within that field.

When the program showed signs of success, the university scaled it up—from an optional pilot program to the norm. This shift resulted in a 32 percent drop in the number of students who changed majors in their sophomore and senior years, which indicated to administrators that stu-dents were finding their fit earlier on in college and corresponded to higher on-time graduation rates.

Today, Georgia State administrators track over 800 indicators every day that are correlated with dropout. Warning signs like getting a C grade in their first course on campus—which has been statistically shown to cor-respond to lower graduation rates down the road—triggers outreach from an adviser who is able to intervene with any necessary targeted supports to promote that student's success. Last year alone, there were over 52,000 one-on-one meetings between students and their advisers and over 100,000 additional contacts (such as through e-mail). They have implemented a suite of sixteen programs focused on retention and graduation. But what is most important beyond isolated programs, explains Renick, is that these interventions mark a different way of doing business, systemically. Programs were started as pilots at a small scale, and if they demonstrated success they would be scaled up, with the desired end result being that "it's no longer a program, it's just the way we do things."[5]

This university-wide shift in focus has reaped incredible results. Since the university started using predictive analytics in earnest, it has begun graduating 1,700 more students each year than it had been just five years earlier. And most notably, in 2016, GSU became the only national university at which black, Hispanic, first-generation, and low-income students graduated at rates at or above the rate of the overall student body.[6] Graduation rates rose from 29 to 57 percent for black students and from 22 to 54 percent for Hispanics and reached 51 percent for low-income students.[7] The university has proved that the achievement gap can be closed—all while significantly increasing the overall representation of these students on campus.[8]

Building up the capacities to collect and interpret data to drive these interventions is not free, but leadership has recognized that they have a high return on investment. What GSU found was that for every 1 percent increase in student retention, the school was receiving over $3 million a year in return on investment. In a nutshell, says Renick, "The best way to increase revenue for a university is to hold on to the students that you already have."[9]

This focus is more necessary than ever to ensure that education remains a pathway for social and economic mobility, especially as changes in the labor market continue to make a postsecondary degree requisite for a well-paying job. In the recovery from the economic crisis, some 95 percent of the jobs that have returned require at least some college education, according to a comprehensive study from the Georgetown Center for Education and the Workforce.[10] Individuals with a college degree make, on average, over 50 percent more than those who attended some college but did not graduate.[11] That adds up to an estimated $1 million more in earnings over the course of a lifetime.[12] And unemployment rates are significantly lower among degree holders.[13]

If college plays such a critical role in improving lifetime income, then we ought to do everything we can to ensure that, at a minimum, those who enroll in college actually finish. Across the country, dropout rates have been quietly rising over the past few decades. During the 1960s, one in five students who enrolled in college did not graduate; by 2005 that number had climbed to one in three.[14]

This is most acute among students of color and lower-income students. Dropout rates for black students, for example, who often struggle to navigate additional obstacles such as culture shock or financial insecurity once arriving on campus, are 15 percentage points higher than for their white counterparts.[15] Some of those same factors contribute to driving up dropout rates for low-income students as well. Although enrollment from lower-income students has climbed substantially, in 2015 only 9 percent of low-income students enrolled in college received a bachelor's degree by age twenty-four. Students from the highest-income bracket, on the other hand, graduate at a rate of 77 percent.[16] Put another way, higher-income adults are eight times more likely to attain a college degree. Altogether, more than 6 million low-income students over the past fifteen years have enrolled in college but not finished.

Even more worrisome, the majority of students—particularly those from lower-wealth households—will be forced to take out loans to finance their college careers. Over the past three decades, tuition rates across the country have doubled at most universities; at others, the spike has been exponential.[17] As a result, 68 percent of college seniors in 2015 were poised to leave school with student loan debt—$30,100, on average.[18] Students who receive Pell Grants are significantly more likely to graduate with debt than those who do not, meaning that, even with assistance, low-income students are often at the greatest risk of shouldering a heavy debt burden.[19]

In addition, a 2016 study from the Brookings Institution revealed the disturbing role that race plays in intensifying the debt burden, even when controlling for household income. Low-income black students are twice as likely as their white counterparts to accumulate student loan debt, and they graduate with an estimated $7,721 more in debt than even low-income white students.[20] The bottom line is that if such students—low-income, first-generation, and students of color, already underrepresented on college campuses—struggle and drop out midway, they are beginning their adult lives with the crippling combination of student debt and no degree.

"As college became a mass institution in America, it started looking like high school. But unlike high school, we didn't build a system that was designed to keep people in," says Anthony P. Carnevale from Georgetown University's Center on Education and Workforce. "If we had a 40 percent dropout rate in high school, we'd think we were in a national crisis."[21]

Well, we are and we have to begin treating it like one. Fortunately, some colleges and universities around the country, such as Georgia State University and others featured in this chapter, are doing something about it. We now know what to do and are seeing it being done in dozens of places; we just need to be doing a lot more of it.

Two studies tell us a lot about what is possible. For the past two years, the *New York Times* has published a College Access Index. The index is the *Times*'s effort to understand which of the nation's top colleges actively recruit and successfully graduate low-income students and why some places are more successful than others in doing so. The index ranks 179 of the country's top colleges based on three factors: the share of the college's students receiving Pell Grants (which typically go to families making less than $70,000); the graduation rate of those students; and the net cost, after financial aid, that a college charges its low-income students. Colleges must have an overall five-year graduation rate of at least 75 percent to be considered.

To understand the index, it is important to understand each of its elements and what each element shows. The first element, "share of the college's students receiving Pell Grants" indicates how serious the college is about recruiting low-income students. The higher the share, the more seats it sets aside for low-income students. The second element, "the graduation rate of the students" tells how successful the college is at graduating *that* targeted population. The third element, "net cost, after financial aid" measures the college's commitment to addressing one of the biggest practical and psychological barriers to enrolling in the first place: cost.

In the 2015 College Access Index, six of the top seven spots belonged to University of California campuses, with the Irvine campus coming in at number one and Berkeley at number seven.[22] But rounding out the top ten were small liberal arts colleges, Vassar, Amherst, and Pomona. Each of these colleges had notably high scores. At least thirty other colleges had scores that demonstrated they were "above average" on each of these factors. It turns out, big public universities are not the only institutions that can increase the number of low-income students it enrolls but also get them to graduate in five years. Of the fifteen highest-performing colleges in the College Access Index, some were rural (Davidson and Knox), some urban (UC Irvine, UCLA, and Harvard), some small (Pomona and Welles-ley), and some large (University of Florida and University of Washington-Seattle). Bumping up representation of historically marginalized students on campus does not have to undercut the competitiveness of an academic institution or require lowering admission standards. One analysis found that such elite colleges could increase the representation of low-income students by another 30 percent without lowering the standards of their SAT or ACT.[23]

More university leaders should be taking a page out of the book of How-ard Gillman, the chancellor of the chart-topping University of California-Irvine. Gillman grew up in California's San Fernando Valley, the only child of working-class parents. As a first-generation college student, he re-lied on the nation's public university system to make the promise of higher education possible. Gillman earned his bachelor's, master's, and doctoral degrees in political science all at UCLA. He also met his wife there, where they were both graduate students mentoring freshmen who needed a little more support to succeed.[24]

So it is not surprising that Gillman, in his role at the head of UC Ir-vine, has made enrolling and successfully graduating low-income students a priority. Their recognition at the top of the *New York Times* index is reflec-tive of the university's sustained commitment to its founding principles. It was established in 1964 with the express purpose of "serving the masses," and for the fifty years since it has taken deliberate steps to attract and gradu-ate students of modest means. Over the years, that has included working to keep control on the cost of tuition, driving available funding toward finan-cial aid, and providing students in need with a network of academic and financial advisers to support them on campus.

Today, UC Irvine's student body includes more students with Pell Grants than all eight colleges of the Ivy League combined. What a college president or administrator has to do is decide that enrolling and graduating low-income students is a priority. UC Irvine's Gillman put it this way in the *New York Times:* "The big challenge for American higher education is that it has to be a gateway through which talented young people can thrive, regardless of their background."[25] Essentially, successfully graduating low-income students isn't brain surgery. But it does "take a lot of systematic effort," Gillman noted. From the *Times* analysis of the highest-performing colleges on the 2014 and 2015 index, it appears that successful efforts require three components in addition to leadership from the top.

First, enrolling low-income students and increasing that number in future years. If you don't enroll them, they can't graduate. The more you enroll, the more you are contributing to solving the problem. However, unless the overall student body grows, enrolling low-income students will mean intentionally taking fewer upper-income students. While the *Times* highlighted a number of schools that have done that, like Pomona College (which increased its enrollment of Pell grantees from 16 percent to 22 percent of its population) it also identified top schools like Dartmouth, Penn, Princeton, and Yale that have kept their low-income populations at 16 percent or even lower.

Second, building and taking advantage of pipeline relationships with community colleges. Community colleges are often the first place that qualified low-income students enroll because their published tuition rates appear to be affordable and, with campuses closer to home, they often are less intimidating places to go to college. While 80 percent of the over 1.7 million students who enroll in two-year community colleges each year have an eye toward transferring and earning a four-year degree, only about 14 percent actually do so.[26] These students are more likely to come from lower-income families, and they often default to community college because they are daunted by the sticker price of a four-year university. The University of California network has built strong relationships with local community colleges and established a robust transfer pipeline, targeting recruitment efforts and setting out clear pathways, offering prioritization, and in some cases guaranteeing admission for students who have demonstrated success at California's community colleges. In fact, nearly one in three graduating University of California students began at a community college.[27]

Third, prioritizing resources to make tuition affordable. Given the skyrocketing cost of tuition everywhere, a college's ability to be competitive in the index rankings boils down to having a competitive net cost, after financial aid. The most common way to have a competitive net cost after financial aid is, unsurprisingly, to be generous with financial aid. Often, that will mean dedicating resources to financial aid or keeping tuition down that could have gone to other parts of the college. Like any business, running a college is, in some ways, a zero-sum game, so prioritizing resources to this will mean giving something up somewhere else.

In addition to the *New York Times* index, the second study that illustrates what is possible comes from the Education Trust, a national nonprofit organization that promotes higher academic achievement, especially for low-income and students of color. The trust study also looked at graduation rates, but instead of focusing on income, it focused on racial and ethnic diversity.

The Education Trust's 2015 report, *Rising Tide: Do College Grad Rate Gains Benefit All Students?*, looked back at ten years of data on four-year colleges to understand which were improving graduation rates, especially among students of color, and why. In particular, the report looked at public colleges, which enroll almost two-thirds of first-time, full-time students. Over the past ten years, graduation rates at all colleges, private and public, improved by 3 percent. But of the 328 public colleges that had improved their graduation rates over this period (out of the 489 reviewed), the average improvement was 6.4 percent.[28]

To better understand the extent to which these improvements specifically impacted blacks, Latinos, and Native Americans ("underserved" students), this study delved even more deeply into a subset of these 328 successful colleges. It looked at 255 of those schools with sizable enrollments of underserved students. In those colleges, graduation rates for underserved students increased slightly more than for white students (6.3 percent versus 5.7 percent), with improvements greatest for Latinos (up 7.4 percent) and smallest for blacks (up by 4.4 percent).[29]

Not unlike the findings of the *Times* College Access Index, the Education Trust study found that colleges actually can increase the graduation rates of targeted populations of students if they really try. Kati Haycock, past president of the trust, put it well: "Institutions turn out to be much more powerful in determining student success than we ever knew."[30]

The Education Trust report independently confirmed what the *New York Times* had also found: success starts with leadership. In an interview with the *Chronicle of Higher Education*, Kati Haycock said, "It really is about presidential leadership. At the institutions that are making real progress . . . the president has made this a real priority in every speech that he or she gives, in every major address to the faculty, to reiterate that successful institutions don't not graduate large numbers of their poor kids or kids of color."[31]

But in addition to the formula for success that can be drawn from the *Times* index of leadership, transfer pipeline, and dedicated resources, the Education Trust study would add focused intervention and vigilance. "The institutions that are really moving the needle are asking the question, how are students doing week one, week two, week five? How many are coming to class? How many aren't? How many are doing OK on their assignments? How many aren't? And acting immediately when they see students falling off the path," says Haycock.[32]

It should not come as any surprise that Georgia State University, a nationally recognized innovator in data-driven interventions, is featured on the leaderboard. Its retention strategies include a University Assistantship Program geared toward integrating low-income and first-generation students into academic life from their very first semester by pairing them with faculty members to work as research assistants. An early-alert system gives administrators a structured way to get help to students who show the warning signs of struggle in the early weeks of their first semester. Those signs can include excessive absences or tardiness, lack of engagement, or poor academic performance. These flags prompt the professor to fill out a report to the Office of First-Year and Transition Programs so that those students can access additional resources and supports.

The program helps empower students who may otherwise have slipped through the cracks or have been chalked up as lost causes to correct course with targeted strategies and additional faculty guidance, without adding a mark to their academic record. Georgia State has also amended its HOPE Scholarship with an additional Keep HOPE Alive program, which enables students who drop just below the academic requirements of the HOPE scholarship to stay at the university and work toward regaining their eligibility.

The Keep HOPE Alive program is just one of the ways that schools can help mitigate the stress of financial insecurity, which can jeopardize students' success. Emergency aid programs exist in universities all over the country—some 75 percent of schools, according to a survey by NASPA: Student Affairs Professionals in Higher Education. These funds provide students with a small amount of money—maybe a few hundred dollars—to help them weather a small financial crisis that could otherwise spell the end of their college career. It might be a utility bill, the cost of a new laptop, medical expenses, or another small but critical payment that threatens the ability of that student to stay on track. The programs can take a variety of forms; some are restricted grants to target food insecurity, others are specifically for book purchases or other academic resources, and still others are unrestricted grants to cover any kind of hardship.[33]

While many schools have some degree of emergency funding available, it is often ad hoc and poorly publicized to students. Furthermore, budget cuts and federal financial aid restrictions can limit an institutions' ability to offer this kind of support. Some external scholarship programs run similar programs. One such organization, Scholarship America, found that 95 percent of students who receive their emergency aid persist through the rest of the semester, and 88 percent enroll the next. These emergency funds may be among the low-cost but high-impact strategies that should be in every school's playbook.[34]

The good news is that Georgia State is far from the only university making progress on this front. The report highlighted twenty-six colleges that were both raising graduation rates across the board and closing gaps in graduation rates between whites and underserved students. It also described the types of focused interventions that the most successful schools in that group, such as San Diego State and University of Nebraska-Lincoln, used to serve underserved students.

San Diego State, for example, engages in outreach to high-performing, underrepresented students as early as seventh grade and helps coach and support these young people throughout their high school careers to prepare them for four-year college. Through their Compact Scholars Program, the university partners with the local district and drives students to meet academic benchmarks throughout their high school career with the offer of guaranteed admission to the university as well as personalized support services.[35]

Educational institutions can take a multitude of steps to support students once they have arrived on campus. That could mean creating a taskforce, as the University of Nebraska-Lincoln did, dedicated to identifying and executing on ways to better serve its low-income, first-generation, and students of color. For the University of Nebraska-Lincoln, a series of small interventions—like ramping up the advising on degree planning and establishing small communities to support students through the transition into college—resulted in a more than thirty-point spike in graduation rates for those underrepresented students over ten years. The university also saw a twenty-five-point decrease in the graduation gap between white and students of color—all the while increasing the proportion of students of color on campus.

The *New York Times* index shows at least forty top colleges, spread out across the country, that are graduating more and more low-income students on time. The Education Trust report shows that more than 255 public colleges, urban and rural, that are already serving tens of thousands of black, Latino, and Native American students are having increased success. We know how to get them to graduate. We just need to make it more of a priority and be doing it everywhere—to ensure that it becomes, as Renick of GSU, aptly puts it, "just the way that we do things."

A NEW NORMAL: GRADUATING ALL ENROLLED COLLEGE STUDENTS

Two ingredients are necessary to make graduation of already enrolled college students the norm, rather than the exception, everywhere in the country.

Leadership from University Executives

Executive-level leadership is the single most important factor in successfully graduating already enrolled students. While the *New York Times* reviewed the performance of low-income students at top-tier institutions and the Education Trust studied the success of students of color at hundreds of public universities, both studies essentially reached the same conclusion: great progress is possible, but it requires presidential leadership.

College and university presidents simply have to make it an institutional priority. They must make it clear to the public and faculty that their institution is a "gateway through which talented young people can thrive regardless of their background," as UC Irvine's Gillman has said. Great institutions today should be measured by the large numbers of poor kids and kids of color whom they graduate, a quality that should be reflected in their speeches and annual budgets. Their leadership is a prerequisite for change.

Adoption of Proven Interventions

Over the course of the past decade, many colleges and universities have been experimenting with different interventions to understand the types and scope of supports needed to ensure student success. The Education Trust's study highlighted some of the different and focused interventions that the most successful schools have used to support students in their journey once they've arrived on campus—from counseling to financial support.

What's so promising is that these proven practices are moving from being hard to find one-offs to the broadly available mainstream, so no institution has an excuse for not adopting them. Efforts like the University Innovation Alliance (UIA) are one way that this is happening. The alliance is a coalition of eleven public universities from across the country that serve large numbers of low-income students, many of whom are the first in their families to attend college. Many UIA members have been aggressively experimenting with interventions like those highlighted in the Education Trust report. They have come together, in UIA, so they can test and improve on one another's most promising practices and speed their spread and adoption to all the member institutions.

Georgia State University's use of predictive analytics to improve its advising of students, as detailed earlier in this chapter, is a great example of what UIA is working to achieve. The University Innovation Alliance estimates that if these same innovations were scaled across the eleven participating institutions over the next five years, they would produce more than 61,000 additional graduates; if scaled across all public universities nationally, an additional 850,000 more students would graduate who would otherwise have dropped out.[36]

The Bill and Melinda Gates Foundation is helping to take this type of collaboration and the broad availability of best practices even further. It is supporting the Frontier Set, a group of twenty-nine colleges and universities across sixteen states and two state systems' colleges and universities, many of which are also in the UIA, that are committed to significantly increasing student access and success and to eliminating racial-ethnic and socioeconomic disparities in college attainment.[37]

Institutions participating in the Frontier Set are working simultaneously to improve their own operations and to drive change in the field, writ large. Internally, they are continuing to implement the most promising practices and to understand how they have to change their long-standing practices, which have not eliminated racial-ethnic and socioeconomic gaps in degree attainment to date. They are thereby actively synthesizing what they are learning and participating in a process where they share those insights with institutions inside and outside the Frontier Set. The expressed intent of the effort is to "share practical and actionable knowledge" focusing on the "what" and the "how" of change not only with the Frontier Set but with the entire field.[38]

3

BUILD A PATH TO A DEGREE
FOR WORKERS ON THE JOB

Detra Wright works in a senior-level position at Anthem, one of America's largest health care companies and the parent of Blue Cross Blue Shield. Just a few years ago, that position felt impossibly far beyond her reach. With only a high school diploma, Wright had transitioned from one low-wage, frontline job to another within the health care field for nearly two decades.[1] She knew that her opportunities to make more money were limited without a college degree, but college never seemed feasible. A single mother since age nineteen, Wright couldn't see a way to shoulder the costs and demands of college courses along with her responsibilities as a single parent.

Wright knew she needed more formal education to get ahead. At the same time, Anthem leadership was also grappling with the fact that, like so many companies across the country, they needed a more highly skilled workforce. Generally, only about a third of Anthem employees have an associate's degree or higher.[2] And while companies like Anthem often prefer to promote from within, it's challenging to do so when employees have neither the competencies to advance nor accessible pathways to gain those skills.

In 2013 Anthem sought a solution to this problem by offering up to 500 of its employees, on a pilot basis, the chance to earn an online, competency-based college degree from Southern New Hampshire University's College for America. Not only was the degree built specifically for working adults to teach the skills that Anthem knew were lacking in its workforce; it could also be attained completely debt free, if employees took advantage of Anthem's already existing tuition reimbursement benefit program.

Wright was one of the first 500 Anthem employees to sign up for the pilot. "The tuition was going to be reimbursed at 100 percent. That was the biggest draw, and, it was just the perfect timing," Wright said.[3] For years, fear and uncertainty had kept her from pursuing a degree. It wasn't until her own child was off to college and this opportunity presented itself that she realized it was time to give it a try. Fortunately, the College for America programs are uniquely designed to position working adults like Wright for success. What she discovered was that there were no courses, no credit hours, no traditional faculty, and no grades. Instead, the program was self-paced, online, and cost roughly $3,000 a year. Wright was matched with an adviser who helped her chart her path to a degree and worked with her throughout the entire process.

Wright was able to prove in just four months that she had the competencies needed for an associate's degree. Eight months later she earned her bachelor's degree in health care management with a concentration in global perspectives—all debt free. Wright has since been promoted to her current senior level position at Anthem. "It turns out," Wright said, "life teaches you a lot. I was already aware of a lot I needed to know."[4]

Detra Wright's success is not an anomaly, even within her own company. After an internal study confirmed that 20 percent of Anthem employees who had participated in the pilot program had not only earned a Southern New Hampshire University (SNHU) degree but had already been promoted, Anthem made the program and tuition reimbursement available to all 51,000 employees across the country. Unlike Wright, Darby Conley, another Anthem employee, had tried several times to complete a college degree. She had climbed the ranks from a customer service representative all the way to a manager but realized she couldn't advance further without a degree. It wasn't until the availability of the College for America program that she was able to earn her associate's degree in a way that was flexible and felt highly relevant to her day-to-day work. It was also what it took to propel her to her current role as a director.[5]

Anthem is far from the only corporation to have embraced this approach. Aetna, the insurance giant, has also long been in the vanguard in offering competitive employee benefits. It provides education benefits that help employees to move up the career ladder and out of low-wage frontline jobs, in part, because it has found a powerful connection between employee personal well-being and customer satisfaction.

What the company looks for in their education benefit programs, explains Kay Mooney, vice president of employee benefits and well-being, is a combination of "affordability and accessibility," so the broadest group of employees can take advantage of them.[6] When Aetna's leadership learned of the SNHU College for America program, especially its cost and online access, it seized on the chance to bring it to its employees.

After completing its own due diligence on the program, Aetna offered College for America to its entire workforce. Immediately, over 200 employees joined. More than half of College for America enrollees within Aetna are people of color, the vast majority are women, and a quarter of them earn less than $35,000 annually (two-thirds earn less than $50,000).[7] And although it's been only a little over a year since the program launched, they've already begun to see some proof points of the impact. Of the 200 enrollees, eleven have received their college degree.[8] One woman received her associate's degree in a mere ninety days. She's since enrolled in a bachelor's program through College for America. Anecdotal evidence shows that those success stories are serving as a source of inspiration for others who may be teetering on the fence about going back to school.

Of the partnership, Mooney reports that implementation was seamless. "[College for America]'s base and expertise was already around health care, and their other major focus areas are around business programs, so it was a natural fit for the skills our employees needed."[9]

Competency-based degrees—like the one offered by SNHU's College for America program that has turned thousands of frontline workers into college graduates—have a few distinguishing characteristics. First, they focus on the real-world skills that people need to succeed in their own workplaces rather than evaluating students based exclusively on number of hours spent in a classroom. The curriculum is shaped by faculty as well as experts in the field, so that students graduate with the specific professional skills necessary to advance within their company.

Second, students advance as they prove that they have mastered certain types of knowledge and skills (competencies). As a result, students can often progress through a degree program in a fraction of the time that it would take at a traditional institution, as Wright did. Students demonstrate their mastery of a specific competency primarily by completing projects that are scored by expert reviewers. The result is that students graduate with something that looks like a traditional transcript, but their transcripts also list projects and associated competencies, which give the employer a more in-depth understanding of the individual's skills. Technology, in particular, allows them to learn at their convenience and more easily balance it with their family and work. The program is online, so as long as employees have access to broadband (addressed in chapter 9), it can be accessed at any time.

Third, tuition is a flat rate, so students pay only for the time they need to prove their competence. This can dramatically reduce the amount of crippling student debt that accrues semester after semester for tuition costs incurred just to accumulate the number of credits required to graduate at traditional universities. In fact, the end cost to the employee, as was the case for Detra Wright, can be nominal, given employer tuition-reimbursement policies—sometimes free, often debt free. What is so attractive to employers is that employees are using this often underused benefit, getting the skills the employee and the employer need.

"This is not merely education for education's sake," says Julian Alssid, who served as College for America's founding chief workforce strategist.[10] Southern New Hampshire University is one of a growing number of nonprofit and for-profit colleges that companies are using to help their employees earn a degree from an accredited school.

I had worked with Alssid for years and considered him one of the country's leading thinkers on workforce development issues; he founded and ran the Workforce Strategy Center for thirteen years, advising states and regions on workforce policy. So when I saw a *Huffington Post* blog post by Alssid, I was surprised to see from his byline that he was working at a place called College for America. I was eager to hear why he would close down his center and go to a university that I had never heard of.

His answers were fascinating. Alssid explained to me that he had become frustrated with the workforce development field. Among other challenges, states move incredibly slowly. Employers and educators often struggled to work effectively together. In fact, we both acknowledged being stunned by a recent study that found 96 percent of university academic officers believed they were educating students with the skills employers wanted, but only 11 percent of employers thought that was the case.[11]

Through a mutual acquaintance, Alssid was connected with the team that had been tasked by Paul LeBlanc, the president of Southern New Hampshire University, to build a college offering that would truly partner with employers to advance the skills of their low-wage employees. Alssid became excited about the idea and ended up merging his Workforce Strategy Center with SNHU to help build the team. Founded in 1932, SNHU is a nonprofit university that started as a traditional school with a residential campus. In 2007 it launched SNHU.edu, an online college with 900 students. Those ranks have now grown to more than 80,000 students, second in size only to Liberty University Online among nonprofits.[12] The university designed the College for America program hoping to build on those strengths and help those employers who want frontline workers— estimated to be more than 24 million people nationwide—to have postsecondary education.[13]

What they landed on was a self-paced, online program that has already helped thousands of employees and employers at the same time. Now in its fourth year, College for America offers associate's degrees in health care management and general studies with a concentration in business and bachelor's degrees in management, health care management, and communications. More than 100 employers, like Anthem, Aetna, McDonalds, Gap, and many more, are partnering with College for America. It holds itself accountable for meeting two types of metrics. The first is student focused: pace of mastery, time to degree, graduation rates, and impact on career. The second is employer focused: retention, promotion, and employee and employer satisfaction.[14]

From the employer perspective, the program has shown promising results at delivering a high return on investment. Companies like McDonald's Corporation, which has adopted this model and is influencing many of its franchisees to do the same, are seeing how the competency-based curriculum helps employees improve their skills in ways that improve their job performance immediately, even before they get their degrees.[15]

Partners HealthCare, which makes College for America available to all its 70,000 employees, believes that it helps employees gain vital, on-the-job confidence. Mary Jane Ryan, the director of workforce development for Partners HealthCare, says the program is "making college graduates out of people who may never have seen themselves as college students before and increasing their professional advancement opportunities."[16]

Today, Partners HealthCare offers not only pathways to associate's and bachelor's degrees but also a certificate program that they co-created with SNHU that helps employees gain communication skills, comfort with Excel, data visualization, and project management, among other competencies.

The data on the return on investment for students is equally promising. It is bringing economic mobility to those often the hardest to help. Of the 14,000 students across the country who have been served by College for America since inception, surveys conducted in 2017 revealed that 67 percent were first-generation college students, and 85 percent are over twenty-four years old. Seventy-three percent of the students report having at least one dependent. On average, students are on pace to complete their associate's degrees in just over two years, significantly faster than community colleges where part-time students are often taking five years.[17] Thirty percent of the students identify as African American, and 15 percent identify as Hispanic, significantly higher concentrations than on most college campuses. What's more, 80 percent of the students expect to graduate with less than $5,000 in debt.[18]

"What's so powerful," Alssid says, "is that I'm seeing this approach eliminate the psychological barrier for low-income people who believe that these degrees aren't within their financial reach."[19] He says that some employers may be reluctant to "endorse" an individual college for their employees, but he believes that the partnership between the employer and the college, whether SNHU or another provider, makes all the difference in the world. "When they make this available in partnership, it raises the completion rate, reduces debt, and has a great chance to result in a promotion."[20]

College for America is just one player in the growing field of competency-based learning. One of the early pioneers was Western Governors University (WGU), which originated in the mid-1990s when a number of governors from Western states, frustrated with the status quo expense and inaccessibility of many of their public higher education institutions, wanted to find a way to give residents better and cheaper access to higher education. The answer they landed on was to start their own university, a nonprofit that would make a meaningful competency-based degree accessible at low cost—a flat rate of just $6,000 a year, with federal financial aid available to help students bear the financial burden. The $6,000 buys as many courses as a student can complete in two semesters, which is often more than a normal academic course load, meaning that the average student completes a bachelor's in two and a half years.[21]

Unlike College for America, which gets the majority of its students through direct relationships with employers such as Anthem and Partners HealthCare, WGU students largely come to it by referral of alumni and other students. Similar to College for America, however, WGU identifies the competencies that are needed for its degrees by working with employers. It has standing committees or external program councils of leading employers like Microsoft and Google that continually inform its degrees in information technology, business, health care, and nursing and teacher education.[22]

Today, WGU is serving 77,000 students nationwide across all fifty states.[23] And it is successfully serving the students that our systems have been failing: students who are enticed to enroll but receive no supports to ensure that they're equipped to actually graduate. The vast majority of WGU students already have tried college and failed at least once. The average student is thirty-seven years old. More than 70 percent of the students come from underserved communities, work full time, and need financial aid to attend at all. Without the explicit ties to employer tuition-reimbursement programs, WGU graduates end up with an average of $17,000 in debt, still considerably less than the national average of $37,000.[24]

The results are impressive for employers and employees alike. In a 2016 Harris Poll survey, 94 percent of employers responded that WGU graduates they had hired met or exceeded their expectations.[25] As to the efficacy of this approach for economic mobility, 87 percent of students who graduated from WGU are employed in their degree field after graduating, and graduates experienced an average salary increase of $19,100 within four years (almost three times the national average).[26]

Based on the successes of institutions like SNHU and Western Governors University, roughly 600 colleges across the country are now in the design phase for their own competency-based education programs. That's up from an estimated 52 institutions last year.[27] More and more employers are aggressively moving in this direction too, often in very public ways. While different from the unique degrees that SNHU offers to corporate partners, new partnerships between major corporations and academic institutions have cropped up to take advantage of the symbiotic advantages of educating the workforce. Starbucks is working in partnership with Arizona State University, Chrysler with Strayer University, and Jet Blue with the online educator, StraighterLine, to name a few.[28]

This is not charity work. American companies, big and small, are in desperate need of a workforce with more skills, and they already employ approximately 24 million frontline workers like Detra Wright and Darby Conley, who are ready, willing, and able to get those skills.[29] In addition, in 2017 alone, an expected 2.5 million new, middle-skill jobs will be added to the U.S. workforce; these are jobs that require some post–high school education, but not a four-year degree.[30] And this trend is not changing; between 2014 and 2024, it's projected that just shy of 50 percent of job openings will be for what's termed "middle-skill workers," with the same education requirements.[31]

Creating these pathways pays, in terms of employee retention, their ability to promote from within (which surveys show most employers prefer to do), and, ultimately, their bottom line. A study from the Institute for Corporate Productivity found that higher-performing companies were two and a half times more likely than low-performing companies to provide opportunities for entry-level employees to move up.[32] Today, thousands of employees all over the country, with dozens of employers paying for their achieving associate's and bachelor's degrees, are improving their economic condition and the company's performance at the same time. We just need to be doing more of it.

A NEW NORMAL: GETTING A COLLEGE DEGREE ON THE JOB

Two ingredients are necessary for getting millions of existing frontline workers in American companies college degrees right now.

Companies Work with College for America and Similar Organizations and Track the Progress of Their Employees

Companies like Anthem, Partners HealthCare, McDonald's, and Aetna have already done what the thousands of other companies who employ the 24 million frontline workers in the America should do: help their employees get a college degree while on the job, for little or no cost. In short, the employees need the up-skilling for economic mobility, and employers want up-skilled employees and are willing to pay for it. This should be a no-brainer. And now, because of employer-led, competency-based education, it can be.

Every employer with frontline workers and an existing tuition-assistance program should create a feeder relationship with a proven online, competency-based, degree-granting university like the College for America at SNHU.[33] They should work closely with the university to ensure that the competencies taught are the competencies that their company needs. And, as Anthem and Partners HealthCare did, they should promote the program broadly with staff, making it as easy as possible to use the existing tuition-assistance programs so the financial burden is minimized, and highlight the successes that employees, like Wright and Conley, have had advancing within the company as a result of their participation.

Effective use of tuition-assistance programs is critical to the success of this approach both for the employee and the company. Detra Wright's statement that the biggest draw to her participation was that tuition was being reimbursed at 100 percent speaks volumes. Many students won't even try to get a college degree because of the very real statistics that they hear about the suffocating debt associated with it. Knowing that the company will pay in advance or reimburse them for the tuition eliminates that fear.

A recent study showed that for every dollar companies spend on tuition assistance, they get $1 back in return and save another $1.29 through reduced employee turnover and lower recruiting costs, yet few companies maximize their efforts to help employees to use this benefit.[34] In 2016 the Institute for Corporate Productivity, in collaboration with the Aspen Institute's UpSkill America, surveyed 365 U.S.-based, nonprofit and for-profit businesses who employ large numbers of frontline workers, to explore what they were doing to develop these employees. The majority of the organizations surveyed employ frontline workers, with 52 percent employing more than 10,000 workers in total.[35] Though 89 percent of the companies surveyed offer tuition-assistance opportunities to frontline workers, almost three-quarters are not even tracking how many of their employees actually take advantage of them.[36] They should.

Employees Must Take Advantage of These Benefits

Ultimately, this approach won't be successful if employees don't take advantage of tuition-assistance programs. While more than 60 percent of employers offer some form of tuition assistance, on average, only 5 percent of employees participate in them.[37] Employee-participation rates will have to keep pace with the growth in feeder partnerships between companies and proven online, competency-based, degree-giving universities. Given the success and very little downside of this new approach, no employee should pass up the opportunity to have their employer pay for their college degree and a better economic future.

4

FIX THE EDUCATION SYSTEM, CRADLE TO CAREER

Nancy Zimpher is one of the most charismatic people you will ever meet. Upon first impression, you know that she is someone special: smart, funny, and impossible to ignore, often dressed in a colorful suit and striking stockings that set her apart from the crowd. Most people associate her with the nation's largest state university system, the State University of New York, of which she served until recently as chancellor. I associate her with the American Dream.

Why? Because she is leading a rapidly growing movement to rethink and reform traditional education systems at every point where they are failing students. For the past decade, Zimpher has been trailblazing a way to create lasting improvements in our nation's public education system so we are no longer forced to triage in high school (see chapter 1) or college (see chapter 2) just to ensure that those who make it that far succeed.

To understand the radical nature of her approach, we need to go back to 2001 in Cincinnati, Ohio. In April of that year, a fatal police shooting of an unarmed African American teenager triggered three days of rioting. It also triggered Zimpher, then president of the University of Cincinnati, and more than 300 other civic leaders to engage in some soul searching. The fate of that young man sparked a collective realization that they needed to chart a new course for Cincinnati's kids, especially those of color.

The leaders amassed a huge amount of data to help them better understand the problem. First, they identified the six key developmental milestones in a child's life, starting with readiness for kindergarten, all the way up to securing a well-paying job—often called the cradle-to-career continuum.[1] Then they charted the percentage of children who were actually performing at passing levels at each milestone. The data were disaggregated by race, income, and geography so the leaders could understand the impact of the current system on young people of color, poor and otherwise. Finally, the names of institutions that were responsible for delivering results at each milestone were overlaid on top.

What community leaders realized, in Zimpher's words, was that kids were "leaking out of the system at literally every milestone."[2] The system was not just failing at one point along the way, but in fact "every one of our institutions, from early child care to the university and the employers, was failing our kids."[3] This also led to the insight that "no one of us could solve the problem ourselves, so we had to figure out a way to commit to something bigger than our own institutions and to hold each other accountable."[4]

Thus the Strive Partnership was established, with Zimpher as its chair, to help these disparate institutions work together toward dramatically better results. Founding members of the new collaborative included executives from the very institutions, or their funders, that were expected to achieve those results. Alongside Zimpher were the presidents of Xavier University and Northern Kentucky University—which together made up the region's three largest teacher-training centers—and the superintendents of the Cincinnati, Ohio, and Covington and Newport, Kentucky, school districts. The partnership also included top executives from several of the area's major employers, such as Procter and Gamble and General Electric, and leadership from charitable foundations along with directors of civic groups, such as the United Way and Urban League.[5]

The partners agreed to pursue a common set of outcomes (based on those developmental milestones) and to regularly track and report out on fifty-three indicators that would tell them whether progress was being made across the milestones. Data, accountability, and transparency were deemed critical for success. Good, reliable data would enable them to assess current performance and identify inequalities in student achievement on each indicator. It would inform them of how to prioritize efforts, to determine whether the expected improvements were being realized fast enough, and if not, to change course.

Fundamentally, they understood that they were not going to get these results by starting yet another new individual program, project, or initiative that addressed one milestone or indicator alone. Instead, they were attacking the entire system. As the tragic death that catalyzed these efforts made undeniably clear, the lives of children were at stake in this work in every sense of the word. It was the Cincinnati town coroner, in fact, who perhaps articulated the general sentiment best: "We are program rich and system poor . . . and until we become system rich, we will not only continue to see low college-graduation rates, we will keep seeing youth who have lost their lives on my tables."[6]

The leaders also realized they needed to work together very differently. First, they had to "lead from the seat of their pants" by personally representing their institutions at monthly partnership meetings. This would enable them to understand the data and how they might need to change their own institution's behavior to get to shared results. Then they needed to actually change their own institution's behavior when the data suggested they should.

That may sound exceedingly simple or intuitive, yet Cincinnati's former approach to kindergarten readiness illustrates how rarely institutions operate that way. Many low-income children were attending preschools funded by local philanthropies such as the United Way, Community Foundation of Greater Cincinnati, and Procter and Gamble.[7] But local-level data revealed that many of these students were not arriving at kindergarten ready to learn. Each philanthropy was essentially providing financial support to its favorite preschools, but none of them were holding any of the schools accountable for sufficiently preparing kids for kindergarten.

But the Strive Partnership prescribed a new way of working. And remarkably, with this data in hand, the funders arrived at a common standard (and training regimen) for all preschools and agreed to fund only those schools that met that criteria and to stop funding preschools that underperformed. Results quickly improved.

The partners also agreed to issue a "community report card" that tracked the partnership's progress in moving the community-level outcomes.[8] The report card served as a public way for the leaders to hold themselves jointly accountable. By 2007, the end of the partnership's first four years, forty of the fifty-three indicators had been trending up year over year.[9]

The challenges that the Strive Partnership took on, up and down the cradle-to-career continuum, are not unique to Cincinnati. Substantially every jurisdiction in this country is failing kids almost every step of the way. Yet few of those places have adopted a coordinated, evidence-based approach that focuses on ensuring students' success. For example, nationally, 65 percent of fourth-graders are not proficient in reading.[10] When you disaggregate that data by race, it tells an even worse story: 82 percent of black children and 79 percent of Hispanic children are failing to read at that grade level.[11] The data are equally troubling further up the continuum. In 2015, 68 percent of eighth-graders nationally lacked math proficiency. That includes 88 percent of black and 81 percent of Hispanic students.[12]

I met Chancellor Zimpher in the summer of 2007 and learned of the Strive Partnership's success for the first time. Knowing that these disparities existed everywhere, my organization, Living Cities, and the Strive Partnership invited a dozen cities to apply for a modest grant and technical support to try to implement the Strive Partnership approach in their own backyards. We picked four places, not knowing whether this way of working would catch on. It has, and faster than we could have anticipated.

Today, sixty-nine cities in thirty-two states, impacting over 8 million students, have adopted this systematic approach and are active members of the StriveTogether Cradle to Career Network.[13] Jeff Edmondson who led the local Cincinnati Strive Partnership was hired to run the national network and served in that role until fall 2017.

Three things about the network make it unique and distinctly powerful. One is that not everybody can get in. To join, communities have to meet certain benchmarks and complete an assessment process that helps them (and the network) identify the strengths and weaknesses of their civic leadership. "If the local civic leaders and their institutions aren't really aligned toward these ambitious goals, they will make very little progress," says Edmondson.[14] The Robert Wood Johnson Foundation's Kristin Schubert, an early supporter of the network says, "It seems to me that systems are made of people. So if people [are committed to] change, the systems change."[15]

The second element is a commitment to using data to drive improvement and eliminate disparities. The network works with communities to equip them to regularly use data to "focus on results, not ideology around interventions," explains Edmondson.[16] If the data tell them that they are not on course to meet their goals, then they have to change course. "Imagine what would happen if we put as much effort into the analysis of data when deciding what to invest in for the success of children as we do when investing in our stock portfolios," says Edmondson.[17]

The third factor is that all sixty-nine communities have adopted the same six education outcome areas. In that way, each community is able to improve its own work based on lessons being learned by others across the country. The network captures and shares these lessons in real time. "The members of the network have been willing to 'fail forward' by sharing not only their successes but also their struggles, using the lessons they have learned to advance the field," says Edmondson.[18] The intentional sharing of results has enabled a leapfrogging effect wherein one community uses the learning from another to get results in a fraction of time. To Edmondson, "This approach has created an optimism that we can get results at a scale not seen before."[19]

Jeff Bradach, a cofounder of Bridgespan, a leading nonprofit consulting firm, calls the network "[a] scaling strategy that centers on the spread of a common process and principles—driven by local leaders. The program isn't replicated, but the process and principles are."[20] "In essence, we're working to define how to achieve the holy grail of systems change," Edmondson states. "There's no cookie-cutter approach that works for everyone, but rather a general framework that respects local context and helps communities face the challenges of moving outcomes at scale."[21]

The Commit Partnership in Dallas is an extraordinary example of how this process is working beyond Cincinnati.[22] Commit was started four and a half years ago by civic leaders who were fed up with the dismal results that they were seeing at every point from cradle to career.[23] The catalyst for the effort was Commit's executive director, Todd Williams, a recently retired executive from Goldman Sachs. Williams was driven by what he heard from local leaders, day in and day out: "People want to solve this problem. . . . It's in our fabric. The day we believe that the American Dream is truly dead is the day America is no longer America."[24]

The group's leadership team comprises the mayor of Dallas, the president of the regional chamber of commerce, presidents of local philanthropies, superintendents from the surrounding school districts, the chancellor of the university system, locally elected officials, community organizations, and key nonprofit organizations, to name just a few.[25] "The only reason that we are all around the same table is to get systemic change," Williams says. "We don't have time to scale individual reading programs, while of course that's part of it, but we need to show we can change the whole system. We can if we break it up into parts, measure it and deploy strategies that people buy into."[26]

Dallas County is not that different from many other counties in America.[27] Its demographics reflect not only why it is so important to fix the whole system but also why it will take an extended commitment from a diverse group of civic leaders to do so. Ninety-one percent of all students in Dallas County attend public school; 70 percent are economically disadvantaged.[28] Fifty-four percent of the students are Hispanic, 23 percent African American, and 17 percent white.[29] The outcomes that the county experiences are troubling at any given stage of students' academic careers. By fourth grade, only one in three students reads on a level on track for college.[30] Only 13 percent of students overall (closer to 4 percent for students of color) complete high school ready to succeed in college.[31] Fewer than 50 percent of higher education students actually graduate with a degree.[32]

Like many other jurisdictions, Dallas needs to build a deeper bench of community leaders reflective of the population who want to advocate for systems change from cradle to career. Members of the local leadership council (not unlike the network of Boards and Commissions Leadership Councils, described in chapter 11) created the Leadership ISD. Leadership ISD recruits and trains forty to fifty citizen leaders a year (now over

200 graduates) that represent all types of Dallasites: white residents and people of color, low-income individuals and multimillionaires alike.[33] "We are building a circle of influencers around the city and state who know how to use our data and scorecard, can direct funding streams and serve on local school boards," says Williams. "Having a great cradle-to-career approach without great governance is like having a heavy weight around your neck."[34]

As is true of the rest of the Strive Network, data drives their work. Annually, they issue a public scorecard designed so that anyone can quickly tell how Dallas County students are performing academically, all the way from kindergarten readiness through postsecondary completion (see table 4-1).

The local leadership looks at achievement gaps based on race, income, and English-language learner status to find out where more focused work needed to be done. Williams notes, "We can now look at triply disaggregated data so we can understand, for example, the number of African American males who are taking Algebra 1 in eighth grade by campus and who is doing a good job in this regard and who is not."[35]

Getting the best results from public funding streams is the group's priority. According to Williams, Dallas area philanthropy annually directs $35—$50 million to K–12 public schools, often to supplement the school day, but the public system itself spends $5 billion—up to 100 times that amount—every year.[36] "We are intently focused on helping to improve education outcomes from "8 a.m. to 3 p.m.," where most of the public dollars go, as well as between "3 p.m. to 6 p.m.," says Williams.[37]

Cincinnati, Dallas, and the other sixty-seven Strive Together communities are showing that there is a framework for implementing sustainable fixes to education at the systemic level, composed of data, leadership, and networks, from all the right places. This just needs to be adopted everywhere.

A NEW NORMAL: AN EDUCATION SYSTEM THAT WORKS FOR ALL

Well-intentioned people have been working on broken parts of the cradle-to-career continuum for decades, so it is important to understand what distinguishes this approach from other efforts and enables it to work. People

TABLE 4-1. Dallas County 2013 Community Achievement Scorecard

Percent of Dallas County Proficient	2012–13 Current year	2011–12 Last year	Since prior year	Movement against the state
Kindergarten readiness	49	52	▼3	n/a
3rd grade reading	35	35	n/c	▼1
4th grade math	29	27	▲2	▲1
8th grade science	32	29	▲3	n/c
Algebra I	30	33	▼3	n/c
Average 10th grade PSAT score (points)	116	115	▲1	n/a
Percent of graduates college ready	14	15	▼1	n/c
Four-year high school graduation rate	84	82	▲2	n/c
Percent of high school grads enrolling in postsecondary education (PSE)	61	62	▼1	n/a
Percent of high school grads returning to PSE after one year	50	51	▼1	n/a
Total two- and four-year degrees conferred	30,684	29,168	▲5	n/a

n/a = not applicable   n/c = no change | Benchmark   Increase ▲   Decrease ▼

Source: The Commit Partnership, "2013 Community Achievement Scorecard" (commit2dallas.org).

who want to make the solution set out in this chapter the new normal in their own community must focus on these three ingredients.

Data

Local-level data are currently available from more sources (both public and private), about more things (from classroom, school, and system-wide student performance to real-time skill needs of employers), and more frequently (often on demand) than ever before in history. In fact, the widespread availability of such robust data is a key reason that this solution is possible at all. But in effectively using data, there are three related obstacles that must be overcome.

One has to do with establishing an understanding of the starting point—the baseline—to set an informed goal for where one wants to go. Getting baseline data for fifty-three indicators, as Cincinnati has, requires gathering information from an enormous number of different government agencies and private, for-profit and nonprofit, institutions that do not share information with one another in the normal course of business. That is why the places with the most success have had executive-level intervention (for example, the mayor and CEO-level executives from the participating organizations) to make sure that the right data sets are made available.

The second obstacle involves understanding what the data mean. Those places most successfully practicing this approach have consistently solicited the help of a local institution, such as a university or research center—usually monthly—to help them accomplish this. Those institutions, often paid for by local philanthropists and government, will "clean" the data so different sets from diverse agencies and organizations can talk to one another. They are also adept at translating the data using formats such as charts and graphs that make it easy to interpret and present on an ongoing basis. This allows for the creation of tools like community report cards so that decisionmakers and the public can easily track progress toward the predetermined outcomes.

The third obstacle is actually using the data to make decisions and drive change. Having the data in hand and a solid understanding of its meaning is one thing. Accepting what it tells and forcing people and institutions to change their behaviors because they are not getting desired results is quite another. It is not unusual for institutions like the philanthropies in Cincinnati to see and understand what the data were telling them about their students' kindergarten readiness—or lack thereof. What is unusual is that they used that information to change and improve their own behaviors. Leaders from each of these independent organizations stopped funding preschools, each in its own way, and adopted a common approach.

Distributed Leadership

The bottom line is that many of today's challenges—such as preparing Americans to succeed in our globalized economy—are too interconnected and complex for any one organization or sector to address on its own. Unfortunately, all too often it takes a tragedy like the death of a young black boy in Cincinnati for local leaders to realize that they have to lead not only their own organization but their communities' change efforts as well. I call what it takes to achieve these larger outcomes, "distributed leadership."

Distributed leadership delivers two things essential to this solution: resources and continuity. Having the right leaders take ownership of the larger outcomes means that they can bring whatever resources—money, political influence, technical expertise—to the table when they are needed. Rip Rapson, the president and CEO of the Kresge Foundation,[38] one of the distributed leaders driving the revitalization of Detroit, thinks of it this way:

> The public, private, and philanthropic sectors work backward from the articulation of a challenge to determine who has the tools most suitable to playing what role, and in what proportion. [They] create a problem-smashing machinery that is sector-agnostic . . . that not only permits us to mix and match the unique qualities of each sector, but also enables a community to tackle a multiplicity of issues at once.[39]

While resources are important, continuity may be even more so because of the long-term nature of this work. Sites like Cincinnati and Dallas that are making great progress all along the continuum have done so by sticking with it, consistently achieving better results over time, year over year.

Distributed leadership has enabled them to do that because the efforts do not have to start over every time a particular leader leaves town. This is especially important given the average terms of many of the important actors at the table—from four years for mayors to three years for school superintendents and university presidents.

When Chancellor Zimpher left Cincinnati for New York and gave up her duties as chair of the Strive Partnership in 2009, the effort did not skip a beat. Other leaders had been leading "from the seat of their pants" and had been deeply engaged. The chair has changed twice more with no adverse effects.

Networks

Networks—people or organizations working together in an intentional way toward a common goal—are a force multiplier. That dynamic is true whether the network is made up of a group of individuals working together as a local leadership council to transform a system from cradle to career or a partnership of cities participating in Strive Together to collectively accelerate their work.

The local network is the glue that binds all of the disparate, distributed leaders together over the long term. It helps them not only to take a balcony view of the whole problem but also to understand the inherent limitations of their own individual organization's approach.[40] It ensures that the leadership council has the right data at the right time, which often involves drawing from and/or contributing to the broader Strive Together network.

Thus the national Strive Together network helps increase the circulation of promising practices to more places. It captures and synthesizes learning that is taking place across these multiple sites so that the next site can build on what has or has not worked already. It helps the sites work together, virtually and in person, in small groups and large to learn from, support, and counsel one another. The network has set an increasingly high bar for membership, requiring sites to adopt proven methodologies and principles if they want to participate.

Networks are not new, but the way in which they enable the viral growth of successful approaches like this is a new phenomenon. The most successful local sites and the continued growth of the national network are the result of individual philanthropists, government, and foundations funding the networking functions described in the paragraphs above. Unfortunately, that type of funding remains the exception, not the rule. Funders still default to looking for a new program that can be taped on to a broken system rather than a new process—the network—that promises to transform the entire system.

Part II

INCREASING INCOME THROUGH JOBS

Many people refer to America between the late 1940s and the early 1970s as the golden age of the middle class. Prosperity was broadly shared, with household incomes for almost all Americans increasing rapidly and roughly at the same rates over that period.[1] But from the 1980s onward, the incomes of the top 1 percent have soared while the incomes of the bottom 99 percent have stayed largely the same.

As has been widely reported, the 99 percent had been making up for this lack of income by taking out a whole lot of easily available, personal debt. By 2007, the beginning of the Great Recession, Americans had $1.35 in personal debt to every dollar in disposable income, up from a little more than $1.00 in 1980.[2] This was bad for the balance sheets of American families, but it fueled the economy overall as personal consumption constituted an ever-increasing share of our gross domestic product.[3] In 2007, the sudden unavailability of personal debt unmasked the fact that the vast majority of Americans could not sustain that level of consumption or quality of life.

A number of factors contributed to the decline in household incomes over this period, from globalization to weaker unions, but none more than this simple fact: the American economy lost its dynamism. Dynamic economies produce a steady stream of new companies that challenge old ways of doing business and create a ton of jobs in the process. Millions, to be a bit more precise. Historically, firms less than five years old have accounted for nearly all the net new jobs created in the country—more than 2 million a year.[4] These new companies have typically been forming faster than others failed. For decades, business "births" outnumbered business "deaths."

The data speak for themselves. The number of start-ups fell by nearly half between 1978 and 2011, as did the share of jobs that start-up companies contributed to the economy. This precipitous decline has occurred all across the country, not just in one region. The deficit in new firms significantly impacts the labor market, reducing both the quantity and quality of new jobs. One estimate has it that the economy would have produced almost one million additional jobs in 2014 alone had the start-up rate been as high as that of 2006.[5]

Places across the country, however, are working to provide entrepreneurs with the ingredients to begin to reverse the downward slope of start-up creation. Nonprofits, private investors, and city governments alike are taking steps to get money and support to businesses that are positioned to grow. They are harnessing local assets, such as university and hospital supply chains, and finding new ways of working together, such as organizing innovation districts so young companies can exponentially grow and hire more employees even faster.

5

SUPPORT PEOPLE WHO WILL START
AND GROW COMPANIES

Five minutes into a conversation with Lula Luu, it becomes very clear that this is a woman with the spirit and grit of an entrepreneur. Luu, who has a doctorate in nutritional science, was in New Orleans conducting research on minority health disparities in rural communities when the Gulf of Mexico oil spill hit in 2010, ravaging the Louisiana coastline and devastating the local economy.

As huge numbers of shrimpers and fishermen lost their livelihoods, Luu began to consider the economic potential of a childhood staple: the Asian carp. In a moment that would set her business on its future course, Luu wondered whether this freshwater fish could be processed into *surimi*, a fish paste that is a common element in Asian cuisine—almost as ubiquitous as ketchup in Asian American households, explains Luu.[1] The problem? Demand for inland fish, like the Asian carp, was almost nonexistent—carp is, in fact, often stigmatized as being a dirty fish. The local fishing industry was skeptical that this new approach would be worth their while.

Soon, Luu and her fellow academic and business partner, John Crilly, were earnestly exploring ways to process this fish, in hopes of proving to local fishermen that Asian carp was a viable and marketable alternative to shrimp and other marine life. In the months that followed, Luu and Crilly would spend their days fulfilling their academic responsibilities and their nights driving to the outskirts of the city for a self-taught crash course in fish processing.

After eight months of experimentation, Luu and Crilly had run through practically all of their savings. But they had developed an entirely new process of pulverizing and organically preparing surimi and had created a product that Luu was proud of. When she went to solicit feedback from her initially skeptical mother, she knew she had landed on something big. "'You've got it,' was all she said. I had impressed my mother, which was a lifetime goal of mine," Luu adds with a laugh. "So I got to check that off the bucket list too."[2]

Luu had a product, but she did not yet have a business. And she might never have, if not for a serendipitous moment at a business event for people of color in Chicago. Luu had flown up in hopes of learning about the nitty-gritty of running a company and making some connections that would help her get FIn Gourmet off the ground. Although she was disappointed with the lack of technical support offered in the program, she met a journalist there whose sister-in-law was a food broker for local wholesale Asian American markets. With nothing to lose, Luu offered the woman all of her samples and returned home.

Two months later, her phone rang. "She said she had never had a surimi product like that—so high-quality—in her life. She immediately ordered 300 pounds. It almost killed the company. I still don't know how we did it."[3] And when the 300 pounds had been sent off and sold (in just one week), the next order came in: a pallet of surimi. "I didn't even know what that meant," admits Luu.[4] It meant 1,700 pounds, she quickly discovered.

Luu and Crilly were still producing surimi just like Luu's grandmother had—in the kitchen, scraping meat off the bone of each fish by hand. But it became clear that that process was not going to work at scale. With both Luu and Crilly still employed at their universities, they needed help. Around that time, Luu received a call from a workforce developer who was trying to help a woman returning home from prison and struggling to find work. They hoped that Luu might know someone within the Vietnamese community who was looking to make a hire. Instead, Luu brought her on as FIn's first full-time employee.

This first hire sparked the company's ongoing commitment to supporting individuals in need of second chances and opened Luu's eyes to the impact that her company could have. "If you're talking about empowering your community," she explains, "you start with your staff person—the one who lives and breathes in that community."[5]

It was also this commitment that won FIn its first investor. One of their earliest customers from Chicago, he believed in Luu's approach of supporting women in need of a second chance. With his support, the team was able to purchase a machine that would separate fish from bone and allow them to dramatically scale up operations. Friends and relatives helped the team move out of the kitchen and rent a warehouse space that they could use as a food-processing facility. By the end of 2012, the company was bringing in about $100,000 in revenue and had grown to a staff of six women.

From the beginning, accessing capital and getting the technical support needed to build and grow her business has been an uphill battle for Luu. "Not a lot of doors open to minority- and woman-owned businesses, particularly in a rural area," she says. "In New Orleans, every bank we went to just didn't take me seriously. They'd look at me, and I knew what they were thinking: What does she know about running a business, let alone a fish business?"[6] One of the most valuable breaks for FIn Gourmet was connecting with Ross Baird and Village Capital. The nonprofit is one of many entities that have cropped up across the country that are dedicated to helping early-stage entrepreneurs overcome the hurdles of starting a business.

Village Capital was founded with the explicit goal of combating the biases that frustrate the growth potential of so many start-ups like FIn Gourmet. In particular, Baird observed that investors, such as venture capitalists, often cannot recognize future high-growth businesses because they do not understand the problem that those companies are solving in the marketplace, such as demand for a new surimi product by millions of Asian American customers, or can't picture a founder of color in charge of such a venture. "Entrepreneurs need investment capital and strategic partnerships to grow," Baird says, "but decisionmakers at firms often invest in and partner with the people they know and understand—whether or not they have the best ideas. If you don't look like the decisionmakers, didn't go to school with them, and don't share the same background, it's really hard."[7]

Village Capital's rigorous three-month training program provided Luu with a crash course in business—everything from building a solid, long-term financial plan to simply reading a financial balance sheet. It offered her a host of opportunities to build relationships with potential mentors, investors, and customers. It exposed Luu to a world of investors interested in supporting companies that seek social and environmental benefits. "It's very comforting to know that there's a movement of people wanting to know that behind every dollar that they invest, there's impact happening. It's helped businesses like ours find our niche," says Luu.[8]

She secured capital for FIn Gourmet through the process, as well. Village Capital helps to overcome the biases that Baird has seen in the capital marketplace, in part, by giving the entrepreneurs who are participating in the Village Capital program the power to award investment capital to the two most promising ventures within their peer group, based purely on merit. FIn Gourmet excelled throughout the process and ended up as one of the two peer-selected winning ventures.

Luu developed a product that was unique. Yet the challenges that she faced in securing sufficient capital at each stage of her business and the support and expertise she needed to grow were not. These are the steep barriers that all early-stage entrepreneurs must overcome today; for lower-wealth and lower-income Americans, especially those of color like Luu, the obstacles are even greater. Faced with these daunting challenges, it is not surprising that Americans are creating fewer start-ups and a lot fewer good, living-wage jobs.

That was not always the case. Young companies historically have played a pivotal role in our economy as the most effective engines of job creation. Over much of the past thirty years, firms less than five years old accounted for essentially all of the net new jobs created in the country—more than 2 million a year.[9] These new companies were forming faster than others failed. Over most of those three decades, business "births" outnumbered business "deaths."

A quick scan of the data reveals the extent to which that has changed. The number of start-ups fell by nearly half between 1978 and 2011.[10] This precipitous decline has occurred all across the country, not just in one region. A Brookings study analyzing business dynamism by geography determined that start-up rates were lower between 2009 and 2011 than they had been between 1978 and 1980 in every state and metropolitan statistical area except one.[11] In 2008 the United States reached a milestone that we had been approaching for years: business "deaths" exceeded business "births" for the first time in thirty years.[12]

As if that was not enough, the start-ups that are surviving are creating fewer jobs. In 1982, 75 percent of all five-year-old firms had fewer than ten employees, and 12 percent had twenty or more employees.[13] By 2010, firms were starting smaller and hiring more slowly than in the past.[14]

There are many hypotheses about the causes behind this change, but one thing seems incontrovertible: our pivot from the "real economy" made it much harder for entrepreneurs to get capital to innovate. The "real economy" is defined as that "part of the economy that is concerned with actually producing goods and services," as opposed to the "financial economy," which is that part of the economy that is concerned with buying and selling on the financial markets.[15]

The traditional role of finance within the larger economy has been to take the savings of households and turn it into investment.[16] But instead of supplying necessary capital to entrepreneurs to fuel innovation and long-term growth, most of today's investment capital is being used to finance existing assets for short-term payoff.[17] As these activities have grown, the amount of money available for new investment in real-economy businesses has shrunk.

Rana Foroohar, columnist and associate editor at the *Financial Times*, wrote extensively about this shift in her 2016 book, *Makers and Takers*. She argues that "rather than funding the new ideas and projects that create jobs and raise wages, finance has shifted its attention to securitizing existing assets (like homes, stocks, bonds, and such), turning them into tradable products."[18] According to Rework America, an initiative led by Markle Foundation president Zoe Baird and former Starbucks CEO Howard Schultz, whether "it is a local restaurant, a corner coffee shop, or a manufacturer that employs 200 employees, most small businesses . . . are experiencing a significant shortage of capital. More than 35 percent of them name access to financing and credit as a major impediment to growth."[19]

The evidence is borne out on the balance sheets of the institutions that we need to be doing this type of lending. In 1995 small business loans made up 51 percent of loan value on bank balance sheets.[20] According to Rework America, "In the boom years in America after 1945, private capital accumulated rapidly. Back then, if people and firms had capital to invest, loans to businesses were a dominant form of credit."[21] By 2013, that same proportion had fallen to just 29 percent.[22] Rework America cited the most comprehensive study to date on this shift, which concluded that

> to a large extent the core business model of banks in the advanced economies today resembles that of real estate funds: banks are borrowing (short) from the public and capital markets to invest (long) into assets linked to real estate. . . . The intermediation of household savings for productive investment in the business sector—the standard textbook role of the financial sector—constitutes only a minor share of the business of banking today, even though it was a central part of that business in the 19th and early 20th centuries.[23]

But there is another dynamic that is compounding this problem and that makes enacting a solution even more important to the long-term health of the U.S. economy: demography. As people of color like Luu become the nation's majority population, it is increasingly imperative that we understand and address the barriers that historically have kept them from succeeding at the same rates as white entrepreneurs.[24]

In many ways, our demography is our destiny. The population of white Americans has shrunk by almost 20 percent over the past forty years, and as a result, so have the number of white entrepreneurs. Twenty years ago, white entrepreneurs were responsible for 77 percent of all start-ups; by 2015, that figure had fallen to 60 percent, resulting in 150,000 fewer white-led firms in 2015 than in 1995. At approximately six new jobs created per startup, that is one million fewer jobs.[25]

Over this same period, start-ups launched by black entrepreneurs rose from 8.4 percent to 9.2 percent of the total; Latino start-ups jumped from 10 to 22 percent and Asian start-ups grew from 3.6 to 6.8 percent. However, these increases only amounted to 15,000 more new businesses being launched by people of color in 2015 than in 1995 or 90,000 new jobs.[26] Persistent barriers, described below, in the systems that support entrepreneurs in starting and growing their businesses must be overcome so we can enjoy exponential growth in the number of successful businesses started by people of color and lower-income Americans more broadly.

We simply must ensure that our growing populations—blacks, Latinos, and Asians—are equipped to launch and grow start-ups at rates that will sustain the economic dynamism we enjoyed in the past.[27]

In fact, if rates of entrepreneurship among communities of color matched their proportion of the overall population, those businesses created could add 9 million jobs and $300 billion in income to the national economy.[28] People like Lula must be able to successfully build real-economy businesses that create jobs.

Three key factors account for the significant racial disparities in successful entrepreneurship that we see today. Lack of sufficient capital at the earliest stages of a company's inception is one. Two simple facts, taken together, help illustrate this clearly. First, firms that have at least $100,000 in start-up capital are 23 percent less likely to fail than firms with $5,000 or less in start-up capital.[29] Second, most firms started by entrepreneurs of color start with $5,000 or less.[30]

The massive wealth gap between whites and people of color, described in detail in chapter 7, is the primary reason for this difference. The median wealth of white households is almost twenty times than of black and Hispanic households.[31] When you consider that more than two-thirds of entrepreneurs rely on personal and family financial resources (friends and family) during the start-up phase, it becomes apparent why entrepreneurs of color systematically face challenges in accessing the capital necessary to start their firms.[32]

Another crucial factor is the limited availability of credit. Access to credit is essential for enabling small businesses to grow and, most important, create jobs. In fact, businesses that get credit are 300 percent more likely to create jobs.[33] However, studies reveal that firms owned by people of color face greater difficulties in accessing loans from financial institutions. That includes having loan applications rejected at higher rates, receiving smaller loans, and experiencing higher borrowing costs.[34]

After controlling for education, credit score, experience, number of owners, and firm age, firms owned by people of color on average received loan amounts 35 percent lower than those offered to white-owned firms.[35] The denial rate for woman-owned firms—white and of color—is twice that of firms owned by white men, according to the 2003 Survey of Small Business Finances.[36]

A third reason has to do with who makes the funding decisions. Data show that women and people of color have been all but shut out of credit and investment decisionmaking positions. Although people of color make up more than 30 percent of the population today and women more than 50 percent of the population, they are rarely the ones determining who receives funding or loans. Recent data also show that on average, senior investment teams of leading venture funds have staff made up of only 1 percent black or Hispanic individuals and only 8 percent women.[37]

The potential impacts on the American economy of these capital gaps are enormous. According to research commissioned by the Minority Business Development Administration, if firms owned by people of color had received credit at rates proportional to their representation in the adult population, they would have employed 11.4 million more workers and would have had payrolls $2.39 trillion larger.[38]

While these obstacles to firm creation and job growth are real and widespread, so too are the efforts to bridge these gaps that are spurring the success of businesses like Luu's FIn Gourmet. All over the country, individuals working on their own and within philanthropy, government, or the private sector are stepping up to meet the capital needs of lower-wealth entrepreneurs, especially those of color, at every stage of their businesses' development. They are assisting young, promising firms in getting the technical support needed to grow and are working to get diverse candidates into fund management and other decisionmaking roles to ensure that racial and gender disparities are not perpetuated into the future.

Take Steve Case, for example. Case was one of the original founders of America Online (AOL), a pioneer in getting Americans on to the Internet. He and a small number of partners began touring U.S. cities in 2014 in search of promising local start-ups and have since invested $2 million of their own money in businesses across nineteen cities.[39] What has motivated him, Case says, is the reality that "most of the attention and most of the capital still finds its way to places like Silicon Valley and Boston and New York City. "But there are great companies and thriving start-up communities being built all across the country."[40] He calls his tour the Rise of the Rest, the rest being everyone *but* Silicon Valley, Boston, and New York.[41] He and his team are pouring capital into real-economy companies like Synek, a homemade beer-tap system, and Fameri, an interchangeable eyeglass-lens manufacturer.

Mitch Kapor founded Lotus Software in 1982 and was instrumental in developing what became the world's leading spreadsheet software, Lotus 1-2-3. Today, Kapor Capital, owned by Mitch and his wife, Freada, have invested in 100 information technology–driven start-ups that bring about positive social impact by "drawing on the lived experiences of their diverse founders."[42] Within their portfolio are companies like Pigeon.ly, founded by formerly incarcerated African American men, which is radically reducing the cost of phone calls between those in prison and their families.[43] In August 2015, the Kapors announced that they will spend $40 million over three years to support companies founded by women and racial minorities.[44]

Case, Kapor, and many other individuals, companies, and foundations are working to institutionalize these new ways of doing business. They are intentionally investing in funds and supporting organizations like Village Capital—the nonprofit that helped Luu succeed—so Americans can drive economic growth in the United States regardless of who they are or where they live.[45] The Impact America Fund, for example, is representative of the type of national funds that are currently growing in number and size that are often run by people of color and/or dedicated to investing in a substantial number of firms led by people of color and other lower-income and lower-wealth Americans.[46] An early-stage private equity firm, the fund has received investment dollars from an A-list of actors, such as Prudential, the Omidyar Network, and Surdna Foundation.[47]

The Impact America Fund is the second venture of this type started by Kesha Cash, one of Forbes's top-five "gamechangers" and an African American entrepreneur herself. Cash previously cofounded an initiative focused on mission-driven entrepreneurs of color called Jalia Ventures. There, she deployed $5 million and built a demonstration portfolio of ten companies.[48] Now, with Cash's leadership, the fund invests between $250,000 and $2 million at a time in high-growth companies often led by people of color generating real financial returns and quality jobs, while at the same time improving the well-being of underserved communities.

In addition to funds with portfolios at the national scale, initiatives like the Propeller–Foundation for Louisiana Fund and the BuildNOLA Mobilization Fund are representative of the types of financial vehicles being created to address an array of capital gaps at the local level. Propeller, a nonprofit business incubator in New Orleans, and the Foundation for Louisiana have raised $5 million from local and national investors to address funding challenges faced by women and entrepreneurs of color starting and growing companies in New Orleans.[49]

The BuildNOLA Mobilization Fund is specifically designed to solve a problem that often keeps small businesses from even bidding on government contracts, much less winning them: cash flow. The fund provides cash-flow loans to successful bidders, allowing them to meet payroll or cover other day-to-day expenses while waiting for payments on government contracts, which often can take weeks or even months. The Build-NOLA Fund was formed in anticipation of $2.4 billion in projected city spending on infrastructure over the next eight years.[50]

And of course, there are a growing number of organizations like Village Capital, acting nationally and in local communities, to provide an array of supports to young businesses beyond just funding. Village Capital's powerful recipe for success includes connecting enterprises with a cohort of peer entrepreneurs, a network of leading industry-specific mentors and investors, and the technical know-how necessary for running a business.[51]

Since 2009, Village Capital's program has supported over 600 companies. They have also provided seed capital to sixty of those companies through an affiliated investment vehicle. Village Capital is specifically committed to supporting businesses with a triple bottom line of positive social, environmental, and financial impact. "We are supporting companies in two major problem-solving areas: access to opportunity for underserved communities (through health, education, and financial inclusion) and resource sustainability of the planet (through energy and agriculture ventures)," says Ross Baird.[52]

Like Case and Kapor, who are among Village Capital's twenty-seven investors, Village Capital looks for companies everywhere in the country, especially outside of California, Boston, and New York. The peer-selection model that they use to determine winning ventures, not unlike the one used for microlending, has not only resulted in more support for companies led by women and people of color but has also helped hone more successful companies.[53]

"Our goal is to democratize the entire process of starting and scaling a successful, purposeful enterprise," says Baird. "What we've learned is that when we invest in a historically underinvested person, they over-perform."[54] Encouraged by the growing energy around local entrepreneurship efforts across the country, Village Capital has set its sights on supporting fifty communities over the next three years.[55]

FIn Gourmet is proof of the transformative impact that capital and technical support can have. Today, FIn Gourmet's operations are based in Kentucky, nearby to where their fish are harvested. The company has maintained its commitment to benefiting the local environment and community. Now, FIn Gourmet employs fourteen people, 80 percent of whom are recovering from drug addiction, returning from prison, or otherwise in need of a second chance.[56] The potential economic ripple effects of growing businesses by entrepreneurs like Luu are enormous. And it demonstrates what can be gained by spreading and scaling efforts to break down the undue roadblocks and allow every entrepreneur with a promising idea a shot at success.

A NEW NORMAL: SUPPORTING THE SUCCESS OF ENTREPRENEURS EVERYWHERE

Three ingredients are necessary for creating a new normal that supports the success of entrepreneurs, especially those of color, in communities nationwide.

Capital

Getting capital to entrepreneurs at all stages of the business-development cycle is paramount. That is why intentionality really matters. Our progress to date has been a direct result of individuals, private and public sector institutions, and philanthropists earmarking their investments (and grant making) to fill these gaps. But more people and institutions need to start or join these efforts to achieve the scale needed for future economic growth.

Individual people, for example, are investing their own money in initiatives like Kiva Zip because those organizations are explicitly working to fill the "friends and family gap" that lower-income and lower-wealth entrepreneurs experience in early stages.[57] Still others are lending money to loan funds, like the Propeller–Foundation for Louisiana Fund, that were formed to give credit where credit is due.

Finally, investors like Steve Case and Mitch Kapor are filling equity gaps left by traditional venture capital. They are investing directly as angel investors early on or through funds founded by people of color, like the Impact America Fund, where investment decisions are made by people of color and capital is dedicated to later stage growth of companies.[58] In December of 2017, Case announced the culmination of his "Rise of the Rest" cross-country speaking tour and pitch competitions: a new fund that may represent, as the *New York Times* aptly put it, "the greatest concentration of American wealth and power in one investment fund." The fund will seek to build an ecosystem like that of Silicon Valley, that will connect potential entrepreneurs in the heartland, outside of coastal hubs, with not only venture capital but also other supports like networking and relationship-building that could be transformative for nascent start-ups.[59]

The other form of intentionality necessary to solve these problems, which is fundamental to the design of the Rise of the Rest Fund, relates to geography. This focus on spreading the wealth beyond traditional hubs like New York and San Francisco is also exemplified by the two New Orleans—based funds described above. Places that are most successfully bridging funding gaps for local entrepreneurs are those that have their own investment vehicles. Often these vehicles are created by local government, a community foundation, nonprofit organization, or community development financial institution or simply a group of local, successful entrepreneurs.[60]

The sponsors of these new vehicles often put their own money in first to attract other investors who have current or former ties to the local community.[61] As evidenced by New Orleans, successful efforts often leverage local resources alongside national funds dedicated to achieving similar results.

Know-How and Networks

Securing capital was not Lula Luu's only obstacle to success. She also faced a formidable knowledge gap that Village Capital helped her to overcome. Many entrepreneurs from "humble means," as many of them often describe themselves, simply do not have the social networks that can address this shortcoming. We are having success as a nation at building and growing real-economy businesses because we are addressing the knowledge-networks and the capital gap at the same time.

Know-how and network strategies have been, and should continue to be, deployed at both national and local levels. Nationwide efforts, like Village Capital, matter because truly high-growth companies do not limit their operations or customers to a single jurisdiction.[62] In fact, what they need to grow are new connections to wider markets and complementary actors all over the globe. They often also need help with nuts-and-bolts business issues, such as talent recruitment, accounting, and law.

These are the types of supports that groups like Village Capital and Endeavor provide. They also can be found in a growing number of incubator-like organizations, such as Tumml and 1776, who convene entrepreneurs in a specific place but seek to help them access relevant networks and customers across the country.[63]

Local know-how and network efforts serve a different but complementary function. They identify future entrepreneurs, connect them with one another, and make it easier for them to start up companies in their own backyards. New Orleans's Propeller is one such initiative. In the most successful places, university leaders, local elected officials, local philanthropy, and successful entrepreneurs use their political, financial, and reputational capital to strengthen the local entrepreneurial ecosystem. The ecosystem builds bridges "between start-ups, established companies, universities, and research institutions, . . . [and] helps ideas flow and people start new ventures, join existing ones, and link innovations together."[64] More and more frequently, local leaders are creating a local organization like Propeller or importing an entity like Endeavor[65] to be a part of their ecosystem.

It is important to recognize that know-how and network activities, nationally and locally, are reliant on grants. They do not generate interest or equity returns like capital investments. While this type of support is as important as capital to many entrepreneurs, as it was to Lula Luu, availability of grants from traditional individual, corporate, or foundation sources has limited the growth of these activities.[66]

Championing

Too many Americans take job creation for granted. Decades of prosperity following World War II seem to have lulled us into the belief that firm creation and economic growth is inevitable. But thirty years of data prove that it is not. Our recent success can be credited, in no small part, to champions like Steve Case and his Rise of the Rest tour, or local mayors like New Orleans's former mayor Mitch Landrieu, who are raising the alarm about this trend, actively supporting entrepreneurship and calling us to action.

Similarly, discussions about the unique barriers that entrepreneurs of color face, while admittedly difficult, are critical to our economic future. It is not always politically palatable to suggest that we must make special efforts targeted at enabling the success of one population specifically. That is why vocal statements and visible investments by mainstream investors and successful businesspeople, like Mitch and Freada Kapor, are so important. Their $40 million, three-year commitment to support companies founded by women and racial minorities speaks volumes and reduces the risk for other high-net-worth individuals and institutions to follow suit.

6

USE ALL THE ASSETS OF PLACE

Eight years ago, when I first met Derek Douglas, he was spending his days in Washington, D.C., grappling with metropolitan and urban issues at the national level, shaping policy that would impact cities across the country from his office at 1600 Pennsylvania Avenue. Today Douglas is at the University of Chicago and one of the best examples in the country of the power of thinking and acting locally.

Back then, Douglas had just been appointed special assistant to President Obama on urban policy. I liked him immediately. There was a certain problem-solving pragmatism about him. Douglas did not seem all that "Washington" to me, though he was trained as a lawyer and had worked at both the NAACP Legal Defense and Educational Fund and the high-profile Washington think tank, the Center for American Progress.

Even so, I have to admit that I was a little surprised when, two years later, he told me he was leaving the White House to become the head of the University of Chicago's Office of Civic Engagement. While Douglas had embraced the chance to create positive social impact through high-level policy work during his time in the White House, "oftentimes," he explained to me, "it just wasn't at a tangible, concrete level."[1]

Then just four years old, the Office of Civic Engagement was charged by the university president to leverage the institution's unique role and substantial resources to positively impact the surrounding community. The neighborhoods in close proximity to the campus, Woodlawn, Englewood, and Park Manor, have poverty rates above 60 percent and high unemployment, particularly among young black men.[2] Impacting these communities right where the university is situated, is certainly "concrete."

"When I came here five years ago," explained Douglas when we last spoke, "we had just a few parts of the university focused on urban issues. Today, it's becoming one of the main priorities of the president."[3] That commitment is reflected in the abundance of programs and initiatives that have flourished under Douglas's leadership. There's the Civic Leadership Academy, which helps nonprofit and public sector leaders with skills development. There's IMPACT, a partnership with the Chicago Urban League to provide leadership development for African American leaders in the private, nonprofit, and public sectors. And there's the Community Programs Accelerator, which aims to support the success of nonprofits serving neighboring communities. At the heart of all of these efforts, the university has increasingly embraced its role as an important economic player in the local community.

"If you're fighting lack of opportunity, you can't leave anything on the field," Douglas says. "You have to use every resource and tool in the arsenal."[4] And perhaps the most powerful tool in the university's arsenal is one that had been largely underutilized until Douglas came aboard: the university's extensive processes of hiring and purchasing. In fact, the university is both the largest employer on the South Side of Chicago, and a major purchaser of goods and services.[5]

Early in his tenure, he pitched the university president a new idea. While the university and medical center together spent hundreds of millions of dollars a year to buy everything from hand soap to high-tech computer software, they never had any conversations about where that money actually landed or who was benefiting from it. What if, Douglas proposed, instead of buying from some company in New York, California, or who knows where, they intentionally directed just some of those millions to businesses in their own backyard, Chicago's South Side? As Douglas explained, "We're going to spend that money anyway, we're still getting the products and services, but now we're investing in the community. We're creating more economic vitality, and people are getting jobs."[6] In a phrase, "it's a no-brainer."

Thus the UChicago Local program was established with a multipronged approach: to leverage the university's procurement process to support local businesses; to focus on efforts to hire locally; to attract other companies to set up their businesses on the South Side; and to work with entrepreneurs to launch new businesses that can serve the university.[7] It is a brilliant recipe for improving local economic vitality. For one thing, a procurement contract with a large institution like the University of Chicago provides the exact type of stable revenue stream crucial for increasing companies' capacity to scale up and bring on more employees. "By getting us as a client, they're getting on a sustainable growth path that will enable them to take on other clients across the city or the country," says Douglas.[8] This suite of new strategies resulted in over $2 million more hyper-local spending by the university and its medical center.[9] With the program up and running, 35 percent of food and goods supplied to these institutions are being sourced from vendors in the South Side of Chicago.[10]

At first, the University of Chicago was operating in isolation. That changed when Douglas participated in a committee meeting of World Business Chicago, a public-private partnership focused on supporting business and economic growth in Chicago. Committee participants were challenged to think about ways that economic opportunities could be directed to the most vulnerable neighborhoods in the city. Douglas mentioned his UChicago Local program. The committee members' response in support was immediate and enthusiastic.

Suddenly, Northwestern, the University of Illinois-Chicago, and Rush Medical Center were on board. Then came the local museums. And then the city's major businesses, like Advocate Health Care, BMO Harris Bank, and ComEd. Ultimately, the city of Chicago and surrounding Cook County joined as well. The purchasing power of the University of Chicago—already substantial on its own—was now magnified by the power of fifteen.

The network of organizations was dubbed the Chicago Anchors for a Strong Economy, or CASE. The network supports these local institutions in more intentionally using all of their assets, especially the money they spend on buying goods and services, to help grow local businesses and create more jobs for Chicagoans. A dedicated staff at CASE plays match-maker, connecting institutions with the right local businesses to meet their needs. They also help participating small businesses navigate the procurement processes of larger institutions and provide advisory and workforce development services out of the University of Chicago.

Derek Douglas's assessment that when it comes to creating economic opportunity, no tool should be left in the arsenal does not mean focusing only on local procurement channels. Though it may sound counterintuitive in an age when globalization and the rise of technology have radically transformed our sense of time and space, better harnessing all the local actors in a regional economic ecosystem and even the unique attributes of the land itself is proving to be an incredibly effective way to drive business growth and job creation. When it comes to creating jobs and increasing business dynamism there is a powerful approach that is all too often overlooked: taking advantage of all of the assets that exist in a place.

This runs counter to the urban myth that a local economy can only grow and create jobs by attracting already existing businesses from other jurisdictions. On the contrary, a recent study showed that recruiting companies, even providing them tax incentives to relocate, does not actually have the desired effect of job creation.[11] Furthermore, the International City/County Management Association reviewed existing literature on the overall effectiveness of using these types of costly financial incentives and came to three conclusions: with few exceptions, incentives do not effectively influence the location decisions of firms; transportation, workforce quality, and the strength of local markets are what really drive businesses' decisionmaking and overall growth; and the best way for government to influence firm location is to create and sustain quality communities.[12]

In fact, analysis of job creation patterns in California over an extended period of time, from 1992 to 2006, found that the overwhelming majority of state job growth came from the birth of new firms or the expansion of existing ones, not from firms moving to the state.[13] Data increasingly shows the importance and power of leveraging your existing assets to the fullest extent possible—keeping place in the forefront as a tool for change.[14]

Clearly, the focus on anchor institutions—universities, hospitals, corporate headquarters, cultural centers, and other organizations—that are deeply rooted and highly invested in their geographic locations is the most obvious of these place-based approaches. It takes no stretch of the imagination to understand why anchor institutions are often motivated, beyond sheer altruism, to invest in their surrounding neighborhoods. Maintaining their success and prestige requires that they compete with peers across the country to attract the best students, patients, professors, doctors, researchers, and other personnel. In particular, for the many anchor institutions across the country located in urban centers, what goes on beyond their gates simply cannot be ignored. Much like the University of Chicago in the city's South Side, Johns Hopkins, the prominent university and hospital system, is situated in an area of East Baltimore that in the early 2000s was plagued with high rates of violent crime, a startlingly high poverty rate, and a nearly 70 percent vacancy rate.[15] None of which looks great on a brochure.

For all these reasons, anchor institutions, including Johns Hopkins, the University of Chicago, other CASE participants, and many others, are increasingly recognizing the varied roles they should play in supporting economic dynamism in their own backyards. They are more than just educators or health care providers. They are employers—oftentimes the single largest in the region. Universities and hospitals alone employ 8 percent of the national workforce; rates are even higher in places like Baltimore, where anchors account for 20 percent of jobs.[16]

The University of Pennsylvania, Philadelphia's largest private employer, has some 37,000 people on its direct payroll, with an additional 53,000 individuals employed through a range of contracts, including construction and professional services.[17] An estimated two-thirds of hospital jobs and one-third of jobs at colleges and universities do not require a bachelor's degree, which opens doors for low- and middle-skilled workers.[18]

Furthermore, these establishments are customers. A single institution, like the University of Chicago, can easily rack up procurement bills of hundreds of millions of dollars. Altogether, universities' procurement constitutes about 3 percent of U.S. GDP.[19] In other words, whether they wield it intentionally or not, anchor institutions carry massive influence within their local economies and can drive business growth and development, employment outcomes, and more.

The opportunity is huge. Like the University of Chicago, approximately one in eight colleges and universities across the country—altogether around 925 institutions—and one in fifteen of the nation's largest hospitals are based in an inner city.[20] Inner-city economies by and large have struggled in recent decades; one analysis from the research and advisory group Initiative for a Competitive Inner City found that, though they make up just 10 percent of the population, inner cities account for 23 percent of U.S. poverty and 15 percent of U.S. unemployment.[21] There is no reason local supply should not pair with local demand.

Many institutions across the country have taken the approach that Derek Douglas introduced at the University of Chicago: harnessing the power of procurement. It is a potent mechanism for building the capacity of local businesses and spurring job creation, but it does require some intentionality. At the University of Pennsylvania, local procurement efforts date back to the 1980s, but initial attempts to execute the plan were fraught. The university put out a blanket call for local suppliers, but most of the businesses that responded had to be turned away because they didn't actually offer goods and services that the institution needed. The frustration and disillusionment incited by this botched attempt did nothing to improve a troubled relationship that had existed between the university and the surrounding community for decades.

This initial, ill-fated effort points to some of the common barriers that pose a challenge to local businesses hoping to partner with larger institutions. Put another way, there are reasons why this hasn't always been status quo. For one thing, local businesses may operate at too small a scale to take on massive, institution-wide contracts or be too cash strapped to service a contract that doesn't offer a paycheck until months into the project. Local entrepreneurs often lack vital business expertise—around marketing, accounting, or responding to requests for proposals—which limits their ability to attract the attention of a big institution.

Such barriers can keep local businesses out of the running when they are pitted up against large-scale corporations during traditional procurement processes. Yet when institutions have recognized these specific hurdles, they have had great success at tweaking procurement systems to level the playing field for local businesses. The University Hospital system in Cleveland frequently breaks up its contracts into smaller components to enable more bidders of various sizes to compete. Henry Ford Health System in Detroit began paying some vendors in advance so smaller local businesses could have the liquidity needed to compete and succeed.[22]

Today, the University of Pennsylvania is a national leader in leveraging procurement channels to support local businesses. When the University revisited its buy-local efforts in 2004, it was with the intention of making it a more comprehensive, institution-wide initiative. Each purchasing department set goals for procurement from local, women- and firms owned by people of color, which were then incorporated into annual performance reviews. Managers who were able to successfully steer the institution toward meeting those objectives were rewarded. They also partnered with the Pennsylvania Minority Business Center to field a more diverse pool of potential local suppliers; often, the university and smaller businesses simply do not have clear pathways to forge those connections.

Managers knew that meeting their ambitious targets would require them to foster the growth and development of local businesses that were not yet fully equipped to be university vendors. So the university began to partner closely with the Enterprise Center—a local organization established through the Wharton Small Business Development Center—which provides access to capital and business education to local entrepreneurs of color and then connects promising businesses with the university and other local buyers.[23] Through these strategies, the University of Pennsylvania has been able to increase its annual spending on local businesses owned by people of color and women from $2 million to over $100 million a year.[24] Today, $122 million of their spending each year goes to businesses not only within the city but actually in the historically underinvested area of West Philadelphia, where the university is located.[25]

To see the payoff of programs such as these, you don't have to look further than the stories of the participants. In Chicago, for example, Jackie Dyess, the owner of Inter-City Supply Co., joined the first cohort of the UChicago Local capacity-building training course. She says that going through the program was critical for getting her company, which provides medical supplies to UChicago Medicine, on the radar of the massive institution. "As a business, you constantly knock on doors, knock on doors, knock on doors, looking for these kinds of opportunities," she explains. "It's absolutely about the relationship, and this program gives you the opportunity to build that relationship incredibly quickly."[26]

To date, CASE has assisted 275 companies and is responsible for the creation of 180 jobs and over $50 million in revenue to small businesses through anchor contracts.[27] The high number of contracts coming out of this program highlights the reality that doing business locally is often simply good practice. It is not charity work on the part of the institutions. "We were able to save [the University of Chicago] a ton of money. No one gives you a special leg up—they just give you an opportunity to get in and show them what you can do. We won the award because we offered the best value," says Dyess.[28]

The growth of this collaborative approach to firm and job creation is spreading everywhere. As a sign of the increasingly important role that anchors play in American economic development and the growth of CASE-type approaches around the country, in October 2016, groups of anchor institutions from more than fourteen cities came together in Chicago at CASE's invitation to share lessons learned and identify further ways to grow this work.

While places are increasingly leveraging the assets of their anchor institutions, they are also taking advantage of "the new geography of innovation" that puts a premium on the clustering of anchor institutions, companies, and start-ups in small geographic areas of central cities.[29] Increasingly known as "innovation districts," these areas within cities are often marked by open collaboration, mixed-use construction or buildings that house incubators, start-ups, open work spaces, and even housing and offer proximity to top-tier universities.

Boston's innovation community is supported by MIT and Harvard, Atlanta's by Georgia Tech, and Pittsburgh's by Carnegie Mellon.[30] As a Fast Company article on innovation districts describes, "The idea is that when you mix all these things together, people, who in the old model of city building might remain siloed, have the opportunity to mingle. And being the social creatures that they are, [they] then spark conversations with those outside of their direct discipline and potentially come up with incredible new ideas."[31] These districts capitalize on making efficient use of land space and urban density to establish cross-sector clusters for innovation.[32]

Innovation districts do not have to be built around or adjacent to traditional anchor institutions. The Boston Innovation District, for example, was the brainchild of former mayor Tom Menino, who in 2010 announced his vision for transforming the isolated waterfront stretch of South Boston's Seaport District. Menino's proposal was less a unified plan than a bold commitment to creating a hub of jobs and creativity by developing clusters around green, biotech, health care, and other industries, experimenting with alternative housing models, and ultimately "invent[ing] a 21st century District that meets the needs of the innovators who live and work in Boston."[33]

Between 2010 and 2013, the Seaport District attracted 200 new businesses and added 4,000 jobs to the area, with 30 percent of the new job growth being driven by technology companies and 25 percent of the new companies having ten or fewer employees.[34] This past year, the Innovation District received another major vote of confidence: General Electric announced in January that it will be relocating its global headquarters to Boston's Seaport District. The move, says CEO Jeff Immelt, is driven by a desire "to be at the center of an ecosystem that shares our aspirations."[35]

While Boston is an example of a major U.S. city leading in innovation, similar efforts are happening in smaller, unexpected cities, across the country. Fargo, North Dakota, has fostered a unique innovation community known as Silicon Prairie. Fargo is home to the third-largest Microsoft campus in the country and 30,000 college students.[36] The Economic Development Corporation and North Dakota State University both played a role in furthering the innovation work in the community.

Local entrepreneur (now governor) Doug Burgum has also been essential to Fargo's growth. Microsoft acquired Burgum's company, Great Plains Software, in 2001, and Burgum has since been working with community members to redevelop the downtown of the city and build an entrepreneurial community with a venture capital group.[37] One outcome of the city's focus on fostering community and entrepreneurship is that North Dakota has become one of the largest hubs for the drone (unmanned aerial vehicle) business. The state has spent $34 million on fostering the $7 billion industry, including a civilian park for drones at an Air Force base.[38]

Greg Tehven, a fifth-generation North Dakotan, cofounded the organization Emerging Prairie in 2013 to create what he calls a "student union" space for the local innovation community. While the co-working model is based on real estate, Tehven found inspiration from universities, where the student union is a gathering place, welcome to anyone.[39] He explains how Fargo got there: "Collaboration is key. Institutions check their institutional ego at the door. It's not about who gets recognition and sponsorship, it's celebrating the work that's getting done and focusing on the experience."[40]

The opportunities for technology transfer, serendipitous connections, and new innovations can be transformative for a local economy, attracting new businesses—particularly in tech-driven and highly creative industries—and subsequently driving employment. In fact, a full half of jobs in the STEM-intensive industries that constitute these innovation districts do not require a bachelor's degree yet offer wages that are on average 10 percent higher than non-STEM jobs.[41]

The model of innovation districts is taking hold in cities across the country, from postindustrial centers looking to spur economic revitalization, like Detroit, to up-and-coming metropolises like Tampa. They are not only appearing in cities where one might expect them—Seattle and San Francisco, for example—but also in Chattanooga, Baltimore, Kansas City, and Austin, Texas. Jane Talkington, a sustainability scholar, attempts to maintain a list of self-defined innovation districts in the United States. As of 2016, she had identified eighty-two examples of communities pursuing the development of an innovation district.[42]

The key to this solution is that it is not a matter of one size fits all. As institutions, municipalities, and local corporations take up the mantle of fueling economic development, their approaches look different depending on the local context. But that is to be expected, because when it comes to implementing these strategies, place matters. As more institutions across the country set their sights local for purchasing, hiring, and investing, my lingering question is the same one that Derek Douglas asked when he raised the idea a few years back: "Why aren't we already doing this?"[43]

A NEW NORMAL: LEVERAGING ALL THE ASSETS OF PLACE

Bold leadership by local leaders and robust, ambitious partnerships are the key to creating a new normal. Two actions alone could significantly insure that all of a place's assets are used to grow firms, jobs, and peoples' incomes.

Bold Leadership and Goals

Like so many of the examples described in this book, huge progress can be made simply when individual local leaders decide to lead and change the behavior of their own institutions. Yes, the successes of Chicago and Penn, described in this chapter, required a lot of work by a lot of people at those institutions, but it never would have happened without the vision and the commitment of the university president. Judith Rodin, Penn's president from 1994 to 2004, set the institution on the course it remains on today. Robert Zimmer, Chicago's president since 2006, has done the same, not the least in recruiting Derek Douglas to lead this work in 2012.

The same can be said for leaders of nonanchor institutions. Serial entrepreneur Doug Burgum used his credibility and personal wealth to help situate a downtown innovation district in Fargo, North Dakota. Former Boston mayor Menino made a bold commitment to creating a hub of jobs and creativity and used an array of city assets to experiment and build success upon success.

Penn's journey is particularly instructive for this work, however. Like other institutions doing this work, the university realized that the old adage, "What gets measured gets done," is right. When the university set goals for procurement for local, women- and minority-owned firms and built them into annual performance review processes, the goals were met. Penn's ability to go from $2 million a year of spending on local, woman- and minority-owned businesses to over $100 million a year can be done anywhere.

Partnerships

Despite the prerequisite of bold leadership, achieving sustained and scaled results from these strategies requires intentional and substantive local partnerships. The places that have leveraged their local assets most effectively have been able to figure out why their strategies weren't working and then recruit and retain the right partners to fill the gaps.

This is especially true with hiring and procurement strategies. For example, when Penn realized that local entrepreneurs needed access to capital and business education, it partnered with the local Enterprise Center. Similarly, when Chicago realized it needed workers with a specific set of skills, it partnered with the Chicago Jobs Council and the 741 Collaborative Partnership to improve the quality of the workforce development training being provided potential employees.

In fact, the most common mistake that places make is failing to intentionally help anchor institutions to solve the myriad of challenges that they face when they adopt these ambitious hiring and contracting strategies. Too often, the anchors are criticized for not doing enough but are then left to do it on their own after they make the commitment to change. Local civic leaders, from the public, private, and philanthropic sectors, must rally around them and help the entire community to succeed in this strategy. Sometimes that means regularly screening eligible contractors and providing capital and training so the anchors can access a pipeline of qualified firms that can do the work successfully. At other times that means ensuring that there is a pipeline of eligible workers and supports to keep them on the job.

Partnerships are no less critical for the establishment and growth of local innovation districts, but they tend to be more organic and fluid, responding to conditions as they change. In many ways, the success of places like Boston was possible because of the willingness of actors to work with one another to watch what was getting traction and to do more of it. For example, the city continually tried to have the district leverage the unique needs and resources of the local entrepreneur community. A 2016 case study on Boston's innovation district concluded that its success was due to the community's ability to thoughtfully align and re-align unique local capabilities with changing realities.[44]

Part III

INCREASING WEALTH THROUGH HOMEOWNERSHIP

Years ago, when I was law professor at Georgetown University and running a housing-development clinical program, I hosted the mayor and deputy mayor of Yaroslavl, Russia, at the request of the U.S. State Department. This was right after the fall of the Berlin Wall, when the city was interested in privatizing housing. I planned to introduce them to the U.S. Department of Housing and Urban Development, Fannie Mae, Freddie Mac, and other housing-related institutions.

About ninety minutes into the day, the mayor asked me a surprising question: "Why is America so obsessed with homeownership? It means nothing to us." My answer to him was almost automatic. "Mr. Mayor," I said, "it means everything to us. It is the ultimate manifestation of the American Dream."

Most Americans would not have wealth if they didn't own a home. Americans who do not have access to pathways to homeownership in essence don't have a pathway to building wealth. More often than not, when people talk about inequality in America today, the conversation centers around income inequality. It was disparities in income that fueled the Occupy movement, illustrating the chasm between the top 1 percent and the rest. And for good reason; it is true that the country's income distribution is disturbingly top-heavy and that on average, black Americans earn only 59 cents and Hispanics only 72 cents for every dollar of income earned by white households.

But the troubling statistics on income inequality are eclipsed by the wealth gap in this country. According to a 2015 report from the Organization for Economic Cooperation and Development, the top 10 percent of Americans have ownership of 78 percent of the nation's wealth. The economist Edward Wolff broke these numbers down further to find that the bottom 80 percent of the population—hardly the "bottom" at all, I think it is fair to say—hold just 12 percent of the country's total wealth.

And that's before disaggregation by race. A recent survey found that people of color have a nickel for every dollar of wealth owned by a white household. The wealth disparity for people of color is actually ten to fifteen times greater than the income gap. A study released in August 2016 made major waves owing to its finding that, if current economic trends and policies continue, it would take 228 years for the average black family to amass the same wealth as its white counterpart. Suddenly, income disparity looks like a molehill next to the looming mountain of the nation's heavily racialized wealth gap.

Why does wealth matter? Wealth, or the difference between the value of a family's assets (such as cash savings, a home, car, business, and so on) and their debt, is the single greatest contributor to future upward mobility and opportunity. A child born into a wealthy family is just over six times as likely to end up a wealthy adult than a child born into a poor family. Of children who grow up in the bottom wealth quartile, fewer than 10 percent will reach high-wealth levels by adulthood.

Wealth offers short- and long-term financial security by providing a pool to dip into in an emergency—be it a car repair or a temporary layoff—or for major investments, such as financing a child's college education or retirement spending. It can enable investment in a friend's or family's business venture (as discussed in more depth in chapter 5).

But low- and moderate-income Americans are grossly underrepresented among the ranks of homeowners: only 49 percent of families making less than the median income own their home, compared with 78 percent of those above median income. Racial gaps in homeownership are even wider—like the overall wealth gaps that they contribute to. These disparities trace back to discriminatory policies and practices that were codified in federal, state, and local laws and regulations and tacitly endorsed through restrictive covenants, discriminatory mortgage lending, and lack of access to credit.

For decades these discriminatory practices restricted access to homeownership and kept households of color from enjoying this fundamental wealth-building mechanism. According to 2016 census data, homeownership rates stand at 72 percent for white families, 47 percent for Hispanics, and just 41 percent for blacks.[1] A 2015 study found that if blacks and Latinos were as likely as white households to own their homes, the median wealth of black Americans would grow $32,113 and the wealth gap between these races would shrink 31 percent. Median Latino wealth would grow $29,213 and the gap with white households would shrink 28 percent.[2]

Chapter 7 not only shows us how to close this gap but also demonstrates that we have already been doing so successfully, for all Americans, low-income, white, black, and brown, for over twenty years. In fact, before the Great Recession of 2007 and related mortgage crisis, one lender, Self-Help Credit Union, alone helped more than 50,000 lower-income borrowers and borrowers of color to become homeowners in forty-eight states. We just need to do more of this, and at a much larger scale. Across the nation, communities and lenders are working to restore safe and affordable pathways for low-income families to homeownership, putting broadly adapted and thriving practices from before the Great Recession back into play.

7

EXPAND ACCESS TO HOMEOWNERSHIP

On any given night, you might find Twin Cities native Jon Li behind a piano, hammering out a spirited rendition of Stevie Wonder's "Sir Duke"—or another of his favorites—for a crowd of partygoers. With degrees in math and music and a mastery of classical piano, guitar, bass, cello, and drums, Jon has been able to turn his passion for music into a successful career that takes him all over the country doing what he loves. Jon is the founder and owner of Rock It Man Entertainment, a full-service music and entertainment production company that puts on shows nationally at weddings, private parties, and other events.

To bring his business to life, passion was not enough; it also required capital. For Jon Li and his wife, Caris, that opportunity came from owning their own home. After graduating college, Jon worked as a freelancer, traveling the country performing at dueling piano bars and other odd gigs. Although he loved what he was doing, he didn't anticipate that he would be able to make a career of it—particularly once he got married in 2012. He and Caris rented an apartment in the Twin Cities, but they hoped that they would not be forced to send in rent checks for long. "I'm a maximizer," says Jon. "I can't stand the idea that I'm spending money on something when I know I could instead be putting it toward something that will actually gain value."[1] They shared the hope that, someday, they would be in a position to buy their own home.

That summer, Wells Fargo and the national organization Neighbor-Works America announced a new program run in partnership—NeighborhoodLIFT—that would offer down payment assistance to Twin Cities residents.[2] The goal was to allow more low- and moderate-income families to purchase their own home. Specifically, Wells Fargo was offering qualifying residents $15,000 in upfront, forgivable loans. Suddenly, buying their own home—what had seemed like a far-off ambition—might actually be possible for the young family. "We got really lucky," says Jon. "We were among the last people to get to sign up before they ran out of slots."[3]

Jon and Caris qualified and were accepted. They received the loans under the condition that they agree to stay in the home for a few years and that they attend a series of financial-counseling courses run through the NeighborhoodLIFT program. They had always had their sights set on a duplex, because they knew they would benefit from the extra income of renting it out. The couple had some savings but not enough to have covered the down payment on a home. Now that they could invest in a home without depleting their savings, it seemed the stars had aligned to do what Jon really wanted to do: turn his music and performance experience into a viable business. Jon began using those savings, along with the supplemental income from renting out a room in the duplex, to invest in sound equipment and advertising. A little over a year later, Rock It Man Entertainment was born.

Today, Rock It Man Entertainment works with a network of sixty musicians and puts on hundreds of shows across the country each year. In the meantime, the Lis have had a child and have since bought a new home to accommodate their growing family. When asked about the impact he has seen of this program, Jon describes it as an investment in the community, rather than a handout. "And I like to think that in some way, we're now able to do the same thing," he explains, "because we're offering full-time work for more musicians in a way we wouldn't have been able to do before." In a phrase, "it's a snowball effect."[4]

The purchase of their first house set the Lis on the path toward long-term financial stability. But it might never have happened without the targeted intervention of a program, like NeighborhoodLIFT, designed to help them side-step barriers. Instead, the Li family might have remained among the millions of low- and moderate-income Americans who, despite being financially equipped for the responsibilities of a mortgage, are unable to achieve the dream of owning their own home. As a result, they would have lost out on one of the most fundamental wealth-building opportunities in our economy.

Homeownership is far and away the most prominent driver of wealth in the U.S. economy. Buying a home is considered to be among the most reliable and savvy long-term investments for three key reasons. One reason is appreciation in value. From 1977 to 2011, home values increased 5.5 percent a year on average; even taking into account inflation, that means steady returns on an investment.[5] The second, and related to appreciation, is leverage. When you buy a $100,000 home with only a $10,000 down payment and it appreciates 5.5 percent, you have earned $5,500 that year—5.5 percent on the entire value of the home, not just the $550 if you had only invested the $10,000 itself.

A final value from homeownership is that it serves as a forced-savings mechanism. Homeowners build equity as they pay off their balance month by month. This equity can be tapped for big purchases or serve as a cushion for unforeseen costs like job loss or medical bills.[6] Homeownership is also said to bring a host of social benefits: owning a home has been correlated with positive education outcomes, better employment opportunities, and stronger civic participation.[7] A recent survey by the Federal Reserve Bank found that, for all these reasons, a homeowner's net worth today is a whopping thirty-six times that of a renter.[8]

Throughout our history, homeownership has been seen as part and parcel of the American Dream. It is also a "concrete way of assessing where we are as a society when it comes to racial justice," says Thomas Shapiro, the director of the Institute on Assets and Social Policy at Brandeis University.[9] That is because homeownership continues to be the single largest driver of the racial wealth gap. Wealth from equity in a home (the difference between the market value of the home and the mortgage debt) on average makes up 92 percent of the net worth of black households, as compared with 58 percent for whites.[10] It is this simple: if you are a person of color and you own a home, you are likely to have wealth; if you don't, then you're not.

Unsurprisingly, racial gaps in homeownership are wide—like the overall wealth gaps that they contribute to. This is largely the fall-out of decades of public and private housing finance policies and practices that denied or severely restricted access to homeownership along racial lines. For example, from the time of their founding in the 1930s through the 1960s, the Home Owners' Loan Corporation (HOLC) and the Federal Housing Administration (FHA) helped to create opportunities for affordable homeownership through new long-term mortgages, while at the same time excluding black Americans and other people of color from reaping those benefits.

Through tacit endorsement of restrictive covenants—private agreements on property deeds to prevent the sale of homes to people of other racial groups, and redlining, or designating entire neighborhoods as "high risk" based on the presence of people of color, regardless of the qualifications of any individuals—these federal policies successfully maintained patterns of segregation, barred investment in communities of color for decades and excluded people of color from owning homes in neighborhoods that greatly appreciated in value.[11] This legacy left households of color with a greatly diminished ability to accumulate wealth, and to pass on the financial security that wealth provides to future generations.

According to 2016 census data, homeownership rates stand at 72 percent for white families, 47 percent for Hispanics, and just 41 percent for blacks.[12] In a 2015 study, Shapiro and his colleagues found that if blacks and Latinos were as likely as white households to own their homes, the median wealth of black Americans would grow $32,113, and the wealth gap between these races would shrink 31 percent. Median Latino wealth would grow $29,213, and the gap with white households would shrink 28 percent.[13]

Low- and moderate-income Americans are also underrepresented among the ranks of homeowners, with only 49 percent of families making less than the median income owning their home, as compared with 78 percent of those above median income.[14] If low-income people and people of color continue to face systematic challenges to this critical wealth-building opportunity, there is no reason to expect that monstrous wealth gaps will not continue to widen.

It is frustrating enough to confront all of these staggering numbers head-on. Even more frustrating is that we know how to address this problem. For decades, we have developed and successfully used reliable methods that enable low-income and low-wealth Americans of every race to become homeowners.

Simple interventions, whether down-payment assistance programs made possible through grant funds like the Lis received or much more scalable approaches, such as the Community Advantage Program (CAP) described later in this chapter, have proved that many Americans who are financially able but struggle to meet the rigid qualifications of traditional lenders can secure a loan without undue risk. But this type of lending has always been limited in scope, and in the wake of the mortgage crisis many banks have clamped down even further on lending to low-income residents, minorities, or anyone considered a risky bet.

This is owing, in part, to a pervasive and destructive myth that has circulated over the past several years, that low-income borrowers were responsible for the Great Recession of 2007 and related mortgage crisis. Those who subscribe to this story have argued that banks were pressured into making bad loans to unreliable borrowers by the strict requirements of the Community Reinvestment Act (CRA) and that it was large numbers of defaults on these government-mandated loans that tipped the country into crisis.[15]

Much has been written to disprove this explanation, but one piece of evidence is particularly powerful. For decades, banks had consistently been making loans to low- and moderate-income homebuyers to meet CRA requirements. This offers an excellent baseline for understanding how these loans perform. A study by the Federal Reserve Bank of San Francisco, for example, found that CRA-eligible loans made in the state during the subprime boom were half as likely to go into foreclosure as loans made by independent mortgage companies.[16] In fact, CRA-motivated loans sold to the Community Advantage Program were at much lower risk of default than subprime loans, even when controlling for income and credit risk.

However, it is true to say that subprime lending was disproportionately concentrated in low-income and neighborhoods of color. In fact, all things being equal financially, people of color were about 30 percent more likely to receive higher-rate subprime loans than their white counterparts.[17] The solution to these problems is to continue to scale up ongoing efforts across the country that connect low-income borrowers and borrowers of color—who disproportionately suffered from the implosion of shoddy securities during the financial crisis—with responsible, affordable loans so that they can enjoy the economic benefits of homeownership.

One of the most exemplary models—a program that today has provided over $3.6 billion in financing to low-income home buyers—got its start almost thirty years ago in the back of a VW Beetle. Martin Eakes, the founder of the Self-Help Credit Union and the Center for Responsible Lending, grew up in Greensboro, North Carolina, and witnessed firsthand how lack of access to financial resources could devastate families and entire communities. North Carolina's economy during the early 1980s made vast stretches of the state look like Rust Belt towns, plagued by high levels of unemployment and disinvestment.[18] Eakes felt compelled to do something about it.

Starting with just $77 raised from a bake sale, Eakes and a small team scraped together a nonprofit loan fund to help disadvantaged entrepreneurs and small businesses that were rejected for loans from other lenders. After five years of supporting the community this way, Eakes says, he and his team stumbled on a fact that they had previously overlooked. "We discovered that black and Latino families had 1/10 the wealth that white families had," explains Eakes, "and that single fact, in my view, is the single most unacceptable fact in the modern US economy."[19]

Self-Help was working to reduce barriers for small businesses, but they recognized that the biggest wealth creator for North Carolina families was homeownership. In fact, they observed, many residents actually drew from the equity from their homes to launch businesses. Eakes realized that he would not be able to achieve the system-level results he was after without addressing the wealth gap directly.

In 1985 the Self-Help Credit Union began making home loans to families that struggled to acquire mortgages from conventional lenders—generally low-income people of color and women-headed households. Most borrowers' profiles had one or more features that would make it difficult to secure a traditional loan, much less one with prime interest rates. For example, the median Self-Help borrower makes only 60 percent of area median income, and most have prohibitively high debt-to-income ratios, low credit scores, and can only afford small down payments on a mortgage.[20]

The Ford Foundation caught wind of the credit union's work and, in 1998, provided it with a generous grant that allowed it to create a reserve fund to guarantee potential losses on loans. This was a missing piece of the puzzle for scaling up operations. With their loans now backed by this capital guarantee, Self-Help was able to launch a secondary-market program[21] in addition to its own direct-lending efforts.

Today, the Self-Help Credit Union predominately purchases home loans originated by mortgage lending partners, like Bank of America and Wells Fargo, through their Community Advantage Program (CAP). By shouldering the financial risk themselves, Self-Help gives other lenders confidence to reach out to underserved markets and offer better terms and lower interest rates to their clients. With their capital reserves as a guarantee, Fannie Mae[22] has been willing to purchase Self-Help clients' mortgages and sell pools of these securities to investors (the secondary market), thereby granting the Self-Help team more equity with which to buy up new loans. And the cycle starts again.

Making loans to lower-income people is not rocket science. It is a matter of identifying the barriers that keep financially equipped homeowners from qualifying for or successfully paying off loans and then mitigating those barriers. For example, Eakes explains, "If you're trying to create opportunities to the middle-class through homeownership and you require a large down payment, but people don't have that much cash, it becomes self-fulfilling."[23] So the CAP program offers home loans with down payments as low 3 percent and allows borrowers to pay for it with an affordable second loan, grant, or cash on hand.

Similarly, many borrowers do not pass the routine credit checks of traditional lenders, so Self-Help allows credit histories to be based on nontraditional forms of credit (that is, utility records or rent payments).[24] High debt-to-income ratios disqualify many borrowers, so Self-Help has developed more flexible underwriting standards based on demonstrated income sufficient to make payments. And mortgages often are uncharted financial territory for first-time home buyers, so Self-Help provides education services and counseling and maintains a relationship with the borrower that lasts through the lifetime of the loan.

With this flexibility, clients can access safe products—predominately thirty-year, fixed-rate mortgages—from Self-Help and their affiliated lenders, such as Bank of America and Wells Fargo, despite not meeting standard underwriting requirements. Most important, these are not subprime mortgages—those loans with skyrocketing interest rates that low-income people were often steered into before the financial crisis.

The results make this clear: CAP loans have performed radically better than subprime (and even many prime) loans. Altogether, CAP has a portfolio of around 46,000 home loans valued at over $4 billion (the median loan balance was $79,000).[25] Between 2006 and 2008, the foreclosure rate for their loans was just 4.8 percent.[26] Two-thirds of borrowers have never missed a payment.[27] As the housing crisis unfolded, subprime loans were between three and five times more likely to default than those originated through Self-Help's program; in 2009, when subprime loans had a serious delinquency rate of 47.7 percent, the CAP portfolio had just a 9.6 percent delinquency rate.

When far more creditworthy Americans were collapsing under the weight of exploding payments, people who had gotten loans through Self-Help's CAP—including their median borrower, making only $30,792—were being outperformed only by prime fixed-rate loans, and even then by a small margin.[28] The Self-Help Credit Union has provided both a case study and a model, demonstrating how responsible lending practices can transform low-income residents into successful homeowners. "My experience has been that a loan to a poor person, a working person, is the best possible risk you can ever take. And all of the past thirty years have simply confirmed that for me," says Eakes.[29]

We actually know how to make homeownership a reality for all Americans who can afford it.[30] Here are just a few more examples. Massachusetts's ONE Mortgage Program was initiated in 1989 by a coalition of public agencies, advocacy groups, and large banks. The loan program was aimed at overcoming patterns of racial discrimination that had long plagued the Boston housing market. Called the SoftSecond Program, it helped borrowers to get a primary home loan from a financial institution and a second "soft-second" loan backed by city and state government resources.[31] Over its first two decades, the program created 17,000 new homeowners in the Boston area.[32] To date, this program has leveraged $3.3 billion in public and private capital and provided affordable mortgages in one of the most expensive real estate markets in the country.[33] Half of all borrowers are households of color.[34]

Like CAP loans from Self-Help, these SoftSecond loans weathered the financial crisis comparably to—if not better than—conventional loans. In 2008 the delinquency rate for SoftSecond loans was 1.8 percent, compared with a 5 percent delinquency rate for all loans in Massachusetts at the time.[35] Over the next few years, delinquency rates for SoftSecond loans remained closer to the prime rate than either the Federal Housing Administration or subprime loan rates. The same was true of foreclosure rates; in 2011 foreclosures stood at just 0.86 percent for SoftSecond loans, compared to 1.88 percent for all prime loans made in Massachusetts.[36]

Homewise, a not-for-profit operating in Santa Fe, New Mexico, is yet another great example of what is possible. Homewise is a full-service mortgage banker that originates, closes, and services loans. One of its key features is the individualized coaching provided to clients to ensure that they are financially prepared to purchase a home. Potential borrowers often engage in months of one-on-one sessions and group classes, offered in both Spanish and English, before they are considered ready to buy.

This intensive approach is credited in large part for the Homewise sterling 0.9 percent delinquency rate during the financial crisis.[37] Between 2008 and 2009, when delinquency rates on prime loans were hovering around 5 percent nationally, the rate for Homewise loans was only 3 percent.[38] Between 2009 and 2013, only 1.1 percent of all loans serviced were seriously delinquent, more than 90 days overdue.[39]

In 2015 Homewise helped their 3,000th client achieve homeownership—a major milestone for the organization that, since 1993, has had the capacity to originate only 150 to 250 loans for new Santa Fe homeowners each year.[40] Homewise recently expanded its model to nearby Albuquerque and helped to bring the NeighborWorks America—Wells Fargo NeighborhoodLIFT program, the one that the Lis benefited from in the Twin Cities—to that community. Wells Fargo supplied the funding for the down-payment assistance, and Homewise added its signature financial-counseling programs.[41]

Jon Li can attest to the power of this partnership. His is one of the 11,000 success stories that have resulted from NeighborhoodLIFT program. And he's among the millions of Americans who have benefited from these and other efforts to bridge the gaps that keep low- and moderate-income residents from achieving the full extent of their American Dream.

A NEW NORMAL: PATHWAYS TO HOMEOWNERSHIP THAT REACH PEOPLE EVERYWHERE

Two ingredients are necessary to enable homeownership to become the new normal and to spread it to even more Americans nationwide.

Expand the Availability of Flexibly Underwritten Home Loans to Millions of Americans

Self-Help was able to prove that we can responsibly ease the rigid requirements traditionally used to underwrite home loans and successfully help lower-income Americans to obtain a mortgage and build wealth. CAP loans made to home buyers with as little as 3 percent down payments, FICO scores as low as 620 and debt-to-income ratios of up to 45 percent performed substantially as well as loans to higher-income borrowers, even during the Great Recession and mortgage crisis. More importantly, because the program demonstrated how Fannie Mae (Fannie), Freddie Mac (Freddie), and the existing secondary mortgage markets can be used to help tens of thousands of people all over the country, we have every reason to believe that we can scale this approach and extend homeownership to millions of eligible Americans.[42]

Scaling this approach from 50,000 homeowners to the 3 million people likely eligible,[43] however, requires two key elements: broad availability of a similar product, and awareness of and uptake by consumers. Unfortunately, the mortgage crisis limited the ability of Fannie and Freddie building a much more robust secondary market that would have made these types of loans widely available at that time.[44] Ten years later, however, that environment has changed. Within the last three years, both Fannie and Freddie have developed new ways to buy as many loans as originating banks are willing to make, under substantially the same flexible down payment, loan to value and debt to equity ratio requirements of the CAP program, and sell them into the secondary market.[45]

This should be a huge wealth-building breakthrough for Americans long denied homeownership. In a short period of time, we already are seeing promising results and increasing originations from some of the nation's largest home loan providers. Wells Fargo's *your*First mortgage, developed for sale through Fannie's Home Ready program, has added terms even more flexible than CAP, for example, allowing earnings from other members of multi-generational households to be counted toward the income required for loan approval.[46] The lender has set a goal over the next five years to channel over $180 billion through this product to Hispanic and black borrowers, creating tens of thousands more homeowners.[47] Freddie already has purchased more than 100,000 mortgages on CAP-like terms from Bank of America and others through its Home Possible program.[48]

The ability of home loan originators to use the flexible underwriting offered under Home Ready and Home Possible, however, does not guarantee that they will in fact offer those terms to borrowers. Some continue to choose not to, adding their own more restrictive terms such as requiring minimum FICO scores as high as 700.[49] The leaders of these financial institutions have to put a stop to this and acknowledge the importance to our long-term economic future of millions of Americans building wealth, starting now. These new programs will only reach their full potential if the nation's largest originators, especially Bank of America, JP Morgan Chase, Wells Fargo, and Quicken, wholeheartedly embrace the most favorable terms in Fannie and Freddie's offerings and aggressively market those opportunities.

Willingness to originate these types of loans is a prerequisite to scaling homeownership for lower-income Americans but it is not the only barrier. Unfortunately, many lower-income people have a misconception of the financial wherewithal that is needed today to get approved for a home loan. Their knowledge simply doesn't match the realities of today's marketplace and often keeps them from even pursuing the opportunity at all.

Researchers have found that some families do not even look for homes because they believe that, even if they found one that they could afford, financing would not be available, and they considered the credit approval process "mysterious and capricious."[50] According to a NeighborWorks survey, the average consumer believes that buying a home requires a minimum down payment of 17 percent.[51] With median home values just over $200,000, it's no wonder that the vast majority of adult renters, and 78 percent of millennials, feel that they "don't" or "probably don't" have enough money saved for a down payment.[52]

It's a similar story when it comes to creditworthiness. More than one in five millennials (ages 18–34) believed that their credit score would not be good enough to get a mortgage.[53] However, while the median credit scores for borrowers vary considerably state by state, the national median FICO score of 700 exceeds the requirements of many lenders and certainly those participating in Home Ready and Home Possible.[54]

We can and must solve this problem. While homeownership isn't for everyone, it should be within reach of at least 3 million Americans who currently don't view it as even possible. Home loan originators and civic leaders around the nation need to mount an awareness campaign focused on overcoming these misconceptions and emphasizing the importance of homeownership to our national economic health. We need more leaders to serve as "cultural brokers," providing a link between their communities and the institutions that hold the keys to homeownership.[55]

Public sector, business, faith or nonprofit leaders are well-positioned to be at the vanguard of an awareness campaign. They have built-in platforms to advocate for these solutions and to encourage members of their communities, whether they are voters, employees, customers, or parishioners, to learn more about the options that may be available to them. Many of these institutions even have their own homeowner assistance programs, as described earlier in this chapter. Foundations and philanthropists can underwrite the costs of these awareness campaigns, locally and nationally.

We must dispel the myths surrounding home buying, dramatically increase the number of Americans who apply for and obtain home loans and utilize the solutions that already exist to their fullest potential if we are to have any hope of closing widening racial wealth gaps, ensuring the stability of our communities and the financial security of the next generation.

Build on Local, First-Time Home Buyer Programs

While we work to build a robust secondary market at a national scale, we cannot forget about the important supports that have proved so successful on a case-by-case and family-by-family basis. Jon Li, and many other hard-working Americans, are just in need of down-payment assistance. Home-owners, like the 3,000 New Mexican families helped by Homewise, have been able to achieve an extraordinarily low 0.9 percent default rate on their mortgages because of high-quality home-buyer counseling and assistance. Down-payment assistance and home-buyer counseling programs have been, and should continue to be, staples of local efforts to promote homeownership. In fact, they are going to need to grow to meet demand.

In places with the most successful programs, funds are provided by government, business, and philanthropy. In place after place, local, county, and state governments provide funding for both down-payment assistance and counseling. In particular, state housing-finance agencies have been essential contributors to this work—and with their vast resources and state-wide research, they need to be a part of these efforts.[56]

As for the private sector, many companies have down-payment assistance as an employee benefit to help them build wealth and live near work. In fact, some of the most effective efforts have been local collaboratives of the business and philanthropic communities. In both Cleveland and Detroit, civic leaders came together to pool resources to give employees and other citizens down-payment assistance and counseling to incentivize their moving into targeted neighborhoods. Unsure of demand, in both cases, the pool of resources was oversubscribed faster than anticipated.[57]

In this case, as in every other case involving experimentation with interventions to make homeownership possible for more Americans, demand is clearly there. It is time we rise to meet it, by building more pathways to this fundamental piece of the American Dream.

Part IV

CREATING OPPORTUNITY
THROUGH ACCESS

Ever since the first personal computers came on the market in 1982, I have been obsessed with technology. No, I am not among those people standing in line in the middle of the night in front of an Apple Store to get my hands on the latest version of the iPhone. My obsession with technology has to do with my unfailing belief, confirmed time and time again, that it is an extraordinary tool that can help lower-income Americans to overcome barriers to economic mobility.

This obsession is what drove me to cofound One Economy in 2000. I was senior vice president at the Enterprise Foundation at the time, working with nonprofit organizations in dozens of communities. While these organizations were some of highest performing in the country, most lacked the resources to provide the customized and time-consuming assistance that people needed to meaningfully improve their economic standing in a lasting way.

At the same time, I was personally experiencing the power of the Internet for the first time through a relatively new tool—the browser. Surfing the Internet from the comfort of my office or the privacy of my own home, I began to realize what it could do that no nonprofit could ever afford to do at a large scale: reduce the isolation often caused by disinvestment or segregation (economic, racial, and otherwise), make the physical distances between places less relevant, and put information at people's fingertips that they could use every day to improve their lives.

Together with three other Enterprise colleagues—and $250,000 from the Ford Foundation—I launched One Economy. Our goal was to get the Internet into the home of every lower-income American and to build and manage online content that would provide them with a gateway to economic opportunity—from learning how to write a check or resume to finding a better job or help in growing a business—in the privacy and dignity of their own home.

Over the years, we learned a lot about the relationships between technology, lower-income Americans, and economic opportunity. We learned that lower-income people, just like everyone else, recognize how indispensable access to technology is for success in today's world. Even with limited means, they prioritize their spending to buy technology that will help them get ahead.[1] We learned that they would not only learn how to use it but would in many cases use it even more regularly and strategically to help themselves get ahead than wealthier people do.[2] We also learned that there remains a huge gap between the number of upper-income and lower-income Americans who have broadband in their homes.[3]

Two technology-rich solutions are spreading across the country and changing the lives of regular Americans, right now. Both are possible today because of technology that did not exist even a decade ago. Smartphones, apps, and public-sponsored high-speed broadband at home are expanding the geography of opportunity available to lower-income workers at a time when it could not be more critical to their economic well-being.

8

HARNESS THE BENEFITS OF
SHARED-USE MOBILITY

When Brad Miller describes his job, it is not quite what one might traditionally expect to hear from the CEO of a public transit authority.
It quickly becomes clear that Miller does not see his responsibilities as
being strictly limited to ensuring that buses are maintained and trains
run on time. His perspective is broader, with an eye toward the future of his
industry. "People aren't disposed to any particular mode of transit. They
want to be transported to their destination, no matter how it's provided,"
Miller explains. In today's day and age, he goes on to say, one trip through
the city could involve catching a bus, using a city bike-share, and then
catching a train. So it's not just about transit. "We have to be 'mobility
managers,'" he explains.[1]

The transit authority that Miller heads in the beachy suburbs of Pinellas County, Florida, has recently made national headlines for a first-of-its-
kind partnership with the private ride-hailing service Uber. Like many public
transportation systems around the country, the Pinellas Suncoast Transit
Authority (PSTA) was grappling with the challenge of how best to provide
service options to residents living off the main transit thoroughfares. The
county had no trouble running regular mass transit in busier, more popu-
lated areas of the city, but it struggled to provide efficient methods that

would connect people living in lower-density areas to the main transit hubs—and, by extension, to job opportunities all over the county. At the same time, Uber was continuing to gain traction across the country as an affordable and efficient way for users to hail a ride in real time to cover short distances, often to and from transit centers.[2]

The inspiration for partnership actually came from nearby Gainesville, where the student government at the University of Florida had signed a contract with Uber to provide $5 rides on weekend nights. Uber could draw a geofence around the campus so that it could identify which users went where in the area, and then students would be presented with a discounted Safe Ride option when they opened the app in late-night hours.[3] The model seemed to work for a college campus. The question was, could it work for an entire county?

In February 2016, Pinellas Suncoast Transit Authority became the first public agency to offer subsidized rides with a pilot program. For six months, in one area of the county, PSTA offered $3 toward any Uber ride that started or ended near a bus station.[4] Now, through the Direct Connect program, PSTA pays the first $5 of any Uber trip to or from one of the bus stops spread across the county, meaning that most of these rides cost the user around $1.[5] Since the program has launched, PSTA has seen participation increase every month.

But the authority didn't stop there. There was still the challenge of providing transportation options to residents after buses stopped running at night—a challenge that is most acutely felt by frontline workers at late-night jobs, such as call centers, explains Miller.[6] The lack of transit options can be a major barrier to getting and keeping a job in places like Pinellas County, particularly for low-income residents who may not have their own cars. Now, the Transportation Disadvantaged Late Shift program offers low-income residents up to twenty-three free Uber rides a month to a place of employment or residence between 9 p.m. and 6 a.m.[7] Miller reports that the program is seeing a lot of regular users. "You hear these testimonials from workers who say that they otherwise wouldn't be able to keep their job and support their families because their shift goes beyond transit time."[8]

The role that physical mobility plays in economic and employment outcomes cannot be overstated. Pinellas County's program is just one of many ways that localities are filling mobility gaps created by the failure of traditional forms of transportation to get everyone where they need to go in a timely and affordable way and to serve all parts of a community in equal measure. A big part of the reason for these gaps is that the spatial mismatch between where the jobs are today and where workers live has grown.

Nationally, job growth has mostly occurred in the suburbs, with more than half of suburban jobs requiring middle and low skills.[9] This is problematic for lower-income workers, whether they live in the city or in the suburbs. Most lower-income workers still mostly live in central cities (and make up the smallest contingent of suburban residents), so their travel distances are disproportionately longer than those with higher incomes.[10]

However, with housing costs in cities growing rapidly over the past decade, the population of lower-income people moving to the suburbs has steadily climbed—up to 64 percent in places like Detroit, Salt Lake City, and Atlanta.[11] The challenge that this poses is that jobs in suburban areas are sprawled over the region—and public transit service outside of the central city is generally even more sparse.

The end result is that job accessibility in many regions across the country has measurably dropped for low-income residents and people of color.[12] These trends, combined with the historical limitations of public transit, has made car ownership the only reliable and timely way to get to and from work (not to mention buying groceries, seeing a doctor, dropping children off at school—the list goes on).

This is especially problematic for lower-income Americans. Owning and maintaining a car today is exorbitantly expensive; on average, AAA estimates, it can cost almost $9,000 a year.[13]

That can translate into a crippling 25 to 40 percent of a low-income person's earnings.[14] A local 2016 study in Rochester, New York, found that residents spent nearly $400 a month to use their cars to get back and forth to work. That means that workers earning $10 an hour ($400 a week before factoring in taxes and withholdings) are spending 25 percent of their earnings on commuting alone, leaving few dollars to spend on other essential expenses like housing, food, clothing, and education.[15] With costs so prohibitive, it is no wonder that low-income households are eight times less likely than higher brackets to own a car.[16]

This state of affairs leaves millions of hard-working Americans reliant on public transit to get to and from work. Yet on average, only 33 percent of jobs in a given metropolitan area can be reached within a ninety-minute commute on public transit. In Kansas City, for example, that figure is 18 percent. This reality is exacerbated by the fact that poor and low-income populations often hold multiple jobs during off-peak times such as nights and weekends, when transit routes are even more poorly served.

What is particularly frustrating for so many commuters is that these long commute times are often the result of infrequent service, unexpected delays, and winding routes on the first and last leg of the commute. It simply takes too long to get from home to the fixed stop where people first board the train or bus (often referred to as "the first mile") and from the fixed stop where they get off the transit and head to the workplace (often referred to as "the last mile").

It is lower-income Americans who suffer the most when affordable and efficient mobility options are scarce. In New York, data collected by the National Equity Atlas revealed that of the 750,000 New Yorkers with a commute of over an hour, two-thirds were from households making less than $35,000 a year.[17] Perhaps most troublingly, a study of Boston found that black commuters traveling by bus spend an extra sixty-six hours a year in commute—waiting, riding, and transferring buses—as compared with white bus riders, most likely reflecting the racialized nature of the city's poverty.[18]

The opportunity costs to families and society are significant. In the Twin Cities, for example, a study conducted by a coalition of local non-profits and NGOs found that over the course of a year, lower-income transit users, especially those of color, will spend 160 more hours commuting than whites who drive to work solo. As the report states, that means that "for a month a year more than white drivers, transit commuters of color are unavailable for working, helping children with homework, helping parents get to the doctor, running errands, volunteering in their communities or participating in their churches."[19]

What is so exciting, today, however, is that an ever increasing number of places across the country are moving from a transit system, built on rigid schedules and fixed stops, to a shared-use mobility system that provides people with a number of ways to efficiently and affordably get from point A to point B, often directly addressing that first- and last-mile problem. The term "shared-use mobility" encompasses "all types of transportation services that are *shared among users*, including public transit; taxis and limos; bikesharing; carsharing (round-trip, one-way, and personal vehicle sharing); ridesharing (car-pooling, van-pooling); ridesourcing/ride-splitting; scooter sharing; shuttle services; neighborhood jitneys; and commercial delivery vehicles providing flexible goods movement."[20] Susan Shaheen, a professor at the University of California-Berkeley, who has been studying shared mobility as it has grown over the past few years, calls it a "renaissance in ride services being driven by real-time information and new service models . . . where sharing a ride no longer requires prearrangement or street hails; mobile technology and social networking can facilitate finding a ride in real-time and less distinction is made between classic ridesharing, ridesourcing, and commercial transportation."[21]

Technology that did not even exist ten years ago is largely what makes this new mobility system possible. Mobile applications, delivered over the smartphone, enable routes to be altered, seats to be filled, and real-time arrival and departure information to be easily accessible.[22] Researcher and New Cities Foundation fellow Greg Lindsay puts it well: "Today, the state-of-the-art in transportation is the smartphone. Its two-way ability to locate, coordinate, and orchestrate both passengers and vehicles is more important than any one mode, including the automobile."[23]

Early results from this new mobility system are promising. For example, a 2016 study of users who combined public transit and shared-use mobility options found not only that 18–30 percent of the users spend less on transportation overall (saving more as they used more) but also that users became even less dependent on expensive cars.[24] In sprawled cities like Los Angeles, where it is hard to get from one point to another, a study showed that people used shared-mobility services to fill gaps in transit accessibility: 33 percent of the time it was when public transit was unavailable and 25 percent of the time to get to and from locations not otherwise accessible by public transit.[25]

The ways that people can replace their cars, address the first- and last-mile challenge, or supplement an insufficient public transit system literally is growing every day. Some of those options, detailed below, have already landed successfully in multiple places around the country.

PEER-TO-PEER CAR RENTAL

Peer-to-peer car rental involves individuals renting out their personal vehicles directly to others. The role of an intermediary company is simply to connect supply with demand. The company does not have to maintain its own fleet of vehicles, which generally translates into lower rental costs for the user. Meanwhile, car owners can turn an asset that would otherwise be depreciating in their driveway into extra cash.[26] With such a clear win-win-win dynamic, it is no wonder that this model has taken hold in cities across the country.

New research shows that as peer-to-peer models continue to expand, they show great promise for positively impacting low-income residents in particular. A study published by New York University's Stern School of Business developed a model for understanding the future of these markets.[27] They found that peer-to-peer rental is correlated with cost savings, as users forgo the many expenses of owning and operating their own cars and also potentially generate new income from renting out their cars.[28] Finally, the study factored in the increased access to opportunities provided by increased mobility, which could result in the highest economic benefits flowing to residents below median income.

This study relied on data collected over two years from Getaround, one of the main players in the peer-to-peer car-rental arena. Getaround enables users to lease out their personal vehicles to other users and offers a hands-off experience by installing technology that allows a user to unlock the car using an app and to access the keys stored inside. Users can rent cars by the hour with no membership fees, and rates start at $5.

Today, Getaround has spread from its home in San Francisco to Berkeley, Oakland, California, Washington, D.C., and Chicago, and membership has grown to more than 200,000 people. When it launched in Chicago in 2015, GetAround received a $715,000 grant from the Federal Highway Administration to participate in a two-year study on the impacts of peer-to-peer car rental. Conducted in partnership with the Shared Use Mobility Center, their research will especially focus on the effects of the service in low-density and low-income neighborhoods.

Sharon Feigon, the director of the Shared-Use Mobility Center, believes that simply expanding the network into neighborhoods that lack a wealth of mobility options can have a major impact. Her confidence stems from firsthand experience. Feigon served at the helm of iGO, a nonprofit car-sharing company in Chicago that was sold to Enterprise Rent-a-Car after ten years of operation. As iGO placed cars in underserved neighborhoods, the resulting ridership revealed the huge unmet demand in those areas. "It fills a need," says Feigon, "and I often think that it's a lot like food deserts. People don't have access to good food, and then you put in a grocery store and everything changes."[29]

RIDESHARING

Another model that boasts both affordability and convenience is ridesharing. Ridesharing is not new. It is a growing umbrella that includes carpooling, a practice that was popular in the 1970s and 1980s. In fact, in 1980 almost one in five Americans carpooled for their commute. But that number has fallen to about one in ten owing to the high coordination costs, the degree of planning necessary, and even the trust that must be built between carpoolers to make the rides work.[30]

The start-up RideFlag and similar companies are betting that it can help resurrect this dying art, using smartphone capabilities to mitigate those barriers. RideFlag prompts users to input their commutes through the app and instantaneously connect with drivers traveling on a similar route. Drivers can pick up passengers along the way and set a price to help offset the cost of the drive—usually around $0.40 a mile—perhaps granting them access to an HOV lane along the way.

RideFlag's founder, Mike Papineau, was inspired to launch the start-up when he observed the broader trends playing out in his own drive to work. "Five years ago, I was driving on Interstate 95 and noticed, 'There are so many people going in the same direction, why are 90 percent of the cars around me single-occupancy vehicles?'" he explains. "So my question was, how can we harness technology to actually improve the lives of people of all demographics by addressing this inefficiency?"[31]

Papineau and his team are based in Montreal, where they first launched RideFlag's services. Recently, they made their stateside debut in Miami, Florida. When they started scouting opportunities to expand, a major factor was the ability to garner the support of municipalities, institutions, and other key players in the local transit space. "We won't go into a market unless we know there's strong partnership in place—we've got limited resources, so where we deploy them, we want to make sure we get enough bang for the buck."[32]

In Miami, that meant partnering with the Florida Department of Transportation and Florida International University to encourage students, staff, and other riders moving to and from campus to coordinate rides. The university has limited parking available on campus and high demand, so identifying new ways to maximize those spaces was also a high priority for administrators.

RideFlag offered an attractive solution to incentivize students to participate by working with Florida International to create a system where a successfully completed carpool results in the user automatically receiving a one-day premium parking pass from the university's parking and transportation office, delivered virtually through the app. During the soft launch in the fall of 2016, RideFlag received 350 new sign-ups and facilitated over one hundred carpools. Ridership was expected to increase when the app officially launched.[33]

App-enabled ridesharing has already grown in popularity around the globe—from SRide in India to BlaBlaCar across Europe to Hitch-a-Ride in Australia. In the United States, in addition to RideFlag, there is Carma Carpooling and Scoop, a new start-up that partners with businesses in the Bay Area (such as Cisco Systems and Kaiser Permanente) whose campuses are not well served by existing public transit options.[34]

Papineau sees carpooling as a powerful tool for bridging the first-mile, last-mile problem—particularly for regions where that "first mile" stretches a longer distance. "If you live a mile away from a transit hub or from your workplace, maybe a service like Uber works well. But for many people, if they're able to carpool for free for the six or seven miles they need to go to get to the rail station, they'd gladly take that over a pay-for-hire service."[35]

BIKE SHARE

Another method that is increasingly part of a local shared-use mobility system is bike sharing. At least seventy cities across the country have an established bike-share program or are in the process of launching one. Bike shares allow members to borrow a bike for a set amount of time and return it at other kiosks in the city. The flexibility makes it a great solution for the first-mile, last-mile problem, helping people connect to transit hubs.

Although bike shares often have been criticized for not being accessible to lower-income people and more isolated communities, many cities are demonstrating that targeted interventions can diminish barriers to access. Reducing membership costs, eliminating the credit card requirement to rent a bike, expanding the bike network into low-income neighborhoods, and working with diverse community members to better market the system are all strategies for ensuring that everyone can participate in the service.

From Pennsylvania to California, cities are experimenting with these initiatives. Philadelphia's bike share Indego began partnering with Pay-NearMe in 2015, which allows people to pay for membership in cash at retail locations such as 7-Eleven. According to the Federal Deposit Insurance Corporation (FDIC), 28 percent of Americans are "unbanked," so this small adjustment could dramatically increase the system's accessibility. Indego also offers free riding lessons and safety classes for students of all ages and works with the Bicycle Coalition of Greater Philadelphia to mobilize bike ambassadors to advocate in their communities.

For residents receiving cash assistance or food stamps, the cost of membership is just $5 a month for unlimited, hour-long trips. Similarly, Chicago's bike share Divvy launched its "Divvy for Everyone"—D4E—program in 2015. Families with an aggregate income up to 300 percent of the federal poverty level pay just $5 for the first year of membership, as opposed to $75. In its first four months, 1,107 people enrolled in the program. However, more than 40 percent of residents below the poverty line live in communities without a Divvy station; expansions of the system aimed at reducing this disparity are planned.

Minneapolis, home of the country's first bike share, also has the longest track record of adapting its system. When NiceRide launched in 2010, no kiosks were located in Near North, a diverse community with a median household income of $32,413 and where 40 percent of residents live below the federal poverty line. Responding to residents' frustrations, the city opened three kiosks in Near North later that year, and a grant from the Minneapolis Health Department enabled the Near North network to expand to eleven kiosks.

NiceRide also hired a staff person dedicated to building relationships with community organizations that serve low-income residents and distributing discounted memberships to capture new riders. After an experimental program to improve pedestrian and biking infrastructure in the city, policymakers discovered that these investments benefited underserved groups most dramatically, expanding bike access to 28,300 residents of color, 2,800 people living below the poverty line, and 922 households without vehicles. Although a strong correlation still exists between higher household income and bike-share use, Minneapolis has shown how significant progress can be made toward disrupting this pattern.

THE GROWTH OF MICROTRANSIT

An important part of these evolving shared-use mobility systems is what many refer to as microtransit. Microtransit enterprises are small, privately operated transit providers that run along select routes, often sourced by the riders themselves. They have greater capacity than single-user modes like private cars, but they are more dynamic than fixed-route public transportation. Current microtransit providers include Chariot, Via, and Lyft Shuttle.[36] Like the other service providers discussed in this chapter, they use technology to link multiple passengers into a vanpool.[37]

While traditional vanpools are not new to cities like New York, where unregulated bus networks have crisscrossed the metro area for decades, the data on mobility patterns and instant connectivity enabled by the predominance of smartphones have created ideal conditions for app-enabled vanpools to flourish. Fleets of passenger vans driven by professional employees are now accessible via apps in six major cities across the United States, and these companies all seem poised to expand.

Vanpools are a relatively cost-effective option. Chariot, available in Austin, Columbus, New York, San Antonio, the San Francisco Bay Area, and Seattle, aggregates pick-up and drop-off spots from all users in an area and then launches routes serviced by their fourteen-passenger "chariots." Reserved seats cost just $3.00. Via is a similar service operating in New York and Chicago, where rides cost a flat fee of $5.95 and $3.95, respectively. Riders can pay with nine different commuter benefit cards, reflecting Via's ambition to be viewed as just another mode in the larger transit network. By 2015, Via had provided 300,000 shared rides to over 40,000 registered users, illustrating the high demand for the promise of their tagline: "Smarter than the subway. Better than the bus. Cheaper than a taxi."

Much like RideFlag and Scoop, many transportation start-ups and microtransit operators have recognized the immense value of forging partnerships with public transit agencies as they expand to new markets. Today, beyond Pinellas County, Uber has coordinated with cities in Pennsylvania, Florida, California, New Jersey, Georgia, and more to offer subsidized rides for users.[38] In Summit, New Jersey, the goal for the new pilot is to reduce congestion at train stations and eliminate the need for more parking spaces by offering free rides to users with parking permits.[39]

The instinct that these new, on-demand transit modes can complement—rather than replace—public transit is supported by research that is come out of the Shared-Use Mobility Center. The organization's analysis found that people who routinely use shared modes are actually more likely to ride public transit and actually spend less overall on their transportation. The most frequent trips taken through ride-sourcing services fell in the late hours of the night and early morning, when bus and rail systems are not in service.[40]

This new take on public transportation is what Brad Miller is seeing play out in his own community, and he is eager to see his peers in other city and county governments begin to innovate with an eye to the future as well. "Almost everyone is seeing a drop in traditional transit ridership. But the reality is, there's always going to be a need for mass transportation;

that's got to be a requirement, especially in our urban centers," he says. "It's incumbent upon transit agencies to partner and figure out how they can be used most effectively, while also making cities easier and easier to navigate."[41]

A NEW NORMAL: ACCESS TO OPPORTUNITY FOR
ALL THROUGH INCREASED SHARED-USE MOBILITY

The growth of shared-use mobility options and their increasing coordination with local public transit systems is making it possible for lower-income Americans to get access to economic opportunities wherever they exist in a region in a timely and affordable manner. Two ingredients are necessary to expand mobility to Americans everywhere.

Willingness of Public Transit Systems to Experiment

It is not hard to envision the following daily experience for a person getting to and from work in the future. But it will take us a lot of experimentation to figure out how to get all of these parts to come together.

> Imagine opening a mobile app, telling it where you would like to go, and allowing it to facilitate the entire trip. A vehicle arrives at your location, not 1/4 mile away at an existing fixed-route transit stop, and takes you to the best fixed-route stop that will fit your trip needs. Your arrival at the fixed-route stop is timed perfectly with the arrival of the bus—no more waiting on the side of the road. You hop on the bus, and are taken the majority of the way on the cheapest possible option: existing fixed-route public transit. At the appropriate time, the app buzzes, letting you know it's time to exit the vehicle where, if necessary, another vehicle is waiting to take you the rest of the way.[42]

Most of the cities and regions that are on the vanguard of building a shared mobility system that will enable this future, like Pinellas County, San Francisco, and Washington, D.C., are leading the way by conducting pilots and experimenting with new partners like Chariot, RideFlag, and Uber. Experimenting with pilots is how cities and private companies are best able to explore one another's unique value added and lower the risk of entering into any new partnership.

Research by New Cities Foundation's Greg Lindsay in 2016 supports this idea. After looking at four of the leading shared-mobility cities around the globe—London, Manila, São Paulo, and Washington, D.C.—he concluded that public transit systems need to reinvent themselves as "mobility orchestrators rather than operators . . . creating new public-private partnerships that create value for all participants while preserving transportation access and equity."[43] Or, to put it in Miller's terms, "mobility managers."

Lessons from Lindsay's study of Washington, D.C., are particularly important to cities and regions looking to expand the geography of opportunity through mobility. Washington planners were willing to try new things, fail fast, reform regulations, and "stop stubbornly thinking of themselves as fleet operators rather than entrepreneurial stewards of a broader mobility ecosystem."[44]

Commitment to Equity

The beauty of many of these shared-use modes is the flexibility they offer compared with static transit systems. They can rapidly bring enhanced mobility to entire areas that have historically been cut off owing to inadequate public transit options. As governments and public transit agencies get involved in these partnerships, they must intentionally make sure that these new options are expanding opportunity for those most in need and historically heavily affected by the time and cost of getting to work, not just making it more convenient for those who can already afford to solve their mobility challenges on their own.

There are already extraordinary examples of this intentional equity focus taking place around the country. Pinellas County's pilot program with Uber specifically addresses both the income and digital divides that can make ride-hailing unfeasible for some residents, by subsidizing rides but also allowing users to hail a subsidized ride by phone call and pay with cash. Philadelphia's Indego bike-share partnership with PayNearMe, which allows people to pay for membership in cash at retail locations like 7-Eleven, is another. Next year, Los Angeles will debut a pilot electric-car-share program specifically designed to serve low-income residents.[45]

A 2016 study conducted for Denver, Colorado, paints the most comprehensive picture yet of the types of things that a local jurisdiction should consider when building an equitable shared-use mobility system.[46] It suggested an array of interventions that would help the region to make first- and last-mile options available to lower-income and underserved citizens. Those recommendations included allocating municipal, county, and regional funding to maintain long-term support for grassroots bike-sharing programs and requiring for-profit car-sharing efforts, like Zipcar, that receive any city parking preference or subsidy to offer cars in every neighborhood. Moreover, the local transit agency should develop a multilanguage geolocation app, en route service Wi-Fi, and data-sharing agreements with Uber and Lyft to understand who uses their services to make first- and last-mile connections.[47]

9

BRING AFFORDABLE HIGH-SPEED
INTERNET ACCESS TO EVERYONE

It all started out as a strategy for a sleepy, southern, municipally owned electric company to modernize its power grid. But when Harold DePriest, then president and CEO of Chattanooga's Electric Power Board (EPB), realized he could bring high-speed, fiber optic cable to every customer's door at the same time, he jumped at the opportunity to do so. Little did he know that this decision to improve his own infrastructure would not only stimulate 3,000 new jobs and $1 billion in local economic growth but also show the country that affordable, high-speed Internet access at home for everyone was indeed possible.[1]

Electric utility companies around the country have been working to upgrade their power grids for years. Generally speaking, the upgrades enable the utilities to better monitor problem areas, locate places in need of repair, and ultimately deploy power more efficiently across the grid. Few, unfortunately, look to leverage the major investment ($330 million in the case of EPB) to establish themselves as an Internet service provider at the same time.[2]

But eight years (and multiple lawsuits by Comcast) later, EPB now provides among the fastest Internet connections to the home at the lowest cost in the nation.[3] By offering high-speed, gigabit connections at $70 a month, half of what it costs in most markets, and providing discounts for low-income residents, EPB has attracted more than half of the area's potential Internet market.[4] That growing number includes tens of thousands of customers from the Internet behemoth Comcast, which offers service that is about 85 percent slower at twice the price.[5]

Far beyond simply saving residents money on their cable bills, Chattanooga's world-class fiber optic network has triggered incredible economic revitalization, prompting the postindustrial town to rebrand itself as the Gig City.[6] Chattanooga has become home to a rapidly growing tech landscape that has garnered national attention. In addition to becoming an incubator for technology start-ups, Chattanooga has also attracted larger companies like Amazon and Volkswagen to invest in new, large-scale facilities within its borders.[7] A study by the University of Tennessee-Chattanooga estimated that the introduction of the fiber optic network has brought the city $865.3 million in economic growth and has helped create at least 2,800 new jobs.[8]

It has also helped to bring broadband to places and households where it was not before. In one nine month period, by partnering with Chattanooga public schools, 1,700 families signed up to get high-speed broadband at home for just $27 per month.[9] "I had a grandmother come up to me and tell me that she no longer has to take her grandchildren to a fast-food restaurant for Wi-Fi access to complete homework assignments," DePriest stated.[10]

The lessons that DePriest has learned about setting Chattanooga on the road to universal broadband, or broadband for all, apply almost everywhere. "We started building fiber in the poorest neighborhoods because that was where we had the most density," DePriest notes, "and we didn't see any difference in take-up rate between the poorest and the richest parts of town."[11] DePriest continues, "Because we already were people's electric company, they trusted us and knew that we would provide great customer service at a fair price; both very different from their experience with the incumbent providers."[12] Finally, DePriest describes building the network so it could serve the entire community, not only the most profitable customers: "We've been able to serve anyone who asks, put computers and free Internet in sixteen recreation centers, and have our school system be the most highly wired system in Tennessee."[13]

It practically goes without saying that the rise of the Internet has been profoundly transformative, influencing almost every facet of society. The benefits of widespread Internet usage are readily apparent at the macroeconomic level. A study in 2009 found that broadband Internet was already responsible for the creation of an estimated $32 billion in annual consumer surplus.[14] The prospects for investment and innovation that will be fueled by wireless broadband access are boundless, and its future is impossible to fully envision. The mobile application industry, for example, rose from nonexistence to a $20 billion industry, responsible for over 300,000 U.S. jobs, in the span of approximately four years.[15] The private investment in wireless infrastructure driven by this new demand constituted $34 billion in 2013.[16]

But quality Internet access has an impact on the individual scale too and is increasingly a requisite for success in daily life. President Barack Obama, in a 2015 address, emphasized this when he said that today, "high-speed broadband is not a luxury, it's a necessity."[17] Using an Internet connection allows for online banking and financial management, provides increased access to medical information and virtual care, enables education at a lower cost through online courses, supports small businesses, creates avenues for entrepreneurship, and potentially even boosts civic participation.[18] In a 2015 survey of people who did not use broadband Internet, 40 percent said that their nonuse posed a "major disadvantage for learning about or accessing government services."[19] The number had risen significantly from 25 percent just five years earlier.[20]

The challenges of lacking Internet access are felt most acutely by students and job seekers. Although an estimated seven out of ten teachers assign homework that requires Internet access, according to the Pew Research Center, 5 million households with school-age children cannot get online from home.[21] This disconnect has been referred to by both President Obama and Jessica Rosenworcel, a former member of the Federal Communications Commission, as the "homework gap," and it is the troubling reality that drives students across the country to flock to McDonald's, sit in their school parking lots, or wait in line at public libraries after school hours to attempt to harness enough free connectivity to complete their basic assignments.[22]

Simply scraping by in today's school system without reliable Internet access is challenging; this does not even begin to address the broader reality that low-income students, white, brown, and black, are disproportionately cut off from opportunities to do outside research, search and apply for scholarships, and ultimately develop the computer skills critical for success in today's economy.[23]

The divide that begins in the classroom extends to the labor market as well. In an age when 60–70 percent of job openings are posted online, lack of Internet access is a significant hindrance for jobseekers.[24] Drafting a resume, searching for vacancies, conducting industry research, filling out applications, receiving job training, and even leveraging social networks are all components of the job search process that have predominately shifted online. A study conducted in 2014 found that from 2005 to 2008, unemployed individuals who used the Internet to conduct their job searches were employed 25 percent faster than those who did not.[25]

Yet despite the widespread recognition of the need for Internet connectivity, quality access remains unattainable for many families. According to the Organization for Economic Cooperation and Development, the United States has among the most expensive broadband services in the world.[26] While a growing percentage of low-income Americans have access to smartphones, these users are subject to more stringent data limits, and accessing the Internet from a handheld device still poses substantial challenges when writing a research paper or filling out a job application.[28]

Research conducted by the White House revealed that less than half of households in the bottom-fifth income bracket use the Internet at home.[27] In fact, low-income households are four times more likely than those in the middle- or upper-income brackets to lack broadband connection at home.[29] In response to a Pew Research Center survey, a full 43 percent of nonusers of broadband cited the cost of either the service or a computer as the predominate reason for their lack of Internet use.[30] This state of affairs constitutes an entrenched digital divide in our country. More and more, communities are realizing that ensuring equality of opportunity will first require getting everyone online.

Chattanooga's success has produced a model for public Internet provision that has been adopted in one way or another by over 450 communities.[31] Wilson, North Carolina, operates an Internet, phone, and cable sub-scription that now services just over a third of the market.[32] The increased competition sparked by the municipal utility company, Greenlight, has been credited with saving residents over $1 million each year. As the local provider, Time Warner Cable, hiked rates in the surrounding region, by even as much as 52 percent, prices for customers of Wilson's municipal util-ity remained constant.[33] This has given Wilson leeway to enter into partner-ships with nonprofits that operate after-school programs and offer free WiFi in the downtown area as the city explores how to better serve all residents.[34]

For those who question whether these communities are merely ex-ceptions, one need only look to Lafayette, Louisiana; Scott County, Min-nesota; Leverett, Massachusetts; or the Choctaw Nation Tribal Area in Oklahoma, they reflect the myriad ways that this model of municipally provided broadband is taking shape, saving citizens money and spur-ring local investment. Communities that never would have associated themselves with the words "futuristic" or "progressive" are being heralded as innovators. Ammon, Idaho, a conservative town of about 14,000, now finds itself in the company of Stockholm and Palo Alto since its construction of a dark fiber network—a subterranean grid of fiberglass that provides high information-carrying capacity, which operators can then compete to use.[35] Ammon's investment in this lasting infrastructure has increased compe-tition, driven down prices, and created a new revenue stream by leasing network access to private operators.

The trend has been especially transformative for rural communities, many of which have grown tired of waiting on improved service from large cable companies that have little incentive to reduce costs or bring cutting-edge fiber optic cables to remote areas. This frustration was the impetus behind RS Fiber, a cooperative formed in south central Minnesota that, when completed, will service twenty-seven cities and townships and an area of over 700 square miles with top-notch, fiber optic Internet access.[36] The idea first materialized almost seven years ago, when slow Internet con-nection was proving to be a serious economic hindrance—particularly for area farmers who were furthest from town centers. As recently as 2015, an estimated 50 percent of students reported having problems connecting to the Internet outside of school.[37] This idea troubled one local resident, Jacob

Rieke, who actually considered moving out of concern that his children were at a disadvantage in their education.

The notion of building and operating their own, cooperative Internet service was so compelling—and the need was so evident—that soon ten small, conservative city governments had banded together to loan almost $9 million to fund the first phase of the project.[38] Construction began in 2015, and by 2016, ninety-six miles of fiber optic cable had been laid.[39] The rest of phase 1, which will connect ten cities, is under way as of June 2017, but the cities have already begun reaping the rewards of the promise of connectivity.[40]

Recently, the Minnesota College of Osteopathic Medicine announced it will set up services in the town of Gaylord, crediting the forthcoming fiber network with offering the necessary technological infrastructure to facilitate its work.[41] According to Phil Keithahn, the chief financial officer of the RS Fiber Cooperative, "A high-speed, affordable, accessible, and reliable gigabit Internet network, such as that provided by RS Fiber Cooperative, is not only essential for economic development, it is also essential for education, health care, and attracting and retaining people who want to live in the area."[42]

A few private sector innovators have taken note of the shifting tides. Among them, Google is earning itself a reputation for helping to both enhance speed and expand accessibility. In 2012 the company began rolling out a new Internet, television, and phone service called Google Fiber. A key part of what Google Fiber touts is revolutionarily fast Internet speeds enabled by fiber optic cables—up to one gigabit per second (Gbps). But Google Fiber also offered high-quality service at remarkably low cost. Initially, customers could receive completely free broadband Internet access for seven years after a preliminary $300 installation fee. While people who signed up under this plan can continue their free service for the duration of the seven-year period, in 2016 Google ceased offering this (non)-payment plan. Even so, users now pay between $50 and $70 a month with no installation costs and no contract—still at or below market average for services with much slower speeds.[43]

To gain Google Fiber access, between 5 and 25 percent of residents in an area (depending on density and other factors) must sign up for the service—creating a "fiberhood," as the company has dubbed it.[44] Thus far, these fiberhoods are established in only ten cities, including Provo, Utah; Austin, Texas; Atlanta, Georgia; Nashville, Tennessee; Kansas City, Kansas; and Kansas City, Missouri.[45] Taking into consideration cities already declared as either "upcoming" or "potential" sites, however, this network is poised to double or triple in size.[46]

Since its inception, Google Fiber has partnered with cities and community groups working to ensure that everyone could take advantage of affordable Internet access. With the roll out of service in Austin in 2013, Google Fiber announced that it would be donating ten years of high-speed Internet access to a selection of 100 local community organizations and nonprofits.[47]

When the Housing Authority of the City of Austin (HACA) launched its Unlocking the Connection initiative the following year, aimed at enhancing technological literacy and computer access among its clients, Google Fiber was among the two dozen national and local partner organizations to contribute.[48] They offered complimentary fiber installation to housing authority properties and guaranteed free connection for residents at basic broadband speeds for ten years.[49] In addition, Google Fiber donated computers and funded Austin Free-net, a local nonprofit, which would provide skills training in these properties.[50]

Our current ways of delivering broadband to all Americans aren't working. From big cities to rural areas, places have proven that there is an array of alternative approaches to solve this problem.

A NEW NORMAL: HIGH SPEED INTERNET ACCESS FOR ALL

I cofounded One Economy Corporation, in 2000, in hopes of catalyzing new and innovative ways of making affordable, high-speed Internet access at home for all Americans, especially lower-income families. In 2012 I helped Julius Genachowski, the chair of the Federal Communications Commission, create a new private-public partnership with existing Internet service providers, EveryoneOn, with a similar goal. Despite these bold efforts, not much has changed. Today, seventeen years after the start of this journey, two things are very clear: most Americans believe high-speed

Internet is essential to the way they live; and market forces alone will not solve this huge barrier to opportunity.

We have only to look at our nation's history with rural electrification for what to do about it. By 1930, while most cities and towns were receiving electricity from privately owned or municipal utility companies, less than 10 percent of rural America was being served.[51] President Franklin Roosevelt and many others saw this "electrical divide," like today's high-speed Internet access gap, as fueling a different standard of living for those with and without the service and hampering citizens' ability to participate in the fast-changing economy. Private utility companies consistently undertook to serve only the more prosperous customers, leaving less favored citizens unserved.

The Congress and country responded then with the Rural Electrification Act of 1936, expanding beyond private operators to enable communities to deliver this service themselves, not unlike what municipally owned power companies like EPB are doing today. About thirty years after electricity began to spread across the country and it was abundantly clear that market forces alone were not going to ensure access to everyone, the nation took action. Now, almost thirty years after the first dial-up Internet access hit the market, it is time that we as a nation do the same with high-speed Internet access.

Three actions would result in the availability of affordable, high speed Internet access becoming the new normal for substantially all Americans.

Local Adoption of Models Like EPB

Just as publicly owned and operated electric companies helped to solve the market failures of rural electrification in the twentieth century, so too can public entities provide this essential service today—often by upgrading their power grids and improving their efficiency at the same time.

Six years ago, Chattanooga was the only city offering publicly owned one-gigabit Internet service. Today, nearly 100 communities do.[52] More than 148 municipally owned electric and gas companies, in the eighteen states that have not restricted them from providing telecommunications services, could and should do exactly what Harold DePriest and the city's

Electric Power Board did to bring affordable, high-speed Internet access to their customers.[53] Hundreds more publicly owned water companies in those states could also use their infrastructure toward this end.[54]

Building these systems will obviously take money, but more important, because the network will ultimately pay for itself through fees and efficiencies, it will take leadership. Local leaders of these utility companies, like Harold DePriest and his board, have to be willing to articulate the importance of providing this service universally and to be prepared to take on the efforts of existing service providers to prevent the competition.[55]

DePriest's experience is a cautionary tale for others who would consider doing this work. Comcast, the larger service provider in Chattanooga, unsuccessfully sued EPB three times to stop the construction of their network. "It turns out," says DePriest, looking back on his experience, "the existing providers don't compete in the marketplace as much as they compete in the courts and the legislature."[56]

Addressing State Laws That Limit Local Provision of High-Speed Internet Access

DePriest's reference to legislatures had to do with the number of states that have enacted laws that limit municipalities from providing high-speed Internet service. After intense lobbying by existing providers in twenty-one states, those state legislatures have adopted laws that prevent or restrict municipal investment in telecommunications.[57] These laws range from a requirement, in Alabama, that cities wanting to build their own networks hold a referendum before actually doing so to a law in Wisconsin requiring municipalities to perform a three-year feasibility study.[58]

While affirmatively taking action right now to build out local systems where no laws currently limit this type of activity will deliver the most immediate results, changing state laws that preempt localities from acting also should be a priority. Like any effort to overturn existing laws, this would be no simple feat. It requires the sustained, often multiyear efforts of individual citizens and civic organizations to educate their elected officials about the law's implications and pressuring them to reverse the action.

Congressional Action

Ultimately, congressional action to close the digital divide, as it acted in 1936 to close the electrical divide, would accelerate the ability of local communities to solve this problem. One way to do that is to explicitly give the Federal Communications Commission authority to preempt state laws that it determines stand in the way of the expansion of high-speed Internet service. The commission's efforts to strike down Tennessee and North Carolina laws limiting municipal efforts to provide access were rejected by the Sixth Circuit Court in 2016, which claimed that the agency needed explicit authority from Congress to do so.[59]

Congress also could undertake legislation, like the Rural Electrification Act of 1936, that provides financial incentives to local communities to build their own networks and close the divide in ways appropriate to their geography and population. The 1936 act enabled the federal government to provide low-cost loans for the construction of local networks and the provision of electricity to communities that the markets could not or would not serve.

The current political environment and dysfunction in Washington makes this approach the least likely of the three actions described in this chapter but one that is not without significant precedent.

Part V

STRENGTHENING THE CIVIC FABRIC AND OUR COMMITMENT TO THE GREATER GOOD

Our nation's ability to achieve a high degree of shared prosperity by the 1970s was no accident. To me, that had been the goal of so many of the earliest European settlers on our shores. Many of them came here, not unlike my own grandparents 100 years ago, seeking relief from a caste system that relegated them to a permanent economic underclass and a political system that provided them no means to change that fate. Armed with those experiences, they set out to create a very different, more egalitarian society, one that encouraged all citizens to be engaged in the "body politic" and to look beyond themselves to the greater good—unlike how they were treated by the landed gentry.[1]

The through line from those early days to the 1970s is pretty clear. Alexis de Tocqueville, in his 1831 masterwork, *Democracy in America*, marveled at that aspect of American civic life:

> I must say that I have often seen Americans make great and real sacrifices to the public welfare; and I have remarked a hundred instances in which they hardly ever failed to lend faithful support to

each other. The free institutions which the inhabitants of the United States possess, and the political rights of which they make so much use, remind every citizen, and in a thousand ways, that he lives in society.[2]

More than a hundred years later, the Harvard professor Robert D. Putnam drew essentially the same conclusions in his seminal book, *Bowling Alone*. Putnam noted that "except for the civic drought induced by the Great Depression, [civic] activity had shot up year after year." He concluded that at the dawn of the 1970s, "there [was] more participation than ever before in America . . . and more opportunity for the active interested person to express his personal and political concerns."[3]

The twentieth century added another powerful ingredient to this civic committment: an effective government able to moderate market forces so economic benefits are broadly shared. Two political scientists, Jacob Hacker and Paul Pierson, make this case in their 2016 book, *American Amnesia: How the War on Government Led Us to Forget What Made America Prosper*:

> Capitalism played an essential role [in growing shared prosperity]. But capitalism was not the new entrant on the economic stage. Effective governance was. Public health measures made cities engines of innovation rather than incubators of illness. The meteoric expansion of public education increased not only individual opportunity but also the economic potential of entire societies. Investments in science, higher education, and defense spearheaded breakthroughs in medicine, transportation, infrastructure, and technology.[4]

Unfortunately, even the formula that worked for so many people, like my own parents, began to unravel after the 1970s. Commitment to building a better society waned, as reflected in a number of indicators. Putnam writes that between 1973 and 1994 the number of Americans who attended even one public meeting on town or school affairs in the previous year was cut by 40 percent.[5] Voting records show that since a record voter turnout for the 1960 presidential election, voting has shrunk across the board. Over the past forty years, voting in presidential elections is down 10 percent, gubernatorial elections down 37 percent, and mayoral elections down, in some cases, more than 50 percent.[6]

Hacker and Pierson track the decline in the constructive role of government as well:

> At a time when we face serious challenges that can be addressed only through a stronger, more effective government—a strained middle class, a weakened system for generating life-improving innovation, a dangerously warming planet—we ignore what both our history and basic economic theory suggest. We need a government strong and capable enough to rise above narrow private interests and carry out long-term courses of action on behalf of broader concerns.[7]

The final three chapters of this book explain how an ongoing civic commitment to taking the long-term actions necessary for every American to have a chance to succeed is returning to communities across the country. Elected officials at the local level are putting the term "public servant" into action, using their cachet to not only rally citizens around a commitment to the greater good, but make government a more effective contributor to it. Extraordinary new efforts, often enabled by technology, are making it easier than ever before for citizens to further strengthen the social fabric by engaging deeply with their government and in their communities. And new groups of cross-sector leaders, many from the business community, are coming together to provide the continuity required to achieve large-scale change and help weather inevitable challenges along the way.

What is particularly encouraging to me and to the long-term health of the nation is that these efforts are intentionally addressing racial disparities and appear, in the words of the Swedish Nobel laureate Gunnar Myrdal, writing in 1944, finally to show "white Americans [living] up to their proclaimed principles" on behalf of people of color.[8] Myrdal traveled the United States for four years in the middle of the twentieth century to understand what made America, America. Like the French sociologist de Tocqueville, who had done the same and written about American democracy, almost one hundred years earlier, Myrdal was impressed with so much of what he saw.[9] He referred to our values as an "American Creed, the most explicitly expressed system of general ideals of any country in the West: ideals of essential dignity and equality of all human beings, of inalienable right to liberty, equality, justice, and fair treatment of all people."[10]

However, Myrdal also wrote extensively about the American creed's failure as to people of color. He wrote that his book was "not a study of the Negroes but of the American society from the viewpoint of the most disadvantaged group." "The predicament," he wrote, "was the conflict between the ideals that white Americans proclaimed and their betrayal in daily life."[11] Myrdal saw America continuously "struggling for its soul" and the creed "act[ing] as the spur forever goading white Americans to live up to their proclaimed principles."[12]

The virtuous interaction of effective government, deeply engaged citizens, and a civic infrastructure of diverse leaders seems finally to be enabling communities to live up to these proclaimed principles and to get consistently better outcomes around the things that truly matter to citizens, particularly, this time, for people of color: education, income, wealth, and access to opportunity for all.

10

FOSTER THE EFFECTIVENESS
OF GOVERNMENT

Two facts about Greg Fischer, mayor of Louisville, Kentucky, may be surprising. One is that much of his public service has been guided by a monk's "epiphany" that happened just a few blocks from his office. The other is that he coinvented the now ubiquitous automated ice-and-beverage dispenser found at fast food restaurants everywhere. Together, these two seemingly unrelated facts go a long way toward understanding Fischer's approach to public service. And they help explain the success he has achieved in both uniting residents around a keen commitment to the good of the entire community and modeling that commitment by leading a high-performing government that works effectively on behalf of all city residents.

Fischer is quick to talk about the epiphany. He is referring to the famous "Fourth and Walnut Epiphany" of Thomas Merton, arguably the most influential American Catholic author of the twentieth century. Merton writes of standing on that Louisville street corner in 1958 and being overwhelmed by a rush of compassion and a heightened awareness of our interdependence to one another, as members of a community and as members of a human race.[1]

So what does that have to do with city government? For Greg Fischer, everything. For Fischer, leading a city effectively requires more than just supporting its economy or maintaining its infrastructure. It also means fostering a healthy sense of community, at the heart of which must be a shared responsibility among members for the well-being of one another and the community as a whole. That sense of commitment to a "greater good" has always been the driving force for individuals to look beyond their own narrow interests and has allowed leaders to take critical steps to advance the prosperity of the whole community.

Such ideas are certainly not revolutionary in the realm of sociology or anthropology. But in recent decades, they have not been considered within the realm of government. In Fischer's view, that is entirely counterproductive. If the goal is a healthy city—one in which residents feel committed to the success and well-being of the wider community—popularly elected officials should be the first to model that behavior. How could citizens be asked to take that wide-angled view if their elected government was not doing the same?[2]

In his first year in office, Fischer signed a resolution officially naming Louisville a "Compassionate City." He also began using his bully pulpit to spread the gospel of interdependence. It may sound trite, but the idea quickly captured residents' imaginations. The result was broad support for a number of actions aimed at benefiting community members most in need, from thousands of volunteers annually participating in city-sponsored service weeks to philanthropists, educators, and community leaders doubling down on their commitment to college graduation for low-income students. "Being a compassionate city is both the right thing and the necessary thing to do," Fischer states. "There's a role for all of us in making sure no one is left behind or goes wanting."[3]

Leading with words was an important component of Fischer's approach, but it was not enough on its own. If the goal was for every member and institution in the city to do its part to serve the broader community, government's role was clear: it had to be functioning at its best, continuously improving and ensuring that it is truly working on behalf of all residents—in particular, reaching those members of the community who were struggling or had been marginalized by government in the past.

Fischer's strategy for improving performance was twofold, as illustrated in figure 10-1. Drawing directly from his experience building a successful

FIGURE 10-1   Fischer Strategy for Performance Improvement

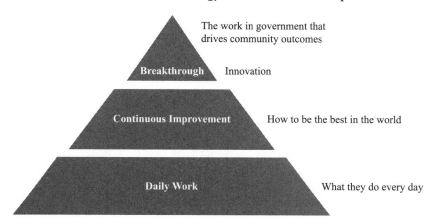

Source: Louisville Office of Performance and Innovation, "Performance and Innovation System," City of Louisville, Kentucky.

company—one that developed innovative products and generated high customer satisfaction—he framed the government's work in terms of continuous improvement and breakthrough innovation.

Continuous improvement was the process by which every department in the city would aim to become best in the world at doing the day-to-day work, rigorously assessing the processes and performance of each to constantly get better. To lead this charge, Fischer hired Theresa Reno-Weber as the city's first chief of performance improvement. She had the right background for the job: a master's degree from Harvard's Kennedy School of Government, six years in the Coast Guard, and three years in management consulting at McKinsey. "The mayor wanted me to bring to government the same data-informed decisionmaking that he felt made him a successful businessman," Reno-Weber notes.[4]

So she did. Reno-Weber executed on a system called LouieStat so that city departments and agencies could use real-time data to evaluate how well they were doing in meeting their missions and identify areas to improve performance.[5] In 2012, when LouieStat launched, city departments met one by one with Office of Performance Improvement staff to clearly articulate the results they were trying to achieve and identify appropriate measures that would enable them to chart performance. Across the board, departments began to measure their performance on the standard processes that most impacted citizen satisfaction—responsiveness to citizen concerns or unscheduled overtime, for example.

With this system in place, Reno-Weber implemented regular Louie-Stat forums, which offered an opportunity for the mayor, his leadership team, and department heads to gather to review performance, identify areas for improvement, and strategize data-informed ways to solve problems, looking across departments.[6] Today, more than 600 employees—10 percent of the city's workforce—are advocates of skilled-performance improvement actively initiating and sustaining improvements within their own divisions and departments.[7]

Reno-Weber also began using that same data-driven approach to attack one of the city's greatest challenges: racial disparities. Decades of housing discrimination and disinvestment had created highly segregated neighborhoods within the city, as well as pockets of concentrated poverty. In West Louisville, where residents are predominately African American, unemployment rates tend to be high, and median incomes in those neighborhoods can be as little as half of those in nearby Jefferson County.[8] Reno-Weber recognized that in efforts to call out and proactively reduce those inequities, government had to lead by example. That resolution spurred Louisville to participate in a new initiative, Racial Equity Here, through which the city is auditing government policies and practices through a lens of racial equity over the course of the next two years.[9]

Building the capacity to innovate—that is, developing breakthrough solutions for seemingly intractable challenges—required another set of skills and processes. For that, Fischer also brought on Ted Smith to serve as the city's first director of innovation. Smith, a Ph.D. in cognitive science and a serial entrepreneur himself, came to Louisville fresh out of the Obama administration, where he had been a senior adviser on health innovation. He set to the task with an understanding that many of the community's problems simply could not be solved by the government working in isolation. "[These problems] often require creative partnerships with different nongovernmental partners," Smith notes. "Sometimes government leads in those partnerships but many other times, we follow."[10]

Smith proudly cites the city's approach to addressing asthma as a key example. Cities will often tell citizens how unhealthy they are, Smith explains, but rarely do they actually take steps to help them get healthier. That is largely because the government cannot actually solve the problem on its own. But in Louisville, "We asked ourselves, could we solve asthma, as a community, if we had hyper-local data about where it is most prevalent?"[11]

The city partnered with a for-profit company that had invented a way to put sensors on respiratory rescue inhalers that would track where they were being used. With that data, the city could identify asthma hotspots, places where the inhalers were used most often. When they recognized that one such location also had a high level of air pollution, a local university scientist was tasked with developing a "green" strategy, calling for the strategic planting of trees and shrubs at the site. The hypothesis was that the vegetation would act as a biofilter to reduce air pollution and the risk of asthma at the same time. "It worked," Smith noted. "As a community, not a government, we were able to get the data, understand what it told us, and work on the mediating factor, air pollution."[12] Participants also realized individual health benefits. The data collected was used by respiratory therapists to teach individuals about the sources of their triggers to change their habits. Overall, participants saw a 74 percent reduction in rescue asthma inhaler usage and 200 percent increase in asthma free days thanks to the coaching from the respiratory therapists.[13]

By marrying a commitment to continuous improvement with a capacity to innovate, Mayor Fischer is leading Louisville to the top of the pyramid in figure 10-1—to a place where government is not merely functioning but is effectively driving positive outcomes for the community at large. His efforts won him well-deserved recognition as *Governing Magazine*'s Public Official of the Year in 2013.

Around the country, as in Louisville, places are embracing innovation to attack real challenges and to continuously improve day-to-day performance. Often these efforts are led by powerful leaders who are calling on their own citizens to hold them and the governments they head to a higher standard. They are modeling how other community members and institutions can use their distinct platforms to benefit the broader community through a variety of mechanisms: strengthening the capacity to innovate, and continuously improve confronting long-standing racial disparities, and using their resources in smarter ways to get better results.

Effective governance alone will not solve our most pressing problems, but, it can help us rise above narrow private interests and carry out long-term courses of action on behalf of broader concerns as we did so well in the twentieth century.[14] It also acts to spur other community members across sectors to do the same and restores people's confidence that our democratic system really can work for all. If we want to reinvigorate our communities, to re-instill a healthy sense of commitment to a greater good beyond our own narrow needs and interests, we should be calling upon our government to do just that. Fortunately, across the country, many cities are already leading by example.

EMBRACING INNOVATION TO ATTACK REAL CHALLENGES AND IMPROVE PERFORMANCE

New Orleans long held the unwelcome distinction of being the murder capital of the United States. For five consecutive years between 2008 and 2012, it had the highest murder rate of any U.S. city with a population greater than 250,000 people.[15] By 2013, the number of murders had dropped almost 20 percent, to the lowest total since 1985.[16] How? Innovation.

A group of city employees, led by a humble former management consultant, Charles West, used crime statistics to identify high-risk individuals, criminal social networks, and the neighborhoods that fostered them.[17] Using an innovation methodology developed by Bloomberg Philanthropies, the family foundation of former New York mayor Michael Bloomberg, West led a dedicated Innovation Team (or iTeam) in deeply analyzing the specific circumstances surrounding each murder that had occurred over the previous three years.

This deep dive surfaced several critical patterns, including that the majority of murders resulted from disputes among groups and that a relatively small set of people were responsible for most acts of violence. Next, the iTeam convened national experts and held focus groups with local young men to understand what motivated their actions and hear their ideas for effective intervention. The result? A comprehensive murder reduction strategy—called NOLA for Life—primarily focused on reducing group violence, which rolled out in the highest-risk neighborhoods first.[18]

The success of this approach owed in no small part to the iTeam's leader. From a glance at his resume, West may appear to be an unconventional choice to lead a crime-reduction effort. He is not an expert on criminology, social work, or law enforcement. Rather, before returning home to his native New Orleans to lead the mayor's iTeam, West spent ten years working at the intersection of business process redesign and technology, leading companies to achieve better results. He had helped the State of Minnesota with performance management and the Centers for Disease Control and Prevention with process improvements and had provided business analysis to companies in a wide variety of industries ranging from health care and insurance to publishing.

What West brought to the table, which proved invaluable to the task, was a deep understanding of statistical mapping and a commitment to using data in a disciplined way to gain the most detailed understanding of the problem. After gathering the necessary data from an array of area experts—including those young men with lived experience in the city—West was best equipped to make sense of that information, hone in on the problem in a way that no one in the city had done before, and work with the team and city officials to develop a strategic solution fully informed by the specific problem.

Just like the causes of violence in New Orleans, the interventions are diverse and involve a range of agencies and departments. For example, in response to the high correlation West and his team uncovered between being unemployed and having a criminal record, NOLA for Life includes programs to support job reentry and youth summer jobs.

Four hundred miles due north, the City of Memphis was seeking a similarly transformative, strategic approach to improving conditions in some of its most blighted neighborhoods. At the helm of its iTeam was Doug McGowen, a twenty-six-year career naval officer and former commanding officer for naval support activity in the mid-South. Their innovative efforts led to a 70 percent reduction in commercial vacancy rates in targeted neighborhoods and the launch of hundreds of new businesses.[19] The City of Boston's iTeam has built a housing lab that is experimenting with ideas for reducing costs to build, own, or maintain housing for middle-income families.[20]

These three cities are part of a seventeen-city initiative from Bloomberg Philanthropies jump-started with a total of $45 million.[21] These places, big and small, from Los Angeles to Syracuse, Albuquerque to Mobile, have deployed iTeams and highly competent iTeam leaders working in ways similar to West's team in NOLA. Altogether, at least seventy-five cities have formally embedded innovation into their operations, whether through the support of philanthropy, as with the iTeam model, or by instituting a formal city position, such as a chief innovation officer, to lead that work.[22] These innovators are taking on issues, as Ted Smith did in Louisville, that effective governments must pursue because energetic markets alone cannot or will not: neighborhood blight, school choice, and affordable housing, to name a few.

These types of bold, top-down efforts are being complemented by equally powerful bottom-up process improvements, like those led by Theresa Reno-Weber in Louisville. The key to this approach is enhancing the competencies of the people who do the day-to-day work and empowering career employees to drive improvements from wherever they sit in City Hall.

Dave Edinger knows a thing or two about that process, which is why he launched a program designed to "blast away roadblocks to bottom-up innovation."[23] Edinger, who spent several years consulting with Eli Lilly's foreign affiliates on productivity improvement and a decade running warehouse and logistics operations, is today the chief performance officer in the office of City and County of Denver mayor Michael Hancock. In 2011 Edinger launched the Peak Performance initiative designed to focus on improving "customer" experience along with its signature effort, the Peak Academy.

The modest goal is quite simply to "transform government from antiquated, bureaucratic, and wasteful systems into a customer-driven, creative, sustainable, and data-oriented government."[24] The Peak Academy is like a graduate school in process improvement and change management for city employees who work on a range of issues, including economic vitality, public safety, the social safety net, outcomes for children and youth, and sustainability. Participants can gain accreditation as "green belts" or "black belts" in Lean Innovation methods—which focus on eliminating waste and improving efficiency. Green Belts receive four hour-long trainings; Black Belts participate in a five-day intensive, hands-on training. As a result, graduates are equipped not only to make small, continuous improvements within their agencies but also to join in building a culture across government in which frontline employees feel empowered to voice their ideas.[25]

Since the academy's founding, more than 5,000 Denver City and County employees have been trained.[26] These employees have identified more than $30 million in potential savings across an array of business operations and have, to date, saved Denver $15 million.[27] Edinger has seen how investing in workers to enable them to lead performance improvements on an ongoing basis enables the government to do more good. "By innovating in those parts of our operations that are 'business-like,'" Edinger notes, "we have more resources to allocate to areas that only government can lead on or handle entirely, like child-protection caseworkers or homelessness."[28]

In the past year alone, Peak Academy has exported its bottom-up approach to ten other jurisdictions around the state and the country, including Texas and California. The State of California and the City of Los Angeles already have eighteen black belts in their ranks.[29]

ADDRESSING LONG-STANDING DISPARITIES

Like Louisville, many local governments across the nation are also addressing long-standing disparities head-on, especially around the nation's third rail: race. "Racial equity isn't just about government, but it must start here," says Austin, Texas, mayor Steve Adler. "We can't avoid that there long has been institutionalized racism at play in city operations. It's a problem we helped to create."[30] Adler, a civil rights lawyer for thirty-five years, is one of a number of mayors—among them New York's Bill De Blasio, Boston's Marty Walsh, former Minneapolis mayor Betsy Hodges, and San Francisco's former mayor Ed Lee—who were swept into office in 2015 in a surge of public will to address inequality.

The changing demographics that are transforming the composition of almost every city in America, taken together with all-too-frequent events like those that recently transpired in Baltimore, Chicago, and Ferguson, have brought to the forefront very real concerns about institutional racism in America. Government has indisputably contributed to these problems through policies, processes, and practices that benefit or harm specific communities in unequal measure. But just so, government has the ability—and the responsibility—to audit itself through a lens of racial equity, as well as implement solutions to turn the curve on long-standing disparities, thereby modeling this behavior for institutions in their own backyards. Adler and hundreds of local government leaders have taken up the mantle of that responsibility.

Adler, a Democrat, was joined by then Albuquerque mayor, R. J. Berry, a Republican, at Living Cities' launch of Racial Equity Here in New York in May 2016. Over a two-year period, Racial Equity Here is helping city officials in Albuquerque, New Mexico; Austin, Texas; Grand Rapids, Michigan; Louisville, Kentucky; and Philadelphia, Pennsylvania, hold a racial equity lens to core government operations. "We are going to take a hard look at ourselves first, then build a blueprint for racial equity," said Berry. "If we can do it in government first, then we can ask everyone to do it too."[31] Adler agreed, adding the process would require them to "look at every department, every program, and have difficult conversations."[32]

Each participating city is receiving help in normalizing the dialogue around race among city employees, standardizing new policies, and organizing decisionmakers inside government to develop powerful solutions to target inequities. A key focus of the work is on reaching young adults age sixteen to twenty-four who have disengaged from school or work and are cut off from the resources, education, and job opportunities they need to thrive. For the mayors involved, ensuring that no residents are disproportionately and systematically underserved by city government isn't just the right thing to do; it's also critical for the sustained economic success and stability of their jurisdictions. These young people represent the future of the city; racial equity is an imperative.

The Racial Equity Here program wasn't pulled out of thin air. It was built on almost a decade of work started by the City of Seattle under Mayor Greg Nichols. Two of Nichols's staffers, Julie Nelson and Glenn Harris, helped to build the Seattle program and now partner in Race Forward's

Government Alliance on Race and Equity.[33] In just three years, the alliance has grown from working in five places in 2014 to twelve in 2015 and now over seventy-five cities throughout California, Iowa, Michigan, Minnesota, Oregon, Texas, Virginia, Washington, and Wisconsin.[34] As these cities undertake this challenging but necessary work, they're setting the example for government at every level.

USING RESOURCES IN SMARTER WAYS AND PAYING FOR RESULTS

Of all of the areas where government can rise to meet a higher standard, perhaps the least controversial—the one that has never failed to rally bipartisan support—is around improving the efficiency of government spending. Tax dollars are limited, and it's tough to mobilize broad public will for investing in programs to benefit the general public good if government can't prove those dollars are having an impact. Today, we have the ability to know more about what works when it comes to improving the lives of young people, their families, and their communities than ever before. But too often, government doesn't use that information to make good spending decisions.

That's the argument made by Results for America, a nonprofit that supports governments in using data, evidence, and evaluation to direct taxpayer dollars toward programs and policies that are proved to be effective and away from those that fail. Through its What Works Cities initiative, they've worked with dozens of cities across the country to build those muscles. In Baltimore, for example, that meant bringing an evidence-based approach to redesign and relaunch comprehensive services for pregnant women and infants. As a result, the city has achieved its lowest infant-mortality rate to date and decreased mortality-rate disparity between white and black infants.[35] To have an impact on long-term challenges, more must be done to drive resources toward high-impact solutions that get results.

By using data to shift the focus to results, government is not only able to be more efficient with its own money, this disciplined approach can also attract additional private capital that can be used for public purposes, often to address inequality or other initiatives for public good that require government resources. The opportunity for this to accelerate the pace of change is enormous.

An innovative model for financing government programs called Pay for Success is helping to channel private capital toward tackling vexing social problems. Pay for Success (PFS) enables state and local governments to tap private investors to cover the upfront costs of the programs. If the programs are successful, governments pay the investors back; if they are not, the investors absorb the cost and governments pay nothing.[36]

It works like this: picture a city where the government spends millions of dollars a year on a particular social program—for example, an initiative that's supposed to reduce recidivism rates for young men in the city. Year after year, the program falls far short of desired outcomes. Not only are peoples' lives not being measurably improved, it becomes increasingly more challenging for government to continue justifying its funding of the program, and it has less political leverage to take a risk on something new.

Now imagine that there's a nonprofit operating in that city with a depth of knowledge on the issue, a wealth of experience, and a battle-tested approach to working with youth that reduces the likelihood they'll wind up back in prison. They have the evidence base to show that their tested intervention works, and that, more likely than not, it will cost less than what the government currently spends trying to solve the problem. With Pay for Success, government can contract with that service provider to deliver the intervention, and private and philanthropic investors can make a bet on its success by essentially fronting the money. If the provider successfully achieves mutually agreed-upon target outcomes, the investors will then be repaid by government, lives are measurably made better, and government has only spent its money on a proven success. A trifecta.

The purpose of Pay for Success is not to supplant existing government-provided services or increase privatization of social services. The aim is to allow local, county, and state governments to innovate and scale what works without bearing the burden of financial risk and failure—something many governments cannot afford to do in today's political climate. Pay for Success also builds in rigorous evaluation to measure actual impact and strengthen the evidence base for the program implemented.

Harnessing these forces through Pay for Success signals an enormous leap forward in bringing private sector discipline and resources to public-purpose activities. These types of partnerships had previously been limited to investments in physical infrastructure, such as affordable housing or community centers. Now private investors can invest in human capital—such as early education in Utah, juvenile justice in Massachusetts, and homelessness in Colorado.[37]

The number of existing Pay for Success transactions (which include social impact bonds) is still small, but the field has garnered a lot of attention, and more investors are getting in the game. Starting from just four deals in 2014, with investment of approximately $50 million, the number grew to twenty-five deals as of December 2016, representing total investment of $250 million.[38] After another three years, it is likely that up to $1 billion will have been invested in these transactions.[39]

A NEW NORMAL EFFECTIVE GOVERNMENT THAT STRENGTHENS THE SOCIAL FABRIC

Effective government can become the new normal everywhere, helping communities to rise above narrow private interests and build confidence that our democratic system really can work for all by focusing on two ingredients.

Leadership

Nothing is more important to the successful implementation of this approach than executive-level leadership. Cities that have had the most success in inspiring residents to shift their focus toward the good of the broader community have been led by committed executives—such as Louisville's mayor Greg Fischer and New Orleans's former mayor Mitch Landrieu. These leaders have used all aspects of their popularly elected positions, whether that means speaking from the bully pulpit or taking meaningful steps, and oftentimes calculated risks, to innovate and continuously improve government performance.

Inspiring words can be a powerful force for shifting the culture of a place. You might think, for example, that Mayor Fischer's designation of

Louisville as a compassionate city was just empty talk, but it is hard to deny that some words on a page have had meaningful impact on how residents perceive their own city, unifying them around a common, articulated set of values. If you spend any reasonable amount of time in Louisville, Kentucky, as I do, you will hear citizens, business leaders, health care professionals, and others refer to their city that way. They are eager to follow the mayor's lead and proud of a distinction that makes their community special and establishes the many ways that residents—just by being residents— are contributing to a greater good beyond themselves.

Governance, on the other hand, is about putting the mechanics in place so the government is equipped to innovate and the executive's inspiring words can be backed by action.[40] Too often, I see executives leading with an inspiring vision but lacking the patience it takes to improve government performance. Mayor Fischer's vision of a compassionate city would have been empty rhetoric if he had not invested in the Office of Performance Improvement and Innovation and directed the capital and human resources necessary for it to fulfill its mandate. Mayor Landrieu's vision for reducing homicides would likely have had the same disappointing results as prior such efforts had he not built his innovation delivery team and tasked them with the painstaking and protracted job of aggregating and deeply analyzing relevant data.

Even so, ultimately the mechanics are only as good as the people doing the work. The most successful executives are able to both recruit and retain extraordinary talent—like Ted Smith, Theresa Reno-Weber, Dave Edinger, and Charles West—and to empower the rank and file of city government to perform at their best as well. A training center for career staff, like Edinger's Peak Academy, may not seem like an obvious function for government, but the results out of Denver—5,000 black belts who have saved $15 million that could then be redirected to drive greater impact— certainly makes the case.[41]

Finally, successful leadership requires a willingness to spend hard-won political capital, to take risks and challenge the status quo. It is one thing for leaders like Louisville's Fischer or Austin's Adler to build political capital through inspiration and improved performance; it is quite another for them to spend that capital by explicitly addressing complex and emotionally charged problems such as deeply ingrained racial disparities and biases. But taking those risky steps helps them gain and sustain the confidence of their entire community.

Philanthropic Grants and Private Investment

Without a doubt, executive leadership is the critical engine driving this approach. A significant amount of fuel for that engine, however, comes from a surprising source: philanthropic grants and private investment. Grant dollars enable executives to overcome a huge barrier to change—using tax dollars to invent or adopt new ways of working, whether that means building an innovation team, instituting a program like the Peak Academy, or building the infrastructure for data-driven decisionmaking. Private investment serves both as third-party validation and a politically possible way to develop and scale promising solutions.

New Orleans's grant from Bloomberg Philanthropies is a great example. Mayor Landrieu was able to use that money to hire Charles West and give him the freedom to develop a new homicide-reduction strategy. Once it was proved effective, Landrieu was able to more easily direct tax dollars to sustain the effort. Given these successes, many more national and local foundations should be following the lead and directing more grant making toward government. Currently, demand from elected officials to lead in new ways greatly exceeds the supply of grant dollars available to help them succeed.

Private investment complements grant making in a number of important ways. One has to do with validation. When a private party, like Goldman Sachs or Living Cities, invests in a government's new approach, such as the Pay for Success transaction with Roca and its youth recidivism program in Massachusetts, it is validating both the executive's leadership and the community's commitment to delivering results.

Private investment can also help scale proven practices, for one thing by helping organizations act sooner, as in the case of Roca in the Pay for Success project.[42] Another way is by helping to improve performance; Omidyar Network, for example, has been investing in social purpose enterprises such as SeeClickFix that provide services to governments that enable them to improve their mechanics and improve performance.[43] Finally, new funds are cropping up, like the GovTech Fund, which provides resources to start-ups dedicated to improving government performance.[44] Private investment opportunities like these will only grow in the coming years.

II

DEEPEN INDIVIDUAL ENGAGEMENT
IN GOVERNMENT AND COMMUNITY

Jennifer Ong was born in the Philippines and migrated to California with her parents in the 1970s. Although Filipinos, like Ong, make up the second-largest group of Asian immigrants in the United States, Filipino-born public officials are few and far between. There have been few Filipino congresspersons and only one Filipino American in the California state legislature. With Filipinos all but absent from public life, it is not surprising that Ong never really considered public service as an option. But in 2012, she ran for a seat in the California State Assembly, winning the primary but losing the general election by only 600 votes. After thirty years in the United States, what changed to prompt her run?

The answer is the Oakland-based Boards and Commissions Leadership Institute (BCLI). The institute is just one of the powerful ways that Americans are increasingly reengaging with their government and their community, whether as leaders, expert staff, or just concerned citizens. Extraordinary new efforts, often enabled by technology, are making it easier than ever for citizens not only to deeply engage in their communities but also to contribute to a high-performing government that works effectively on behalf of all city residents.

The BCLI's focus is on increasing the number of public sector leaders so their numbers more accurately reflect the population. Today, though people of color and women make up more than 50 percent of the population, 65 percent of officeholders are white men.[1] The institute recruits and trains people from underrepresented populations, like Filipinos, and places them in leadership positions on local boards and commissions. Placement is focused on those boards and commissions that unduly influence and impact the equality of opportunity available in the region, especially concerning economic development, health, housing, transit, and workforce development.[2]

Training involves more than 100 hours of face-to-face and online classroom time. Fellows learn about the issues that have the strongest impact on equitable opportunity, develop the technical skills required by commissioners, such as *Robert's Rules of Order*, messaging, and media, and fine-tune their political skills through interactive trainings that cover topics such as negotiation, persuasion, and leadership styles.[3]

Classes are most often taught by alumni, especially those who currently sit on boards and commissions. Ong participated in the first BCLI cohort of leaders in 2009. After her training, she was placed first on the Alameda Commission on the Status of Women, and then on the Alameda County's Workforce Investment Board. Those experiences gave her the confidence and networks to believe that she could run successfully for the State Assembly just three years later.

Since that first BCLI cohort in 2009, Oakland has sponsored seven more, achieving successes similar to Ong's. Over those years, 37 percent of the fellows have been African American, 29 percent Latino, 19 percent Asian/Pacific Islander, and the rest multiracial, South Asian, and white.[4] Many places around the country are now adopting this approach. In the past three years, BCLI has spread quickly to Minneapolis—St. Paul, Minnesota; multiple towns in Texas; Detroit, Michigan; Washington's Puget Sound; and the Central Valley, Marin County, Sacramento, and San Diego in California.

"The democracy we have actually works, we just haven't intentionally pushed to utilize all of its muscles," says Terri Thao, the program director for the Nexus Community Partners' BCLI, the sponsor of the Twin Cities program.[5] Graduates of Thao's program already are shaping policy across an array of areas critical to leveling the playing field for all low-income people in the Twin Cities, from health (Roxxanne O'Brien sits on the Public Health Advisory Committee) and transportation (Jamez Staples sits on Metropolitan Council's Transportation Advisory Board) to workforce training (David Martinez sits on the Ramsey County Workforce Investment Board) and equal economic opportunity (Maggie Lorenz sits on the Human Rights and Equal Economic Opportunity Commission).[6] A graduate of the first BCLI class in Minneapolis, Ilhan Omar, a Somali immigrant, was elected to the Minnesota legislature in 2016.

NEW WAYS TO ACTIVELY CONTRIBUTE UNIQUE SKILL SETS

While BCLI is broadly engaging many more citizens in local policymaking, other efforts are enabling citizens to apply their unique skills and talents to helping government get consistently better outcomes for everyone. In many instances, they are powering improvement efforts in government performance similar to those being led by mayors in places like Louisville, Denver, and others described in chapter 10. Organizations like Code for America and Civic Consulting USA, described below, are leading the way and putting a new twist on President John F. Kennedy's challenge to the American people to "ask not what your country can do for you—ask what you can do for your country."

Since Kennedy's 1961 inauguration speech and the subsequent creation of the Peace Corps, many organizations provide Americans with the opportunity to serve the public good. But few have been dedicated to making government work better and focused on bringing the user-centered, iterative, data-driven approaches of the consumer Internet to government operations. Code for America (CfA) is one of these new generation organizations.

In a number of ways, CfA provides governments with access to the resources and tech talent they need so that together they can meaningfully impact tough societal challenges. From making it easier and faster for people to apply for food assistance to giving people a second chance at jobs and housing by clearing past convictions, the CfA is helping government serve the public and helping the public improve government.[7]

For example, over the years the CfA has offered a one-year fellowship to individuals who might not otherwise take a public service job, modeled, in part, after the Peace Corps and Teach for America. What is different about CfA fellows, however, is that they are highly skilled technologists who spend that year helping government improve the way it delivers services to lower-income citizens, focusing, like the private sector does, on the user experience.

"The way that most people experience government erodes their faith in the institution," says the CfA's founder, Jen Pahlka. "That experience becomes even more severe the farther down you are on the socioeconomic ladder."[8] Former CfA fellow Jake Solomon captures that issue perfectly in describing what he observed as part of his work with the City and County of San Francisco to understand the user experience involved in applying for food stamps: "So there I was: In San Francisco—one of the greatest and most prosperous cities in our country—watching a man on his knees, struggling to hear through bullet-proof glass, trying to access nutrition assistance from our federal government."[9]

Despite San Francisco's ambitious efforts to increase enrollment in food stamps and many other services, Pahlka has found that "fixing the experience for the user is really the only way to improve enrollment." She continues, "The process needs to remove barriers and be intuitive to the way people think. What citizens are required to do is too technical, time consuming, and in competition with so many other priorities in their lives."[10] Working with San Francisco, they have reduced the time to apply for food stamps from forty-five minutes to five minutes and reduced time to process the application from almost four hours to less than thirty minutes.

Solomon's story is a great example of the power of this approach. Solomon applied for a CfA fellowship after spending years doing government policy work at the Rand Corporation and software development at Palantir, a tech start-up at the time. "I wanted to learn what it takes to solve real problems in the real world," Solomon said in explaining why he applied to CfA. "I knew that software and government both were highly scalable but not whether together they could highly impact people."[11]

As noted above, Solomon spent his one-year fellowship working for the City and County of San Francisco to help them transform the user experience around food stamps. In the process he helped San Francisco change the way it does business for citizens most in need, but the experience also changed him: "I got to appreciate that government should move deliberatively because it is dealing with the largest and most important parts of people's lives. But in some circumstances, when transformational changes in the world, like the proliferation of software, reduced costs of storage, and mass penetration of mobile phones, far outpace what government can absorb, people like me can help."[12]

Solomon agrees with tech guru Tim O'Reilly's admonition that "now is a great time to seize the moment and commit ourselves to create government services that give all citizens services that are simple, effective, and easy to use."[13] "It turns out," Solomon says, "that the health of a democracy lives in the accumulation of highly individual transactions."[14]

Since its founding, CfA has partnered with over forty cities, placed 135 fellows, and supported 127 "Brigades," or local chapters, around the country made up of thousands of volunteers. The CfA has also incubated eight civic technology companies and developed a network of government staff advocates.[15]

EMPLOYEES AND THEIR COMPANIES HELPING SOLVE PROBLEMS FOR FREE

What the CfA is doing to enable citizens to improve the user experience for their fellow citizens, Civic Consulting USA is doing for overall government operations. Civic Consulting enables citizens to engage deeply in their government by bringing their expertise and their employer's expertise to government's day-to-day challenges. "When a city works with a network of skilled volunteers, they are able to solve seemingly intractable issues like doubling community college graduation rates, creating urban-analytics programs, and turning around public health systems," says Alexander Shermansong, the CEO of Civic Consulting USA.[16] He should know. He's been helping cities and counties do that for almost two decades.

Shermansong has been working with this model since his time at the Civic Consulting Alliance in Chicago. The alliance dates back to 1985, when more than seventy Chicago-based companies came together on a pro bono basis to write a financial turnaround plan for the City of Chicago and then helped the city execute it.[17] Today, it continues to build pro bono teams of business experts to help government solve problems from "redesign[ing] workflow for the police department that resulted in the equivalent of adding dozens of officers to the force" to helping "county agencies to establish countywide goals and metrics in areas such as public safety and economic development."[18]

In 2013 the alliance spun off Civic Consulting USA to meet demand of local companies to help governments solve problems through pro bono services around the country. Ambitious efforts are already under way in the District of Columbia, Los Angeles, Minneapolis, New Orleans, New York, San Francisco, Silicon Valley, and St. Paul. "We have found that there is extraordinary interest from the business community in having a meaningful engagement with government," says Shermansong.[19]

This is how it works. Civic Consulting helps local government leaders scope the issues, secure the right local pro bono staff from local companies with relevant expertise, and collaboratively solve the problem. Pro bono employees are assigned to the work full-time on the project as they would any other consulting assignment. The key, as described by Shermansong, is to be an outstanding "matchmaker." In other words, outline the project and its components and define what type of help is needed so the companies can identify the right skill sets within their companies. Shermansong explains that "different companies work on the same big picture issue, but the scope is generally discrete for each company."[20]

Why do companies want their employees to engage in this type of pro bono work? Shermansong says more and more companies view it as a critical strategy for attracting and retaining talent. In fact, according to the Committee Encouraging Corporate Philanthropy (CECP), 56 percent of companies are willing to pay staff for skilled volunteer projects.[21] "We are talking to one company that is looking to launch employee social impact programs in a number of places simultaneously," Shermansong says. "This approach often allows companies with staff who want to give back the chance to do so without losing them or to offer alternative new volunteering pathways."[22]

The benefits to the cities can be enormous because they are getting the specific skills they need from people who have years of experience applying those exact same skills for paying clients. Civic Consulting USA's work in New York is a great example. The State of New York wanted its employees to be trained on lean innovation, like Denver's Peak Academy is doing.[23] Private sector consultants have been trained on lean innovation for years and have adapted it across many different sectors, so Civic Consulting could identify exactly the type of help that was needed.

It proved to be the perfect private-public partnership. The pro bono lean coaches had the opportunity to grapple with a very different mindset and explore how learning from that work could inform their next engagement. Thousands of state employees have been trained on lean methods. More than 100 process improvements have already been documented that are allowing the state to improve the citizen user experience in ways that matter to them, like getting a driver's permit, opening a restaurant, or starting rehabilitation on a home.[24]

Cities and counties also are seeing that these relationships are helping keep their own staff happy and engaged. "Interestingly," Shermansong states, "cities and counties today have been able to hire much more diverse and highly skilled staff who come with the expectation that the city has capacities in-house that it doesn't have. We help to solve that problem."[25]

MORE WAYS FOR VOICES TO BE HEARD

In the 1980s, as a young lawyer in Washington, D.C., I represented community residents who were trying to have their voices heard by the local government on issues ranging from affordable housing and the crack epidemic to neighborhood redevelopment and jobs. It was really hard to help them do that. Essentially, they had one option: they could take a day or night off of work, put their name on a list to speak at a public hearing, and wait for their turn. It was not uncommon to wait four or five hours before you were asked to give remarks, often limited to five or ten minutes. It was also not uncommon to have that "day off" cost a lot in lost wages or unhappy bosses.

Most of the time, the people speaking for the first four or five hours were the same people who came and spoke at every one of those hearings. Few public officials appeared for the sessions, in large part, because they already knew what the "usual suspects" who came to speak were going to say. It was not American democracy at its best, and there seemed to be no alternative.

That has all changed. In large part, that change is the result of technology.

Technology-powered tools are complementing the new wave of citizen engagement that the BCLI, the CfA, and Civic Consulting have made possible and making it even easier for regular citizens to contribute to the greater good of their community. SeeClickFix and Change.org are just two examples of new and extraordinary ways that individual citizens across the country are able to stay aware of and communicate with their leaders, holding elected officials accountable and helping make government, in Abraham Lincoln's words, uniquely "of and by" the people.

Ben Berkowitz founded SeeClickFix in 2008, to "serve as a public feedback loop for residents and a means for holding government officials accountable for their actions or inactions."[26] SeeClickFix calls itself "a communications platform for citizens to report nonemergency issues, and governments to track, manage, and reply—ultimately making communities better through transparency, collaboration, and cooperation."[27]

Here's the problem that SeeClickFix set out to solve. Historically, when a citizen tried to communicate with city hall, they first had to figure out who was responsible for whatever problem they wanted to report, like a broken streetlight, abandoned car, or pothole. Then they would have to contact that person. Even if those barriers were overcome, there was no system that confirmed that the report had been received and no way to track the status of the request. There also was no way to know if a neighbor had reported the same thing.

SeeClickFix turned the problem into a solution. Cities subscribe to the service and when a citizen files a request, not only is it publicly documented but the government's responses are, as well. This simple change in protocol has made an enormous shift in how citizens communicate with their government. "We sometimes forget just how much our local government has to do with our quality of life," Berkowitz said.[28]

The proliferation of smartphones and a SeeClickFix app has only made its use easier and more robust. Citizens can use their smartphones to instantly report nonemergency issues via the app, which are then automatically directed to the appropriate agency. Then, they can track and engage with government employees in real time as they work to address the problem.

In April 2015, Detroit launched its Improve Detroit app, powered by SeeClickFix. By October 2015, Detroit mayor Mike Duggan reported, 10,000 issues had been submitted by citizens, resulting in cleanup on more than 3,000 illegal dumping sites, repair of 2,092 potholes, water shut off to 991 abandoned structures, removal of 565 abandoned cars, and more.[29] To Duggan, "The Improve Detroit app has ushered in a new era of customer service and accountability in City government. It's never been easier for Detroiters to get their voices heard and their complaints taken care of."[30]

A surprising result of SeeClickFix has been how it has helped the governments who use it to improve their own internal operations. "What governments found out," said Berkowitz, "was that what was happening on the other side of the citizen request was not a perfect communication or a frictionless system."[31] SeeClickFix has caused and helped governments to solve communications between one part of government and another allowing them to better allocate resources, identify persistent problems or trends, and to observe friction in how agencies work together. "It turns out," Berkowitz says, "that technology is a bridge, not a barrier," for citizens to government and government agency to agency.[32]

SeeClickFix has been adopted by more than 250 cities, spread evenly throughout the country, adding from five to fifteen new cities every month.[33] They add to an increasing number of cities that are providing this function either through in-house, 311 services, or other online providers, like Public Stuff, serving more than 200 local government clients.[34]

Online petition tools, like Change.org, are another resource giving citizens the power to connect with more people—and catalyze greater change—than ever before. "We're not perfecting democracy but we are democratizing democracy": that's what Change.org founder Ben Rattray calls the impact of tools like Change.org.[35] Change.org manages an online petition site, and a petition is a time-tested way to make change. At its simplest, it's a clear request to a decisionmaker, signed by many supporters. With these types of powerful, online petition tools, you have power to connect with more people—and make more change—than ever before. This is how Change.org describes it:

> Think of it this way: What if your company received thousands of emails from valued customers asking you to use a different supplier for your parts? What if you started to receive emails from each of your neighbors asking you to stop playing loud music at night? How quickly would you act? That's the unique thing about creating an online petition on Change.org. Governments, companies, and individuals value their reputations and feel accountable to their neighbors, constituents, and customers. When hundreds or even thousands of people raise their voices about an issue they care about, the message is very hard to ignore.[36]

Sounds simple. Anyone can go online, start a petition, get others to sign it and have people in power change their behaviors. Believe it or not, it works. Change.org adds a million users every six days, with more than 150 million users to date.[37] Nearly 25,000 new petitions are launched each month, with 1,200 petitions a quarter "winning" or resulting in what the petitioner wanted.[38]

What is so interesting is that tools like Change.org are perfect complements for making strong, effective local governments even stronger. They give citizens, like those residents of the District of Columbia who I used to represent, an alternative way to have their voices heard. Rattray initially thought that the online site would mobilize people around big national issues and incite large-scale change. It turns out that it is way more successful when the petition involves a personal story, a more modest, early win that people can understand and get behind.

The median number of signatures on a winning Change.org petition is 388.[39] "Small, personal, and rapid" is the formula, Rattray says.[40] He compares that approach to Rosa Parks's role in the civil rights movement. "One of the most important civil rights battles was a simple walk to the back of a bus. Her personal story sparked a national movement."[41]

Take these two examples for the power of the personal story. In 2012 Abby Goldberg, a thirteen-year-old girl living in the Chicago suburb of Grayslake, Illinois, was fighting to have her small town adopt a ban on plastic bags owing to the damage they do to the environment and ocean life. She found out in the process that legislation had just been passed in the Illinois legislature that would preempt cities and towns in Illinois from banning plastic bags and imposing fees on their use.

Outraged at this, she filed a petition on Change.org decrying "the devastation that millions of plastic bags have caused the environment and ocean life."[42] A month later, with more than 174,000 signatures in hand, she traveled to Springfield and urged Governor Pat Quinn to oppose the industry-backed bill.[43] Two months later, he did, calling her on the phone to tell her personally.[44]

In 2014 Spencer Collins was nine years old and lived in Leawood, Kansas. He loved to read and wanted to spread his love for books to his community by setting up a Little Free Library in his front yard. This small library could hold a few books and had a note "take a book, leave a book" on its bookshelf. However, the city of Leawood decided the Little Free Library was illegal and ordered the family to take it down. Spencer's Change.org petition asking the City to reverse this action received thirty-three signatures (out of the 32,000 people who live in Leawood).[45] The signatures and related press resulted in Leawood City Council's decision to exempt little free libraries from a city ordinance that prohibits structures in front yards.

An exponentially increasing number of individuals already are engaging with their governments and helping to strengthen their own civic fabric for the greater good in hundreds of places. New leaders like Jennifer Ong and Ilhan Omar are stepping into community leadership roles, elected and otherwise. New ways to engage through almost universally available tools, such as the smartphone, suggest that there is little reason that deep citizen engagement can't and shouldn't be happening everywhere.

A NEW NORMAL: DEEPER INDIVIDUAL ENGAGEMENT
IN GOVERNMENT AND COMMUNITY

What is so fascinating to me about the extraordinary increases in individual engagement in government and communities that I have seen over the past decade is that they are largely made possible because of social enterprises. Code for America, a non-profit organization, and SeeClickFix, a for-profit organization, for example, were both created to harness "civic tech" or the use of technology to improve civic life—and they both are successfully doing so. Therefore, it's not surprising that these types of entities play a substantial role in the following four actions that we as a nation should be taking so citizens deeply engaging with their local government and democracy becomes the new normal everywhere.

Give to or Invest in Social Enterprises Like the BCLI,
Code for America, and SeeClickFix

All of these social enterprises need capital to grow and to make their services available everywhere. Nonprofit entities, like Code for America, or programs like the BCLI need grant funds from philanthropy to do that. They have been able to scale as far as they have because of substantial grants from high-net-worth individuals, like LinkedIn cofounder Reid Hoffman, in the case of CfA, and investor George Soros, for the BCLI. Scaling to meet the demand of the entire country, however, will require not only their sustained financial commitment but participation from a much broader group of donors including more traditional, established foundations, many more family offices of high-net-worth individuals, and even individual contributions. Donations will be needed to help bring their products and services to targeted locations but also to fund the organization's core operations so they have the capacity to meet demand. We have to figure out how to make it easier and less time consuming for leaders like Jen Pahlka and Terri Thao to raise the money they need to do this work.

For-profit entities, like Change.org and SeeClickFix, have the potential to raise capital more easily because they can attract private investment. However, even these for-profits often face challenges because of perceptions that their social purpose will compromise their ability to achieve appropriate financial returns.

That is why the path being blazed by a new generation of investors, like Omidyar Network and, more recently, the Chan Zuckerberg Initiative, is so important. Their approach, detailed more fully in the epilogue, is unlike what has been done by any single entity in the past. They are setting out to change whole systems or "markets" and letting the circumstances determine which tool (grants, loans, equity) to use based on potential impact, not the other way around.

Bring SeeClickFix and 311–Type Services to Your Community

Tools like SeeClickFix and similar 311 services have spread to hundreds of cities incredibly fast because they are relatively inexpensive and easy to adopt. There really is no reason that these engagement tools shouldn't be everywhere. Local government officials in jurisdictions that have yet to do so simply need to make it happen.

Have Your Company Engage with Civic Consulting USA

Alexander Shermansong and Civic Consulting USA have made it relatively easy for local companies to not only retain their most valued employees and promote deep citizen engagement in local government but also to help government solve its most challenging problems, all at the same time. The first step, however, is for local companies to make a commitment to make their staff available to government on a pro bono basis. Civic Consulting USA will then work with local government leaders to scope the issues and ensure placement of their pro bono staff with relevant expertise.

In the growing number of cities where it already has a presence, Civic Consulting USA's ability to make the match between employees and government projects should be a slam dunk. It is more complicated in places where Civic Consulting USA doesn't yet have a presence. In those situations, companies should reach out to Civic Consulting to understand what's possible. As a grant-driven organization, local funders and companies that want Civic Consulting's services available in their communities could provide them with grants sufficient to build a local Civic Consulting USA office.

Participate in These Types of Activities as Citizens

Ultimately, none of these approaches will be successful if citizens don't participate. Today, there are an extraordinary number of options for citizens to shape their government and community, from being placed on local boards and commissions to improving government performance and holding elected officials accountable through SeeClickFix. Citizens need to take this responsibility and engage in the ways that make the most sense to them. Given the array of options, there is no excuse for staying on the sidelines.

12

ENABLE THE LONG VIEW

In the mid-1990s, I was the senior vice president for the Enterprise Foundation, a national housing and community nonprofit started by Jim Rouse, the legendary real estate developer, civic activist, and philanthropist. Our goal was to build thriving communities across the country for low-income families by supporting the financing and development of affordable housing. In that capacity, I served on a funding collaborative in Cleveland, Ohio, alongside other local leaders, making grants to neighborhood housing organizations. During one of my initial visits there; I had the opportunity to meet the leaders of Cleveland Tomorrow, a group of CEOs from more than twenty-five Fortune 500 companies. The organization had been founded a decade earlier by the executives from some of the city's biggest companies, such as TRW, Premier Industrial Corporation, and Eaton Corporation, who called Cleveland home and were dedicated to the long-term health of the city.[1]

These CEOs saw themselves as civic leaders and took that role and responsibility seriously. Cleveland Tomorrow provided them a place to put aside their parochial interests to discuss, debate, and take action to promote the long-term health of their shared community. Almost everyone I spoke to in the city shared the belief that Cleveland Tomorrow played an outsized and critical role in preserving and advancing the economic and civic vitality of the region.

Fast forward ten years and Cleveland Tomorrow had all but disappeared. Globalization and economic forces beyond the city's control resulted in those twenty-five Cleveland-based, Fortune 500 companies—once major economic drivers and pillars of the community—dwindling to little more than a handful. Premier Industrial, for example, was sold in 1996 to a British company; TRW was bought a few years later by Northrop Grumman. One by one, the leaders of Cleveland Tomorrow left with these companies.

Organizations like Cleveland Tomorrow, local groups of civic leaders often anchored by home-grown but national companies, once were mainstays of our communities. While they were far from perfect—in fact, usually made up only of older, white businessmen—they nonetheless served an important civic function. They shared a commitment to the quality of life and economic health of their respective hometowns. They wore their business hats and their community hats at the same time, looking to maximize on the healthy interactions between energetic markets and effective governments. They were anchors in the storm, forming what I think of as "civic infrastructure" that holds the public sector accountable and helps the community survive the inevitable business cycles and turnover of elected leaders, superintendents, university presidents, and other local leaders.

My instincts told me that this type of civic infrastructure was critically important. But it wasn't until I met Eric Rosengren, the president of the Federal Reserve Bank of Boston, that I realized that others were studying this phenomenon, that there was actually research to support my hunch. This research was conducted in 2008 as part of the Boston Fed's efforts to better understand how it could help reinvigorate the city of Springfield, Massachusetts. The decline of manufacturing had left Springfield with one of the highest rates of concentrated poverty in the country: one-third of the city's poor lived in neighborhoods where the poverty rate exceeded 40 percent.[2]

For decades, an array of efforts designed to revive Springfield were tried, but none made any meaningful difference. Similar cities, like Winston-Salem, North Carolina, had had impressive success in turning themselves around. The question on everyone's mind—the question that so many of the city's leaders and disadvantaged residents desperately needed answered, was, why not Springfield?

In search of an answer, the Boston Fed conducted a study of twenty-five "peer" cities that most closely matched Springfield's profile. Peer cities were identified based on population, employment in manufacturing, and the role of the city in the wider region from 1960 to 1980. The cities that fit the profile—including Winston-Salem, North Carolina; Grand Rapids, Michigan; and Providence, Rhode Island—all were located in the Northeast, Midwest, or Upper South.[3]

What they found was that ten out of that group of twenty-five cities had fared substantially better than the others in the decades since 1980. "The research illustrates that a big part of the answer to these complicated and persistent challenges facing mid-size cities is people in multiple sectors working collaboratively with a common vision," said Rosengren. I was fascinated by their findings. Their research suggests, in Rosengren's words, "that civic infrastructure is a prerequisite to physical infrastructure, requiring active leadership of cross-sector 'muscle,' spirited consensus, and passion and perseverance over the long haul. Put another way, it may take 10 to 15 passionate but collaborative visionaries pushing for some 10 to 15 years to achieve transformational change."[4]

Initial leadership in these ten resurgent cities, as they termed them, came from a cross-sector of key institutions and individuals. In some cases, "the turnaround started with efforts on the part of the public sector, while in other cases nongovernmental institutions or even private developers were at the forefront."[5] Resurgent cities all had multiple instigators, not just the business-executive-type founders of Cleveland Tomorrow, who recognized that it was "in their own interest to prevent further deterioration in the local economy, and . . . took responsibility for bringing about improvement."[6]

One of the most promising things happening in our democracy today is the rapid growth of this type of civic infrastructure all over the country. Together with a more effective government and a highly engaged citizenry, it is completing the virtuous circle that has been needed to restore our ability to take forward-looking, bold actions that benefit the community at large rather than appeasing short-term, private interests.

The city of Minneapolis is an instructive case study. That story revolves around Rip Rapson, the head of the Kresge Foundation, based in Troy, Michigan. Ten years ago, Rapson stepped into his current position and transformed the foundation from a sleepy institution that had funded building construction for eighty years into one of the most dynamic philanthropic institutions in the nation. He was a central figure in the "Grand Bargain," an unprecedented partnership between the philanthropic community, city pensioners, the State of Michigan, and the Detroit Institute of Arts that propelled the City of Detroit's successful emergence from municipal bankruptcy in 2014. But in my mind, the Itasca Project, launched in 2004, may be his greatest success.

In the early 2000s, when he was president of the Minneapolis-based McKnight Foundation, Rapson recognized that a few fundamental changes occurring in the region threatened its well-being. One had to do with leadership. For decades, the CEOs of the Twin Cities Fortune 500 companies, like General Mills and Pillsbury, were home grown and actively engaged in the community. But as these companies grew more global and there were fewer leaders with strong local ties, civic engagement waned. The second important dynamic was the impact of this leadership void. Rapson recognized that there was simply no one left who was interested in or willing to focus on challenging issues. The problems that Minneapolis needed to tackle as a city, like improving education or addressing income inequality, would have to be solved on a much longer timeframe than the normal political cycle, or even a CEO's term in office.

So in the fall of 2003, Rapson invited a small group of business and community leaders together to explore how they might go about changing that trajectory. With the help of McKinsey and Company, that group interviewed over eighty CEOs and civic leaders. They learned what other communities have learned since then: that many leaders had a lot of interest in becoming more civically engaged, but few knew how to get involved. Many didn't even know what the most pressing issues were.

The Itasca Project, now made up of sixty local executives, was born from those humble roots. Unlike traditional business-led efforts, its agenda doesn't center on lowering taxes, reducing regulation, or working around government. Rather, its progress as a task force is gauged in improved quality of life, overall economic competitiveness, and more widespread prosperity. "They take a long-term view—one that is not dependent on the election cycle," Rapson explains.[7] Itasca sets its sights on the region's greater good: working through issue-specific task forces to address the region's toughest problems. The challenges that Itasca prioritizes during its meetings—issues like infrastructure, inequality, and higher education, to name a few—are not the kind of issues that traditional chambers of commerce want anything to do with.

The results have been extraordinary—from increased savings for low-income workers to small local companies creating more jobs by connecting to the large supply chains of Itasca members. Pressure from Itasca members, who were willing to work with local government officials, even helped to override a governor's veto that would have limited the availability of state funds to rebuild roads and transit.

Building on the lessons learned from Itasca, six years ago Living Cities launched the Integration Initiative (TII) in part to help support the creation of new civic infrastructure in the cities of Albuquerque, Baltimore, Newark, New Orleans, San Francisco, and Seattle.

For example, in Albuquerque today, leaders from the mayor's office, the University of New Mexico, New Mexico Educators Federal Credit Union, Nusenda Credit Union, Central New Mexico Community College, Sandia Labs, ABQ Community Foundation, and more are working together to accelerate economic mobility through the creation of 10,000 good jobs, especially for the growing immigrant community. Their coordinated effort includes entrepreneurial education, a district-type innovation effort called "Innovate ABQ," and coordinated multi-institution supply-chain efforts, not unlike CASE in Chicago, discussed in chapter 6.

In 2013, after learning and partnering with Living Cities through this process, Rosengren's Boston Fed launched a new initiative called the Working Cities Challenge. Today, eleven mid-sized cities in Massachusetts, five in Rhode Island, and more to come throughout New England are building out their own civic infrastructure to help solve seemingly intractable problems.

Lawrence, Massachusetts, is a great example. Lawrence, one of America's first industrial cities, is home to 77,000 residents. Today, a little under one-third of residents live in poverty.[8] In response, a coalition of the mayor, the public school system, leading nonprofits like Lawrence Community Works, and employers such as the Greater Lawrence Family Health Center, New Balance, and Merrimack Valley Federal Credit Union have jointly committed to working to increase parent income for students in the public school system by 15 percent over a ten-year period.[9] In two years, they've more deeply engaged over 600 parents in schools across the district, connected 240 of those parents to job training and placed 70 in jobs. To top it off, they've formed a new CEO group called the Lawrence Partnership that is bringing in the perspective of employers and driving local employment efforts across the city.

Similarly, the Aspen Forum for Community Solutions is working to strengthen civic infrastructures in twenty-three cities with a specific focus on addressing a huge problem in the country: the more than 5.5 million young people, ages sixteen to twenty-four, who are neither enrolled in school nor participating in the labor market. In rural Maine, for example, the Southern Maine Youth Transition Network is working to connect students with relationships, skills, and opportunities for future job success. Staffed by the University of Maine's Muskie School, it weaves together a network of partners—including those representing K–12 education, workforce development, community-based organizations, juvenile justice, and the state child-welfare agency—all of whom have a stake in supporting the region's young people. Likewise, Philadelphia Youth Network's Project U-Turn includes a network of over 100 employers who work closely with government and agency partners to ensure that everyone is aligned in the shared goal of equipping young people with the skills that the employers need.

Interestingly, the same forces of globalization that led to the disappearance of Cleveland Tomorrow have given rise to a new generation of civic infrastructure across the country. They are coalescing in places that see the dangers of persistent short-termism and narrow private interest, and a leadership void for combating them. They are a response to the growing recognition that civic infrastructure is just as important to economic vitality and the health of a community as physical infrastructure.

A NEW NORMAL: THRIVING CIVIC INFRASTRUCTURE

Two ingredients are necessary for ensuring the local civic infrastructure that is necessary to enable the long view becomes the new normal everywhere.

Distributed Leadership

My experience watching the growth and impact of local civic infrastructure in more than 100 places around the country confirms, over and over again, what the Boston Fed found in its study of resurgent cities: when multiple instigators from different industries and sectors come together and take responsibility for bringing about improvement, it happens. Kresge's Rapson, whom I've spoken with in depth about this, would most likely add the caveat, "after a slow and difficult aggregation of trust among the participants." There is no question that he's right; collaboration, especially over the long term, is an intentional act that has to be nurtured and supported.

Distributed leadership is discussed in chapter 4, where the Strive Network and others have recognized that bringing cross-sector actors to the table is critical to the execution of long-term change in the education system, from cradle to career. Essentially everything outlined in chapter 4 is relevant to this solution as well, but a few additional points are important.

The first has to do with individual choice. The success of local civic infrastructure as a whole rests on the commitment of individual citizens who are going to choose to lead from wherever they sit. There really is no magic to this work, and no substitute for leadership. Every time a foundation CEO like Rapson, a university chancellor like Zimpher, or a community leader like Lawrence Community Works CEO Jessica Andors puts his or her political capital toward the greater good, the chances of success improve dramatically. That's part of why Rapson's efforts in Minneapolis are so instructive for other local leaders around the country. If Rapson hadn't taken the personal risk involved in bringing other leaders together, Itasca literally never would have happened.

Second, the importance of collective action and peer pressure can't be overstated. While individual decisions to lead are a precondition to the building of civic infrastructure, the collective commitment from multiple leaders from multiple sectors to work together is what makes it a success. Not only does this ensure that every part of the community has a vested interest in the future, but it also harnesses the powerful force of peer pressure to keep people at the table.

Finally, the most successful instances of civic infrastructure are sustained through continuity. As noted in chapter 4, distributed leadership is a prime way of ensuring that a partnership does not hinge on any one individual. Because the community's efforts don't have to start over every time a particular leader leaves town, this factor enables much more progress toward reducing deeply rooted, highly complex disparities. This is especially important given the average terms of so many key local actors at the table—from four years for mayors to three years for school superintendents and university presidents.

Support of the Backbone Function

No matter how committed leaders are, the reality is that busy people with other full-time jobs can't work together effectively unless it is someone's or some organization's job to help them do so. This function is often referred to as the "backbone" of a collaborative. It's a concept that comes from the world of collective impact, but the features are highly relevant to the work of supporting strong civic infrastructure.

The backbone function essentially provides six types of support: it guides the group's vision and strategy, supports the selected activities, such as Itasca's task forces, establishes shared measurement practices, builds public will, advances policy, and mobilizes funding.[10]

The backbone function for the most successful local civic infrastructures around the country often are executed by participating companies, individual philanthropists, and foundations. The Itasca model, where McKinsey and Company provides the backbone support, has become a model for many communities. A backbone like McKinsey provides not only stable ongoing support but access to an array of information, data, and reports that McKinsey interacts with around the world. Regardless of the source of support, no civic infrastructure can be sustained and serve its function as the long-term fiduciary for the community without a highly functioning backbone.

EPILOGUE

THE URGENCY OF NOW

O ver the past forty years, we have failed to take the steps that would have led to the revival of America as the land of opportunity—to reclaim the American Dream for all. The signs of major systems failure have been evident. We've long known that our high schools haven't been preparing all of our children adequately for the future. But we have done very little to fundamentally change how the K–12 system works so that it actually produces better results. Study after study has confirmed that college completion is critical for an individual's long-term economic success, but we have been complacent about low levels of educational attainment—only 42 percent of Americans have a post–high school degree. And while a recent survey reported that 46 percent of Americans don't have enough money to cover a $400 emergency expense, we continue to do very little to help qualified people become homeowners—the primary way that wealth is built in America.[1]

Our current systems are failing to position millions of Americans of all races for success but failing spectacularly when it comes to people of color, the fastest growing segment of the population. We won't be able to profoundly improve the economic trajectory of millions of Americans unless we broadly adopt approaches, like the solutions described in this book,

179

that already have been proved to work at scale for these populations and white people, too.

When implemented together, this set of solutions provides us with a blueprint for creating a "new normal" that addresses the biggest barriers to restoring and reinvigorating the American Dream: better education, more income, increased wealth, greater access to opportunity, and the restoration of a civic commitment to a greater good—especially for those who are rapidly becoming the most significant drivers of our economy.

Creating the new normal is not about adopting any one individual program; it's about changing broken systems that were perhaps suited for the majority population in 1970 but aren't getting the results that we need now. A new normal would mean, for example, that getting a high school diploma and a college degree at the same time would be the norm in every one of the 26,000 communities that has a public high school, not just the 280 that now make that possible. It would mean permanently changing how we provide tuition assistance to our employees, how people become homeowners, how we get broadband into homes, and more.

This is not essentially different from the new normal that we created at the turn of the twentieth century, when we made public education open to all to meet the needs of our fast-industrializing country or when we enacted the GI bill after World War II to scale college and homeownership for the millions of returning veterans who never thought that either would be possible for them. We've learned and relearned the lesson throughout our history: if our system doesn't work for all of us, then in the long run it's not going to work for any of us.

Unfortunately, this view of how and why we need to change is rarely the dominant narrative. Despite the clear economic imperative that we face and the opportunity that our growing population provides for our future, as the Brookings demographer William Frey aptly points out, less than a quarter of baby boomers and seniors view the increasing populations of color, including immigrants, as a positive for the country. More than half said it threatens traditional American values and customs.[2]

The sooner we are able to change that narrative, disrupt our current failing systems, and get all Americans fully contributing to our economy, the better for all of us and our children.

LEADING FROM WHEREVER YOU SIT

I'm confident that we can establish this new normal all across the country. But it will require that each of us lead from wherever we sit, whether that is as an elected leader, an engaged resident, a corporate CEO, philanthropist, or investor. Believe it or not, there are actually no laws or regulations that have to be changed for these solutions to be adopted everywhere. The barriers to implementation, more often than not, are simply resistance on the part of individuals and a failure to change our own behaviors.

Each of us must take the future into our own hands and stop waiting for permission, or for someone else, to act. We have to ask ourselves the following four questions to determine how we can contribute to the adoption of these approaches in our own community, or across the country.

Can I Get People to Work Together Differently?

So many of the success stories in the previous chapters were catalyzed simply by leaders reaching out to other leaders in their communities and urging them to partner with them in new ways to accomplish their goals, whether they actually had any real authority to force them to change their behavior or not. For example, Daniel King of the Pharr—San Juan—Alamo Independent School District, and essentially all the other superintendents who have implemented early-college high schools in their districts, were able to do so by building new relationships with their local community colleges and universities. Once they had a goal in mind, they identified the community members that needed to be at the table to make change happen.

The same can be seen throughout the book, from leaders in Strive Together cities who are reengineering education from cradle to career (chapter 4) and those building new civic infrastructure, as Rip Rapson did with Itasca in the Twin Cities (chapter 12), to local elected officials facilitating the placement of BCLI graduates on boards and commissions (chapter 11) and public transit agencies partnering with shared-mobility companies, as Brad Miller did in Pinellas County, Florida (chapter 8). With formal and informal authority, motivated individuals are achieving real, systems-level change simply by identifying the other players who need to be involved and forging new, untried partnerships where there are shared interests.

Can I Use the Assets of My Own Organization Differently?

Similarly, many of the solutions are made possible in large part because institutions have decided to make them an organizational priority and to direct their assets accordingly. Georgia State University would not have achieved such a dramatic success in graduating low-income students and students of color had they not made it an institution-wide priority (chapter 2). Companies like Aetna that have helped their frontline workers get college degrees at no cost did so by undergoing a company-wide shift to make competency-based degrees part of their education benefit programs (chapter 3). Networks of anchor institutions like CASE and Chicagoland companies are showing what's possible when you intentionally harness existing supply-chain spending to grow businesses owned by people of color (chapter 6). These organizations have stepped back to assess their unique assets, then asked themselves how they can leverage those assets creatively toward a particular goal.

A growing number of companies are taking this approach to the next level by applying the same line of questioning to their core business model. Prudential Financial, for example, has recognized that America's changing demographics will present new business imperatives and opportunities in the future, as their customer base and workforce pipeline become more diverse. Today, Prudential is taking steps to ensure that the company is effectively attracting and retaining employees of color, so that the company will be positioned to create and market products that truly meet the needs and interests of its future majority customers.

Seizing the competitive advantage of inclusion has led Prudential to reevaluate everything from their internal policies and work environment to their products and services. Perhaps most importantly, the company has recognized that future success hinges on their customers' ability to buy Prudential's products sustainably over their lifetimes, which has informed new strategies and investments geared toward boosting peoples' incomes and advancing financial security.

This way of "future proofing," or reassessing the entire company from the inside out so it can respond to and thrive in America's changing demographic landscape, is one of the most exciting trends that I see in the U.S. economy.[3] As Georgia State University provost Timothy Renick expressed it, what it takes is putting a mirror to your own institution and asking candidly, "In what ways are we the obstacle?"[4] And then the next question becomes, "In what ways can we be part of the solution?" More often than not, they end up seeing those benefits pay out in their own bottom line.

Can I Put My Personal Credibility on the Line to Make a Difference?

An extraordinary amount of progress toward creating a new normal has been achieved by people putting their own personal credibility and moral authority on the line. This behavior was modeled throughout the book. University of Cincinnati's then-president Nancy Zimpher's candor and vulnerability about her own institution's failure to graduate 50 percent of its students pushed other local, educational institutions to hold themselves publicly accountable for getting better results for low-income students (chapter 4). Harold DePriest's willingness to withstand multiple lawsuits and attacks by incumbent Internet providers resulted in the building of a high-speed fiber network in Chattanooga that began offering service first in the poorest neighborhoods (chapter 9). Louisville Mayor Greg Fischer not only spread the gospel of interdependence, but also consistently modeled the behavior he hoped other organizations would follow by auditing government policies and practices with a lens of racial equity (chapter 10).

You don't have to be an elected official or senior leader, however, to lead by example. Extraordinary things happen when people across sectors and levels of an organization use their own credibility and moral authority to advance the change they want to see.

Can I Take Action on My Own Behalf?

Ultimately, if you build the new normal, people have to seize the opportunity. Much of the success of these solutions rests on people taking advantage of the new opportunities that they provide. For example, students must stay in college until they graduate when provided the appropriate supports (chapter 2); people of color and women must start up and grow their own businesses if capital, contracts, and supports are available (chapter 5), and lower-income Americans must apply for home loans under flexible terms that they can meet (chapter 7).

Individuals also have to push for the change needed. Once you've seen what's possible, it's much easier to demand that relevant stakeholders adopt those proven solutions in more places. If a neighboring district has adopted the early-college high school approach, the pressure of parents who want their children afforded the same opportunities can be a powerful force to encourage a school board to pursue new partnerships. If a peer company provides competency-based education degrees, it may be that your employer hasn't yet heard of these programs. If SeeClickFix is available two towns over, raise it with your representatives at a council meeting. Changing old ways of working is challenging work; often it takes meaningful pressure to shift the cost-benefits analysis and overcome resistance.

DRIVING ADOPTION OF THE NEW NORMAL THROUGH INTENTIONAL GRANT MAKING AND INVESTMENTS

Philanthropic and private investment dollars, as highlighted in virtually every chapter, have been a critical driving force behind the development and rapid spread of the solutions. Thus far, these funds have been sufficient to prove that this new normal is possible but insufficient to have them spread everywhere. Nationwide adoption will require commitments commensurate with the economic imperative and urgency of the problem from grant makers and investors who have been supporting this work already and from many who have not. New and existing grant makers and investors should follow the following six principles when doing so.

Supply Flexible Funds That Enable Organizations to Experiment

Even when people are willing to change, more often than not, they don't have the flexible dollars available to them to experiment with working in new ways. This is as true for a billion-dollar city as it is for a million-dollar nonprofit organization. When flexible dollars are made available to risk-taking leaders, change happens—whether they are superintendents adapting the early-college high school model to their own communities (chapter 1), corporate human resources departments offering tuition reimbursement for untested competency-based degree programs (chapter 3), or cities, like San Francisco engaging Code for American fellows to transform the user experience when applying for food stamps (chapter 11). Often, the initial dollar amounts necessary to test and experiment aren't huge, yet the long-term payoffs can be incredible. What is needed is the flexibility to pilot new approaches and even adapt solutions, like those in this book, to local circumstances.

Stop Constantly Chasing the Shiny New Penny: Fund Proven Approaches and Organizations

The allure of the shiny new object or idea is often a lot more exciting to a philanthropist or investor than the often unglamorous but critical work that goes into scaling that idea everywhere once it matures and is shown to work. In my experience, grant makers and investors have a bias toward earlier stage efforts, move on too quickly, and leave organizations that have developed successful, scalable strategies without the capital they need to see them spread. Almost every one of the solutions highlighted in this book has an intermediary organization—such as StriveTogether (chapter 4), Village Capital (chapter 5), NeighborWorks (chapter 7), the Shared-Use Mobility Center (chapter 8), and Code for America and the Civic Consulting Alliance (chapter 11)—who could help that solution land all across the country if it had sufficient and sustained grants.

The same can be said for for-profit companies who need adequate private capital, like Kesha Cash's Impact America Fund (chapter 5) and Change .org and SeeClickFix (chapter 11). These intermediaries may not provide the grabby headlines of some new, untried initiative, but they offer something that should be more attractive: a strategy that has changed lives and changed systems and a hunger to bring that model to more places.

Move Away from Individual Programs toward Processes
That Can Achieve Results at Scale

There is an old adage, "Systems get exactly the results that they are designed to achieve." According to that adage, then, a K–12 education system with a high school dropout rate of 30 percent is designed to achieve just that. Therefore, we should never expect that result to change until the underlying system itself (and each of the actors in that system) is redesigned to get a different result. In fact, that is what I have seen play out, time and time again. We regularly throw a new program at a problem until that program's money runs out instead of doing the really hard work of changing the underlying system and holding people and institutions accountable for better results.

To achieve a new normal across the country, grant makers need to acknowledge that so many of our current problems can't be fixed by attaching a new program onto a broken system. They must pivot away from privileging the majority of their grant making to individual program interventions and instead prioritize the funding of new processes that force institutions to work together differently to actually achieve different results. This work may not garner headlines or ribbon cuttings, but it's the only way that lasting change actually happens. The extraordinary results highlighted throughout this book point to what's possible when we do so locally, from early-college high school (chapter 1) and cradle-to-career initiatives (chapter 4) to the building of new civic infrastructure (chapter 12).

But the same approach is also incredibly powerful at a national scale. More and more funders are helping to resource non-traditional, new problem-solving entities, rather than individual organizations or specific programmatic interventions. Networks, for example, can enable ideas to be shared and spread more quickly, such as Gates' Frontier set of colleges (chapter 2). When it comes to increasing homeownership, we need investment not only in new loan products, but also in large-scale campaigns that enable the mass take-up of transformative opportunities (chapter 7). And when funders and investors pool resources and actively engage in longer-term collaboration, the new entities that can result—such as my own organization Living Cities—can bring about results that are far greater than the sum of the parts.

These funder/investor collaboratives are less common, but are often uniquely equipped to influence systems in need of change. Typically, these collaboratives are created when a group of organizations (foundations, private investors, or financial institutions, for example) acknowledge that the problems that they are all trying to solve—like poverty or climate change, for example—are complex, need multi-faceted interventions, and require patience and persistence to start seeing results.[5] These collaborators break the old mold of individually designing and implementing their own strategy that they fund for a limited amount of time. Instead, they pool their resources and create a new entity charged with taking on the daunting, systems-level problems that all participating members want to see solved, taking risks and experimenting with new approaches in ways that no one member could do on its own. Each member makes a longer-term (often multi-year) commitment to support the work, and the group regularly stops, reflects on their results, and pivots as that data suggests, continually scouting for new partners to fill gaps identified along the way.

In all those cases, funders made, what I call, process the new program, by either providing sustained support to a backbone organization whose only job was to help make each actor's role in a new system stick; create a network effect among network members; or change a long-held narrative.

Capitalize Social Enterprises and New Business Ventures to Solve Problems and Create Jobs

Investors of private capital need to look for opportunities to invest much more heavily in two types of for-profit entities. The first is social enterprises. These organizations give leaders tools and solutions that they need to create the new normal. One of the most exciting trends of the past decade has been a wave of entrepreneurs who are intentionally trying to contribute to solving social problems while building successful, for-profit ventures. These are companies like SeeClickFix and Change.org (highlighted in chapter 11) who are helping local leaders to re-define community engagement as never before.[6] There's an ever-growing number of these types of social ventures. But demand for capital far outstrips supply.

Secondly, we must direct more capital to entrepreneurs who don't have ready access to capital, especially people of color, who we need to be starting and growing companies to create new jobs. There is a serious mismatch between the capital needs of entrepreneurs of color, at every stage of their business, and access to that capital. Despite the fact that we will be relying on these entrepreneurs for the vast majority of our future job creation, as detailed in chapter 5, we have not yet been able to overcome the barriers that keep us from fully unleashing this potential. Solving this problem has to be an economic priority for our country.

Obviously, private capital can be provided to these types of enterprises through direct investment or through funds built to source, invest, and manage a portfolio of similar investments. The growth of funds such as the Urban Investment Fund (for urban-serving social enterprises) and the Impact America Fund (for entrepreneurs of color), both highlighted in chapter 5, make it much easier for investors to find quality investments and to ensure that people making the investment decisions have the necessary cultural competencies. Flowing investment capital through these and similar funds will dramatically grow the field and spread the new normal.

Develop New, Potentially Transformational Applications of Technology

Technology is not a silver bullet that can reverse inequality and bring economic opportunities to all, but it is a huge ally in the fight. Its lack of geographical boundaries and its color blindness can free the human imagination from the laws of physics, or the often more pervasive laws of society. It already is fueling innovations that enable us to overcome barriers to opportunity, link lower-income people to the economic mainstream, and deliver products and services at incremental marginal costs, in ways not imaginable even a decade ago.

The potential of technology to accelerate the adoption of the new normal is evident throughout this book, in the use of predictive analytics to keep students in college until they graduate (chapter 2), enabling self-paced, online competency-based college degrees (chapter 3), powering smartphones to create seamless connections among shared-mobility options on demand (chapter 8), improving delivery of food stamps and public benefits and facilitating new and powerful ways for citizens to hold their elected officials accountable (chapter 11).

My conviction in the power of technology for accelerating positive social outcomes has been a constant throughout my career across sectors; it's part of what led me to cofound One Economy Corporation, a technology-led nonprofit, in 2000. Yet over all that time, I have continuously been baffled by the reality that there is still very little philanthropy, as a percentage of the whole, dedicated to developing technology-led solutions to many of our most challenging problems. Over the same period, technology investment has been the darling of Silicon Valley, competing only with biotechnology and clean tech for the greatest amount of investment.[7] With billions of dollars in assets, philanthropy needs to make a more systematic, sustained, and substantial commitment to funding technology solutions, broadly defined, that will take the new normal to scale.

I am certain that we would see unimaginable applications of technology that would drive a new normal if the top 100, more general-purpose foundations set aside only 0.1 percent of their $10 billion in annual giving ($100 million) to technology innovation. This could be accomplished in a number of ways, but I look to the Robert Wood Johnson Foundation's Pioneer Fund for a real life example. The foundation has been setting aside a very small percentage of its grant budget to support innovations that "wade into uncharted territory in order to better understand new trends, opportunities, and breakthrough ideas" that don't necessarily fit in its current funding categories.[8] They are forging a path that more philanthropic institutions need to follow if we hope to fully leverage technology— one of the greatest assets we have to create a new normal everywhere.

Blur the Lines between Grants, Loans, and Equity Investments

Historically, there's been a fairly rigid divide between institutions and individuals who only provide grants to nonprofits and those who invest capital (meaning debt or equity) only in for-profits. Today, that line is blurring, and for the better. Increasingly, foundations and high-net-worth individuals seeking to accelerate a new normal are realizing that they should let the circumstances determine which tool (grants, loans, equity) to use, not the other way around.

That is the path that a new generation of investors, like the Omidyar Network, cited in chapter 11, are defining. Pierre Omidyar became a billionaire at the age of thirty-one when his online auction site, eBay, went public. Since then, he and his wife, Pam, have been using their wealth to invent a new way of supporting large-scale social change. Unlike much of philanthropy, they are not looking simply to invest in companies or programs. Instead, their aims are to achieve scale by fundamentally altering how whole "markets," like government, financial services, and education, function.

Their philanthropic organization, the Omidyar Network, includes a traditional grant-making foundation and a for-profit equity-investing corporation, so it can invest in the right change maker, whether it is a for-profit or a nonprofit entity. Of the $850 million that the Omidyar Network has committed to date, an unprecedented $400 million has been in "impact investments"—investments in for-profit companies that will achieve both a social and a financial return.

Their investments in "civic tech" are a perfect example of how powerful this approach can be if you want to change how government works. Omidyar made for-profit investments in companies like SeeClickFix and Change.org, to provide tools from outside of government to make it better, but also grants to Code for America, which helps increase capacity within government itself. While the Omidyars, and now others such as the Chan Zuckerberg Initiative, Emerson Collective and the Ballmer Group, who are essentially addopteding this model, are on the vanguard of this approach, they do not have to be alone. Any institution or individual can decide how many of these solutions they want to help to spread, understand the gaps in making that a reality, and then, as appropriate, fill those gaps with grants, loans, or equity.

This is the moment. I wrote this book because I wanted everybody in America to see what I have seen for the past ten years: the promise of America is alive and well. I wrote this book so everyone who loves this country and wants to be a part of reclaiming the American Dream for their children and neighbors can more easily see what they can do about it. We can do this. We really can if we each play our part—starting now!

NOTES

Sources for epigraphs on p. vii are James Truslow Adams, *The Epic of America* (Boston: Little, Brown, 1931), p. 404; Michelle Alexander, *The New Jim Crow: Mass Incarceration in the Age of Colorblindness* (New York: New Press, 2010); Jerry Blackburn, retired Virginia coal miner (quoted in *VOA News*, "For Many Supporters, Trump is a Thing Called Hope," November 11, 2016 (www.voanews.com/a /ap-for-many-trump-supporters-trump-is-a-thing-called-hope/3591957.html); and Langston Hughes, "Let American Be America Again," *Let America Be America Again and Other Poems* (New York: Vintage Books, 2004).

INTRODUCTION

1. James Truslow Adams, *The Epic of America* (Boston: Little, Brown, 1931), p. 404.

2. See, for example, Roger Cohen, "We Need 'Somebody Spectacular': Views from Trump Country," *New York Times*, September 9, 2016; and Josh Feldman, "Poll: Trump Leads Clinton among Non-College-Educated White Men by a Whopping 59 Points," Mediaite.com, September 25, 2016 (www.mediaite.com/online/poll-trump -leads-clinton-among-non-college-educated-white-men-by-a-whopping-59-points/).

3. Ann Case and Angus Deaton, "Rising Morbidity and Mortality in Midlife among White Non-Hispanic Americans in the 21st Century," December 2015 (www.princeton.edu/faculty-research/research/item/rising-morbidity-and-mortality-midlife-among-white-non-hispanic).

4. "New Research Identifies a 'Sea of Despair' among White, Working-Class Americans," *Washington Post*, March 23, 2017.

5. Terry Gross, "A 'Forgotten History' of How the U.S. Government Segregated America," *NPR*, May 3, 2017, https://www.npr.org/2017/05/03/526655831/a-forgotten-history-of-how-the-u-s-government-segregated-america. See also Amanda Tillotson, Race, Risk and Real Estate: Federal Housing Administration and Black Homeownership in the Post World War II Home Ownership State, 8 DePaul J. for Soc. Just. 25 (2014).

6. Edward Humes, *The Journal of Blacks in Higher Education*, no. 53 (Autumn, 2006), pp. 92–104. See also Ira Katznelson, "Making Affirmative Action White Again," *New York Times*, August 12, 2017, https://www.nytimes.com/2017/08/12/opinion/sunday/making-affirmative-action-white-again.html.

7. There is considerable literature on this topic. See Noel Ignatiev, *How the Irish Became White* (Routledge, 1995) and Karen Brodkin, *How Jews Became White Folks and What That Says about Race in America* (Rutgers University Press, 1999). See also Nell Irvin Painter, *The History of White People* (W. W. Norton & Company, 2011) for a discussion of the invention of race and its frequent use for economic, scientific, and political ends.

8. D'Vera Cohn and Andrea Caumont, "10 Demographic Trends That Are Shaping the U.S. and the World," March 31, 2016 (www.pewresearch.org/fact-tank/2016/03/31/10-demographic-trends-that-are-shaping-the-u-s-and-the-world/).

9. Ibid., p. 26.

10. William H. Frey, *Diversity Explosion: How New Racial Demographics Are Remaking America* (Brookings Institution Press, 2014). Frey documents that between 2010 and 2050, the Hispanic, Asian, and multiracial populations are projected to more than double. The black population, the largest minority group for most of American history, is also expected to increase faster than the population as a whole. From 2000 to 2010, the total U.S. population grew by less than 10 percent, compared with a black population (those who indicated they were black or African American, or multiracial in combination with black) that grew by 15 percent. Meanwhile, the white population is expected to decline by approximately 6 percent by 2050.

11. Ibid., p. 73.

12. Ibid.

13. Consumer spending accounts for a majority of GDP in all advanced nations. See William R. Emmons, *Don't Expect Consumer Spending to Be the Engine of Economic Growth It Once Was*, Federal Reserve Bank of St. Louis, January 2012 (www.stlouisfed.org/publications/regional-economist/january-2012/dont-expect-consumer-spending-to-be-the-engine-of-economic-growth-it-once-was). The World Economic Forum's Global Agenda Council on Aging believes that rapidly aging populations around the world will result in a myriad of economic and social issues, from financial well-being and public health to maintenance of the social safety net (www.weforum.org/agenda/2016/02/japans-population-is-shrinking-what-does-it-mean-for-the-economy/).

14. Gross domestic product is the best way to measure a country's economy. GDP is the total value of everything produced by all the people and companies in the country. "What Is GDP? Definition of Gross Domestic Product," March 7, 2017 (www.thebalance.com/what-is-gdp-definition-of-gross-domestic-product-3306038). Consumer spending's share of GDP was already high, but it increased substantially further during the 1980s, 1990s, and 2000s. See Emmons, *Don't Expect Consumer Spending to Be the Engine of Economic Growth It Once Was*.

15. Terence P. Jeffrey, "7,231,000 Lost Jobs: Manufacturing Employment Down 37% from 1979 Peak," May 12, 2015 (www.cnsnews.com/news/article/terence-p-jeffrey/7231000-lost-jobs-manufacturing-employment-down-37-1979-peak).

16. Anthony P. Carnevale, Nicole Smith, and Jeff Strohl, "Recovery: Job Growth and Education Requirements through 2020," Georgetown Public Policy Institute, Center on Education and the Workforce, June 2013 (https://cew.georgetown.edu/wp-content/uploads/2014/11/Recovery2020.ES_.Web_.pdf).

17. Jesse Bricker, and others, *Changes in U.S. Family Finances from 2007 to 2010: Evidence from the Survey of Consumer Finances*, Federal Reserve Bulletin, June 2012, vol. 98, no. 2 (www.keepingcurrentmatters.com/2015/10/26/2016-home owners-net-worth-will-be-45x-greater-than-a-renter/).

18. Brooke Torres, "Job Seekers: Social Media Is Even More Important Than You Thought," The Muse, n.d. (https://www.themuse.com/advice/job-seekers-social-media-is-even-more-important-than-you-thought).

19. Raj Chetty and Nathaniel Hendren, "The Impacts of Neighborhoods on Intergenerational Mobility," Harvard University, April 2015 (www.equality-of-opportunity.org/images/nbhds_exec_summary.pdf). See also Gillian B. White, "Stranded: How America's Failing Public Transportation Increases Inequality," *The*

Atlantic, May 16, 2015. In a large, continuing study about upward mobility, the longer an average commute in a given county, the worse the chances of lower-income families there moving up the economic ladder.

20. The rise of the "gig economy" means that a growing share of Americans are getting or supplementing their income through short-term, contract- or freelance-based work. Data from the Brookings Institute showed that the number of nonemployer "businesses" (a Census Bureau designation that's mostly made up of self-employed freelancers and contractors) grew from 15 million in 1997 to nearly 24 million in 2014 (See Ian Hathaway and Mark Muro, "Tracking the Gig Economy: New Numbers," Brookings Institute, October 13, 2016 (https://www.brookings.edu /research/tracking-the-gig-economy-new-numbers/). This work is often made possible by digital platforms that enable them to contribute labor (e.g., Uber or Task-Rabbit) or rent or sell assets (e.g., AirBnb). A 2016 study of Americans' income patterns by JPMorgan Chase found that although only 1 percent of adults were participating in the "Online Platform Economy" each month, the cumulative percentage of adults who had ever participated was 4 percent—a 47-fold growth over a three year period. What these numbers reveal is that while the gig economy still constitutes a relatively small share of the overall economy, it's a significant force and growing fast.

21. "Employee Tenure in 2016," Bureau of Labor Statistics, U.S. Department of Labor, September 22, 2016 (www.bls.gov/news.release/pdf/tenure.pdf). This short duration is even more astounding when you take into account that Americans are now moving less frequently than they have since the Census Bureau has been tracking mobility. The percentage of people who changed residences between 2010 and 2011—11.6 percent—was the lowest recorded rate since the Current Population Survey began in 1948.

PART I

1. Thomas Kochan, David Finegold, and Paul Osterman, "Who Can Fix the 'Middle-Skills' Gap?," *Harvard Business Review* 90 (December 2012), p. 85.

2. "American Public Education: An Origin Story," *Education News*, April 16, 2013 (www.educationnews.org/education-policy-and-politics/american-public-edu cation-an-origin-story/).

3. See Neil G. Ruiz, Jill H. Wilson, and Shyamali Choudhury, "The Search for Skills: Demand for H-1B Immigrant Workers in U.S. Metropolitan Areas," Brookings, July 2012 (https://www.brookings.edu/wp-content/uploads/2016/06/18-h1b-visas -labor-immigration.pdf).

4. "The Rising Cost of Not Going to College," Pew Research Center, February 11, 2014 (http://www.pewsocialtrends.org/2014/02/11/the-rising-cost-of-not-going -to-college/).

CHAPTER 1

1. See Texas Education Agency, "2016–2017 Economically Disadvantaged Students: Statewide Totals, by County," 2017 (https://rptsvr1.tea.texas.gov/cgi/sas/broker).

2. Luis Silos, interview with author, March 7, 2017.

3. Orlando Ochoa, interview with author, March 7, 2017.

4. Silos, interview.

5. Scott Jaschik, "The Missing Low-Income Students," *Inside HigherEd*, November 25, 2015 (www.insidehighered.com/news/2015/11/25/study-finds-drop -percentage-low-income-students-enrolling-college).

6. Thomas Kochan, David Finegold, and Paul Osterman, "Who Can Fix the 'Middle-Skills' Gap?," *Harvard Business Review* 90 (December 2012), p. 85.

7. See Bureau of Labor Statistics, "Unemployment Rates and Earnings, by Educational Attainment," October 24, 2017 (www.bls.gov/emp/ep_chart_001.htm).

8. Anthony Carnevale, Nicole Smith, and Jeff Strohl, *Recovery: Job Growth and Education Requirements through 2020*, report (Washington: Georgetown Public Policy Institute, Center on Education and the Workforce, June 2013), p. 15.

9. Ibid.

10. See Jobs for the Future, "Reinventing High Schools for Postsecondary Success," 2017 (www.jff.org/initiatives/early-college-designs).

11. Alexandria W. Radford and others, *Persistence and Attainment of 2003–2004 Beginning Postsecondary Students: After Six Years*, report (U.S. Department of Education, National Center for Education Statistics, December 2010) (https://nces.ed .gov/pubs2011/2011151.pdf).

12. Marlene Seltzer, interview with author, December 22, 2016.

13. See Jobs for the Future, "Early College Designs: A Jobs for the Future Initiative" (www.jff.org/initiatives/early-college-designs).

14. See Jobs for the Future, *Early College High Schools Get Results*, report (2014) (www.jff.org/sites/default/files/services/files/ECHS_get_results_021014.pdf).

15. Ibid.

16. Ibid.

17. Seltzer, interview.

18. See Pharr—San Juan—Alamo Independent School District, "Inside PSJA ISD," 2017 (www.psjaisd.us/site/Default.aspx?PageID=53).

19. Daniel P. King, "Is There Any Way You Can Start Now?," *School Administrator* 70 (June 2013), p. 16.

20. Daniel P. King, "You Didn't Finish High School? Start College Today!," *EdTech*, Winter 2013 (www.edtechmagazine.com/k12/article/2013/01/you-didnt-finish-high-school-start-college-today).

21. See "Hidalgo ISD," *Texas Tribune*, 2016 (https://schools.texastribune.org/districts/hidalgo-isd/).

22. Cecilia Le, "Launching Early College Districtwide," Jobs for the Future and Educate Texas (March 2012), p. 5 (www.jff.org/sites/default/files/publications/ECDS_PSJA_LaunchingECdistricts_032212.pdf).

23. Ibid., p. 2.

24. Karina Quintana, interview with author, March 7, 2016.

25. Joel Vargas, interview with author, December 22, 2016.

26. Jordan Brown, interview with author, December 21, 2016.

27. See KnowledgeWorks, "More Than a Decade of Success," 2017 (www.knowledgeworks.org/schools/early-college).

28. Ibid.

29. See U.S. News: Education, "Youngstown Early College," 2017 (www.usnews.com/education/best-high-schools/ohio/districts/youngstown-city-schools/youngstown-early-college-15362).

30. Silos, interview.

31. Camille L. Ryan and Kurt Bauman, *Educational Attainment in the United States: 2015*, Report P20-578 (U.S. Census Bureau, March 2016) (www.census.gov/content/dam/Census/library/publications/2016/demo/p20-578.pdf).

32. Joy Coates and Michael Webb, "Partners in Innovation: How a High School and College Are Improving Outcomes for Youth in San Diego," Jobs for the Future, November 2013 (www.jff.org/sites/default/files/publications/materials/PartnersInInnovation_112013.pdf).

33. John Reinan, "College Courses for High School Kids Become a Touchy Subject in Small Minn. Districts," *Fulda (Minn.) Star Tribune*, November 2, 2016.

34. Seltzer, interview.

35. 2016 Minnesota Statutes, Chapter 122A: Section 122A.61 "Reserved Revenue for Staff Development" (www.revisor.mn.gov/statutes/?id=122A.61).

36. Jennifer D. Zinth, "Dual Enrollment: A Strategy to Improve College-Going and College Completion among Rural Students," Education Commission of the States, June 2014, p. 3 (www.ecs.org/clearinghouse/01/12/61/11261.pdf).

37. Jennifer D. Zinth, "Increasing Student Access and Success in Dual Enrollment Programs: 13 Model State-Level Policy Components," Education Commission of the States, February 2014, p. 14 (www.ecs.org/clearinghouse/01/10/91/11091.pdf).

38. See P-TECH 9–14 Model, www.ptech.org/model.

39. Michael Webb and Carol Gerwin, "Early College Expansion: Propelling Students to Postsecondary Success, at a School near You," Jobs for the Future, March 2014, p. 17 (www.jff.org/sites/default/files/publications/materials/Early-College-Expansion_031414.pdf).

40. Ibid.

41. See Education Commission of the States, "Dual Enrollment: Statewide Policy in Place," March 2016 (http://ecs.force.com/mbdata/MBQuestRTL?Rep=DE1501).

42. Serve Center, "Smoothing the Way to College: Impact of Early College High Schools," University of North Carolina at Greensboro (www.serve.org/uploads/docs/Genpercent20Documents/Smoothing_the_way_to_college.pdf).

43. See more about Performance-Based Funding for Higher Education at National Conference of State Legislators: Education (www.ncsl.org/research/education/performance-funding.aspx).

44. U.S. Department of Education, "Fact Sheet: Department of Education Launches Experiment to Provide Federal Pell Grant Funds to High School Students Taking College Courses for Credit," press release, October 20, 2015.

CHAPTER 2

1. Georgia State University, "Complete College Georgia: 2015 Status Report," 2015, p. 3 (http://enrollment.gsu.edu/files/2015/08/Georgia-State-University-CCG-Report-2015.pdf).

2. Timothy Renick, interview with author, April 21, 2017.

3. Ibid.

4. Ibid.

5. Ibid.

6. Georgia State University, "2016 Status Report, Georgia State University, Complete College Georgia," p. 3 (http://success.gsu.edu/files/2017/01/Georgia-State-University-2016-Complete-College-Report-with-Appendix-10-26-16.pdf).

7. Nick Chiles, "At Georgia State, More Black Students Graduate Each Year Than at Any U.S. College," *The Hechinger Report*, November 25, 2016 (http://hechingerreport.org/at-georgia-state-black-students-find-comfort-and-academic-succes/).

8. GSU increased the number of black, Hispanic, and low-income students by 10 percent over the same period that they increased graduation rates. See Chiles, "At Georgia State."

9. Renick, interview.

10. Anthony Carnevale, Tamara Jayasundera, and Artem Gulish, "America's Divided Recovery: College Haves and Have-Notes," Center for Education and the Workforce, Georgetown University, 2016 (https://cew.georgetown.edu/cew-reports /americas-divided-recovery/).

11. Bureau of Labor Statistics, "Employment Projections," March 15, 2016 (www .bls.gov/emp/ep_chart_001.htm).

12. Department of Education, "Fact Sheet: Focusing Higher Education on Student Success," July 25, 2015 (www.ed.gov/news/press-releases/fact-sheet-focusing -higher-education-student-success);

13. Bureau of Labor Statistics, "Employment Projections."

14. David Leonhardt, "The College Dropout Boom," *New York Times*, May 24, 2005 (http://www.nytimes.com/2005/05/24/us/class/the-college-dropout-boom.html?_r=0).

15. Emily Tate, "Graduation Rates and Race," Inside Higher Ed, April 26, 2017 (https://www.insidehighered.com/news/2017/04/26/college-completion-rates-vary -race-and-ethnicity-report-finds).

16. The Pell Institute, "Indicators of Higher Education Equity," p. 31.

17. Department of Education, "Fact Sheet."

18. Institute for College Access and Success, "Project on Student Debt: State by State Data," 2016 (http://ticas.org/posd/map-state-data).

19. Institute for College Access and Success, "Quick Facts about Student Debt," March 2014 (http://ticas.org/sites/default/files/pub_files/Debt_Facts_and_Sources.pdf).

20. Michal Grinstein-Weiss and others, "Racial Disparities in Education Debt Burden among Low- and Moderate-Income Households," Brookings Institution, April 29, 2016 (www.brookings.edu/research/racial-disparities-in-education-debt -burden-among-low-and-moderate-income-households-2/).

21. Ylan Q. Mui and Suzy Khimm, "College Dropouts Have Debt but No Degree," *Washington Post*, May 28, 2012 (www.washingtonpost.com/business /economy/college-dropouts-have-debt-but-no-degree/2012/05/28/gJQAnUPqwU _story.html?utm_term=.1d46b2be2614).

22. See "Top Colleges Doing the Most for Low-Income Students," *New York Times*, September 16, 2015 (www.nytimes.com/interactive/2015/09/17/upshot/top -colleges-doing-the-most-for-low-income-students.html).

23. U.S. Department of Education, "Fulfilling the Promise, Serving the Need," March 2016 (www2.ed.gov/about/overview/focus/advancing-college-opportunity .pdf).

24. David Leonhardt, "California's Upward Mobility Machine," *New York Times*, September 16, 2015.

25. Ibid.

26. Paul Bradley, "Report: College Transfer Pipeline Badly Leaking," *Community College Week*, January 19, 2016 (http://ccweek.com/article-4981-report:-college -transfer-pipeline-badly-leaking.html).

27. University of California, "Admissions: Transfers," 2014 (http://admission .universityofcalifornia.edu/transfer/index.html?PHPSESSID=5f0dfe5a9f66b556f81 f49cc58488d5f).

28. Education Trust, *Rising Tide: Do College Grad Rate Gains Benefit All Students?*, December 2015, p. 1 (https://edtrust.org/wp-content/uploads/2014 /09/TheRisingTide-Do-College-Grad-Rate-Gains-Benefit-All-Students-3.7-16 .pdf).

29. Ibid., p. 2.

30. "Getting Traction in Closing the Inequality Gap," *Chronicle of Higher Education*, March 18, 2016 (www.chronicle.com/article/Video-Getting-Traction-in/235713).

31. Ibid.

32. Ibid.

33. Kevin Kruger, Amelia Parnell, and Alexis Wesaw, "Landscape Analysis of Emergency Aid Programs," NASPA *Student Affairs Administrators in Higher Education*, 2016, p. 16 (www.naspa.org/images/uploads/main/Emergency_Aid_Report .pdf).

34. Emma Kinery, "Emergency Aid Helps Keep Students in College," *USA Today College*, May 2, 2016 (http://college.usatoday.com/2016/05/02/emergency-aid -helps-keep-students-in-college/).

35. See San Diego State University, "Compact Scholars Program," 2017 (http:// csp.sdsu.edu/dus/compactscholars/).

36. Ibid.

37. The group is supported by the Bill and Melinda Gates Foundation explicitly for the experimentation, iteration, and sharing of the most promising practices to improve college completion (http://postsecondary.gatesfoundation.org/frontier-set -fact-sheet/).

38. Ibid.

CHAPTER 3

1. Frontline workers are the "employees who are closest to serving and supporting the customer." See Anthony Tjan, "Listen to Your Frontline Employees," *Harvard Business Review*, April 4, 2012 (https://hbr.org/2012/04/listen-to-your-frontline-emplo.html). They often have less than an associate's degree and make less than $40,000. See Anadelia Fadeev, "You Need to Invest in the Frontline," *Inkling*, March 23, 2016 (www.inkling.com/blog/2016/03/clos-need-to-invest-frontline-employees/).

2. College for America Staff, "Why Anthem Is Willing to Pay for 51,000 Employees to Go to College," *College for America*, November 10, 2015 (http://collegeforamerica.org/why-anthem-is-willing-to-pay-for-51000-employees-to-go-to-college/).

3. Detra Wright, interview with author, September 29, 2016.

4. Ibid.

5. CFA Staff, "Proof That There Is a College for Working Adults with Busy Lives," Southern New Hampshire University College for America, June 20, 2015 (https://collegeforamerica.org/student-case-study-darby-conley/).

6. Kay Mooney, interview with author, March 30, 2017.

7. Ibid.

8. Ibid.

9. Ibid.

10. Julian Alssid, interview with author, February 2016.

11. Julian L. Alssid, "A New Gallup Survey Says Colleges and Employers Disagree about How Workforce-Ready Graduates Are—Who's Right?" *Huffington Post*, April 29, 2014 (www.huffingtonpost.com/julian-l-alssid/a-new-gallup-survey-says-_b_4862669.html).

12. Boston.com for Knowledge Connection, "SNHU Reinvents Itself as National Online Hub," Boston.com, January 10, 2017 (http://sponsored.boston.com/knowledge-connection/snhu-reinvents-national-online-hub).

13. Institute for Corporate Productivity and UpSkill America, "Developing America's Frontline Workers," report, 2016, p. 2 (www.nist.gov/sites/default/files/developing_america_s_frontline_workers_i4cp_upskill_america_2016.pdf).

14. Alssid, interview with author, January 2016.

15. College for America Staff, "Caspers Company McDonald's and Its Employees Get Extra Value Out of Tuition Assistance," College for America, February 26, 2015 (http://collegeforamerica.org/caspers-company-mcdonalds-and-its-employees-get-extra-value-out-of-tuition-assistance/).

16. Mary Jane Ryan, interview with author, March 27, 2017.

17. Complete College America, "Time Is the Enemy: The Surprising Truth about Why Today's College Students Aren't Graduating . . . and What Needs to Change," 2011, p. 12 (http://completecollege.org/docs/Time_Is_the_Enemy.pdf).

18. College for America student surveys, 2017.

19. Alssid, interview, January 2016.

20. Ibid.

21. John Gravois, "The College For-Profits Should Fear," *Washington Monthly*, September–October 2011 (http://washingtonmonthly.com/magazine/septoct-2011/the-college-for-profits-should-fear-2/).

22. Fred Hurtz, WGU vice president for institutional advancement, interview with author, April 21, 2017.

23. Ibid.

24. Ibid. See also Student Loan Hero, "Student Load Debt Statistics for 2017," May 17, 2017 (https://studentloanhero.com/student-loan-debt-statistics/).

25. See Western Governors University, "Graduate Success," 2017 (www.wgu.edu/about_WGU/graduate_success).

26. Ibid.

27. Paul Fain, "Keeping Up with Competency," Inside Higher Ed, September 10, 2015 (www.insidehighered.com/news/2015/09/10/amid-competency-based-education-boom-meeting-help-colleges-do-it-right).

28. Alssid, interview, January 2016.

29. Institute for Corporate Productivity, "Developing America's Frontline Workers," p. 2.

30. Randy Task, "Meeting the Demands of the Job Market with Education Opportunities for Frontline Workers," *Huffington Post*, April 12, 2017.

31. National Skills Coalition, "United States Middle-Skill Fact Sheet," February 6, 2017 (www.nationalskillscoalition.org/state-policy/fact-sheets).

32. Institute for Corporate Productivity, "Developing America's Frontline Workers," p. 18.

33. Or create a tuition assistance program if you don't already have one. The data noted earlier in this chapter shows that is what the highest-performing companies have.

34. Kaitlin Mulhaire, "Paying Their Workers' College Tuition Can Pay Off for Companies," *Time Magazine*, April 26, 2016.

35. Institute for Corporate Productivity, "Developing America's Frontline Workers," see "The Study." The majority of the organizations surveyed employ frontline workers with 52 percent employing more than 16,000 workers in total.

36. Ibid., p. 3.

37. Mulhaire, "Paying Their Workers' College Tuition."

CHAPTER 4

1. Other milestones include early-grade reading, middle-grade math, high school graduation, and postsecondary enrollment and completion. See Strive Together, "Roadmap to Success," 2017 (www.strivetogether.org/our-approach/student-roadmap-success/).

2. Nancy Zimpher, interview with author, July 13, 2016.

3. Ibid.

4. Ibid.

5. See Strive Together, "The Strive Together Story," 2017 (www.strivetogether.org/vision-roadmap/strivetogether-story).

6. Jeff Edmonson and Nancy Zimpher, *Striving Together: Early Lessons in Achieving Collective Impact in Education* (State University of New York Press, 2014).

7. Allen Grossman and others, "StriveTogether: Reinventing the Local Education Ecosystem," Harvard Business School, January 9, 2014, p. 2 (www.strivetogether.org/wp-content/uploads/2017/03/StriveTogether-Reinventing-the-Local-Education-Ecosystem-314-031.pdf).

8. See StriveTogether, "Community Reports," 2017 (www.strivetogether.org/impact/community-reports/).

9. Lillian Pace and Jeff Edmondson, "Improving Student Outcomes through Collective Impact: A Guide for Federal Policymakers," report, Knowledge Works and StriveTogether, October 2014, p. 7 (www.knowledgeworks.org/sites/default/files/Improving-Student-Outcomes-Through-Collective-Impact.pdf).

10. See The Nation's Report Card, "Mathematics and Reading Assessments: National Results Overview," 2015 (www.nationsreportcard.gov/reading_math_2015/#reading?grade=4).

11. Annie E. Casey Foundation, "The 2016 KIDS COUNT Data Book, State Trends in Child Well-Being," June 21, 2016, p. 16 (www.aecf.org/resources/the-2016-kids-count-data-book/).

12. Ibid.

13. See Strive Together, "The Network," 2017 (www.strivetogether.org/the-network/).

14. Jeff Edmonson, interview with author, June 2016.

15. See Jeff Edmondson, "Systems Change: More Than a Buzzword," Bridgespan Group, January 27, 2016 (www.bridgespan.org/insights/blog/transformative-scale/systems-change-more-than-a-buzzword).

16. Edmondson, interview.

17. Ibid. Communities in the network must publicly disaggregate local data by race, income, and geography. These disaggregated data help communities identify inequalities in student achievement and make decisions about how best to differentiate services to eliminate locally defined disparities. Data on reading proficiency at the third-grade level might tell you that 80 percent of the students, systemwide, are reading at grade level. But when you disaggregate the data by race, income, and geography, you are likely to see that the "deficient" 20 percent actually come from from schools in two neighborhoods. Those schools would then get a targeted intervention, and attention would be paid to see if it is making a difference.

18. Edmondson, interview.

19. Ibid.

20. See Edmondson, "Systems Change: More Than a Buzzword."

21. Edmondson, interview.

22. Report cards issued by forty-five of the sixty-nine communities show the progress each is making against its declared outcomes. See Strive Together, "Community Reports," 2017 (www.strivetogether.org/results/community-reports).

23. See Commit, "About the Commit Partnership," 2017 (http://commit2dallas.org/about-us/).

24. Todd Williams, interview with author, June 23, 2016.

25. See Commit, "About the Commit Partnership."

26. Williams, interview.

27. Dallas has approximately 900,000 school-age students spread over fifteen different independent school districts, fourteen four-year colleges, seven community colleges, and more than 300 nonprofits. See Commit, "Dallas County Snapshot," 2017 (www.commit2dallas.org/about-us/Dallas-county-snapshot/).

28. Ibid.

29. Ibid.

30. Ibid.

31. Ibid.

32. Ibid.

33. See Leadership ISD, "Our Program," 2017 (http://leadershipisd.org/program/).

34. Williams, interview.

35. Ibid.

36. Ibid.

37. Ibid.

38. For more about Rip Rapson, see chapter 12.

39. Rip Rapson, "From Detroit to Memphis: The Imperative of Bold Leadership for the Future of American Cities," speech, Memphis, Tenn., August 23, 2016 (http://kresge.org/library/detroit-memphis-imperative-bold-leadership-future -american-cities).

40. Professors Ronald Heifetz and Marty Linsky framed this term in their work on adaptive leadership. They refer to "getting off the dance floor and going to the balcony," or the ability of a leader to step back from the action and ask, What's really going on here? For more, see Ronald Heifetz and Marty Linsky, "A Survival Guide for Leaders," *Harvard Business Review*, June 2002 (https://hbr.org/2002/06/a-survival -guide-for-leaders).

PART II

1. A Guide to Statistics on Historical Trends in Income Inequality, Center for Budget and Policy Priorities, October 11, 2017 (www.cbpp.org/research/poverty-and -inequality/a-guide-to-statistics-on-historical-trends-in-income-inequality).

2. Household Debt Service Payments as a Percent of Disposable Personal Income, Federal Reserve Bank of St. Louis, January 9, 2018 (https://fred.stlouisfed.org /series/TDSP).

3. By 2013 personal consumption had risen to 73 percent of GDP, up from just 62 percent in 1970.

4. In fact, companies less than one year old had regularly created an average of 1.5 million jobs a year over the past three decades. Jason Wiens and Chris Jackson, "The Importance of Young Firms," Entrepreneur Policy Digest, Kauffman Foundation, September 13, 2015.

5. Dynamism in Retreat: Consequences for Regions, Markets and Workers, Economic Innovation Group, February, 2017 (http://eig.org/dynamism).

CHAPTER 5

1. Lula Luu, interview with author, November 4, 2016.

2. Ibid.

3. Ibid.

4. Ibid.

5. Ibid.

6. Ibid.

7. Ross Baird, interview with author, May 19, 2017.

8. Luu, interview.

9. In fact, companies less than one year old had regularly created an average of 1.5 million jobs per year over the past three decades. Jason Wiens and Chris Jackson, "The Importance of Young Firms for Economic Growth," Kauffman Foundation, September 13, 2015 (www.kauffman.org/what-we-do/resources/ entrepreneurship-policy-digest/the-importance-of-young-firms-for-economic-growth).

10. Ian Hathaway and Robert E. Litan, "Declining Business Dynamism in the United States: A Look at States and Metros," Brookings Institution, May 2014, p. 2 (www.brookings.edu/wp-content/uploads/2016/06/declining_business_dynamism _hathaway_litan.pdf).

11. Ibid., p. 3.

12. Benjamin Ryan, "Starved of Financing, New Businesses Are in Decline," Gallup, September 4, 2014 (www.gallup.com/businessjournal/175499/starved -financing-new-businesses-decline.aspx).

13. E. J. Reedy and Robert E. Litan, "Starting Smaller; Staying Smaller: America's Slow Leak in Job Creation," Kauffman Foundation, July 2011 (www.kauffman .org/~/media/kauffman_org/research%20reports%20and%20covers/2011/07/job _leaks_starting_smaller_study.pdf).

14. In 2010, the number of new but small companies grew to 80 percent while the companies with twenty or more employee shrunk to 8 percent (Reedy and Litan, "Starting Smaller; Staying Smaller").

15. See Longman Business English Dictionary Online, 2017 (www.ldoceonline .com/).

16. Rana Foroohar, *Makers and Takers: Rise of Finance and Fall of American Business* (New York: Crown Business, 2016), p. 6.

17. For more on the reasons behind this shift, read Foroohar's *Makers and Takers.* Foroohar details how the U.S. economy has "financialized" over the past thirty years. The term—coined in the early 2000s to describe the current phenomenon— refers to an economy in which the finance sector has become highly profitable at the expense of the rest of the economy.

18. Foroohar cites research by Roosevelt University's Ozgur Orhangazi that has found that investment in the real sector of the economy actually falls as these types of activities rise as well as research by the former British banking regulator Adair Turner— now chairman of the Institute for New Economic Thinking—who estimates that a mere 15 percent of all financial flows now goes into projects in the real economy. Ibid.

19. Baird and Schultz brought leaders from business, academia, government, and nonprofits together over an eighteen-month period to propose an action agenda for America. They published their recommendations in a book in 2015. Rework America, *America's Moment: Creating Opportunity in the Connected Age* (W. W. Norton & Company, June 2015). See a description of the process in the book's acknowledgments. The book provides a thoughtful discussion of the current incentive structure that makes it more attractive (and less risky) to provide capital for mortgages, student loans, and consumer debt, in large part because they either cannot be discharged in bankruptcy (mortgages and student debt) or are historically easy to sell through securitization (mortgages and consumer debt), p. 102.

20. Karen Gordon Mills and Brayden McCarthy, "The State of Small Business Lending: Credit Access During the Recovery and How Technology May Change the Game," Harvard Business School, July 22, 2014, p. 5 (www.hbs.edu/faculty /Publication%20Files/15-004_09b1bf8b- eb2a-4e63- 9c4e-0374f770856f.pdf).

21. Rework America, *America's Moment*, p. 91.

22. Mills and McCarthy, "The State of Small Business Lending," p. 37.

23. Rework America, *America's Moment*, p. 90.

24. According to research conducted by the Kauffman Foundation, the performance of businesses started by people of color is very different from that of white-owned businesses. For example, black- and Hispanic-owned enterprises have higher failure rates than white- and Asian-owned firms. White-owned firms have at least twice the average sales of Asian, Hispanic, and black-owned businesses. See Kauffman Foundation, "Including People of Color in the Promise of Entrepreneurship," December 5, 2016 (www.kauffman.org/~/media/kauffman_org/resources/2016 /including percent20people percent20of percent20color percent20in percent20the percent20promise percent20of percent20entrepreneurship percent20pdf.pdf).

25. Robert W. Fairlie and others, "The Kauffman Index of Startup Activity: National Trends," 2015, p. 12. See also Economic Innovation Group, "Dynamism in Retreat," February, 2017, p. 29 and Reid Wilson, "Aging White Population Speeding Diversity," The Hill, December 2, 2016 (http://thehill.com/homenews /news/308357-decline-of-americas-white-population-accelerating-study-finds).

26. Ibid.

27. It is not just that the number of white start-ups has fallen but that the total number of start-ups overall has fallen. As noted earlier in the chapter, the number of annual start-ups ranged from 400–500,000 annually for more than thirty years but have largely been under 400,000 since 2007. The U.S. economy needs people of color and

women to continue to make up a large part of the start-up population, but even more simply we need many more people engaging in entrepreneurship.

28. Algernon Austin, "The Color of Entrepreneurship: Why the Racial Gap among Firms Costs the U.S. Billions," Center for Global Policy Solutions, April 20, 2016 (http://globalpolicysolutions.org/report/color-entrepreneurship-racial-gap -among-firms-costs-u-s-billions/). Women of color are the fastest-growing segment of the woman-owned small-business community. From 1997 to 2013, while the total number of female-owned firms in the United States grew by 59 percent—one and a half times the national average—a closer look at the statistics shows that women of color are the catalyst behind much of this growth, with businesses owned by African American women growing by 258 percent, Latina women by 180 percent, Asian American women by 156 percent, Native American women by 108 percent, and Native Hawaiian and Pacific Islander women by 216 percent. Maria Cantwell, "21st Century Barriers to Women's Entrepreneurship," Majority Report of the U.S. Senate Committee on Small Business and Entrepreneurship, July 23, 2014 (www .sbc.senate.gov/public/?a=Files.Serve&File_id=3f954386-f16b-48d2-86ad -698a75e33cc4).

29. Kaufmann Foundation, "Including People of Color."

30. According to the Annual Survey of Entrepreneurs, among firms that started with at least $100,000 in capital, 82 percent are white owned, 13 percent are Asian owned, 4 percent are Hispanic owned, and 1 percent are black owned. Ibid.

31. Rakesh Kochhar, Richard Fry, and Paul Taylor, "Wealth Gaps Rise to Record Highs between Whites, Blacks, Hispanics," Pew Research Center, July 26, 2011 (www.pewsocialtrends.org/2011/07/26/wealth-gaps-rise-to-record-highs-between -whites-blacks-hispanics/?beta=true&utm_expid=53098246-2.Lly4CFSVQG 2lphsg-KopIg.1&utm_referrer=https%253A%252F%252Fwww.google .com%252F).

32. Research suggests that approximately 15 percent of the difference in start-up rates among black and white Americans can be explained by differences in assets. Kauffman Foundation, "Including People of Color."

33. Josh Silver, "Small Business Loan Data: Recommendations to the Consumer Financial Protection Bureau for Implementing Section 1071 of the Dodd-Frank Wall Street Reform and Consumer Protection Act of 2010," National Community Reinvestment Coalition, 2014, p. 16 (www.aba.com/Tools/Economic/Documents /NCRCRecommendationsToCFPBonSmallBusinessLoanData.pdf).

34. Cantwell, "21st Century Barriers to Women's Entrepreneurship," p. 15.

35. Silver, "Small Business Loan Data," p. 14.

36. John Paglia, "Small-Business Lending Has a Diversity Problem," *American Banker*, February 13, 2017 (https://www.americanbanker.com/opinion/small-business-lending-has-a-diversity-problem). See U.S. Census Bureau, "QuickFacts: People," 2017 (www.census.gov/quickfacts/table/PST045216/00).

37. This is important because we know that those in decisionmaking positions are more likely to lend to borrowers who look like themselves. Those entrepreneurs are then likely to hire employees that look like themselves, too. A recent Babson College study documented that just 2.7 percent of the 6,517 companies that received venture funding from 2011 to 2013 had women CEOs and 1 percent were led by African Americans. Other groups, including Hispanics, receive so little funding that numbers are hard to come by. Candida G. Brush and others, "Diana Report Women Entrepreneurs 2014: Bridging the Gender Gap in Venture Capital," Arthur M. Blank Center for Entrepreneurship, Babson College, September 2014, p. 14 (www.babson.edu/Academics/centers/blank-center/global-research/diana/Documents/diana-project-executive-summary-2014.pdf). See also Kim-Mai Cutler, "Here's a Detailed Breakdown of Racial and Gender Diversity Data across U.S. Venture Capital Firms," October 6, 2015 (https://techcrunch.com/2015/10/06/s23p-racial-gender-diversity-venture/).

38. Silver, "Small Business Loan Data," pp. 15–16.

39. Herbie Ziskend, "Four Observations about Startup Ecosystems after 4,000 Miles on the Road," December 17, 2016 (www.huffingtonpost.com/herbie-ziskend/four-observations-about-s_b_8826198.html).

40. J. D. Harrison, "With a Bus and a Checkbook, Steve Case Tries to Remap American Entrepreneurship," *Washington Post*, April 3, 2015 (www.washingtonpost.com/news/on-small-business/wp/2015/04/03/with-a-bus-and-a-checkbook-steve-case-tries-to-remap-american-entrepreneurship/?utm_term=.ec81c44a7ce1).

41. Ibid.

42. Mitchell Kapor, "Bio," 2017 (www.kapor.com/bio/).

43. See all companies in Kapor Capital's portfolio at Kapor Capital, "Honor," 2017 (www.kaporcapital.com/portfolio/).

44. Nathan McAlone, "Silicon Valley Philanthropists Will Invest $25 Million in Startups That Help Diversify the Tech World," *Business Insider*, August 5, 2015 (www.businessinsider.com/silicon-valley-philanthropists-will-invest-25-million-in-startups-that-help-diversify-the-tech-world-2015-8).

45. Funds are stand-alone investment vehicles where investors either lend the fund money, at a certain rate of interest for a certain period of time, so it can be

re-lent to entrepreneurs or invest equity that is only returned if the investments made by the fund are profitable.

46. The number of similar funds and firms is extraordinary, including Urban Innovation Fund and Bridges Ventures to Groundwork Equity, LLC, which is focusing on the very risky, but important, early-stage friends and family capital gap.

47. A private equity firm aggregates funds from wealthy individuals or institutions for the purpose of buying all or part of a company. The firm then helps the company grow, selling its ownership interest in future years for a profit, then returning the original equity investment, plus profit, to the investors.

48. Impact American Fund, "Management," 2017 (www.impactamericafund .com/management/).

49. Chapter 6 addresses incubators.

50. NOLA.com, "BuildNOLA Launches Loan Fund to Help Small Businesses Access City Contracts," October 28, 2016 (www.nola.com/business/index.ssf/2016 /10/buildnola_launches_loan_fund_t.html). The $1.5 million pilot fund includes $1.25 million from my organization, Living Cities, and $250,000 from NewCorp, a local community-development financial institution. If the pilot fund is successful, as similar funds have been across the country, the city intends to raise capital for a $10 million loan fund—$8 million from private banks and $2 million from city and philanthropic sources.

51. While Village Capital works at the earlier stages of a business's life, other organizations, like Endeavor, work at the growth stage. Endeavor (www.endeavor .org) has been wildly successful around the globe and has just begun expanding in the United States. Endeavor requires the support of five to ten top local business leaders to fund local operations, form a board of directors, and build a local network to mentor Endeavor entrepreneurs. It looks for strong macroeconomic conditions that enable entrepreneurship (for example, stable economic growth, low corruption levels). While it operates in countries and cities that possess structural barriers to entrepreneurship, its approach intentionally seeks to reduce them.

52. Baird, interview, June 2016.

53. For example, 40 percent of Village Capital's investments are in companies with women cofounders (who are, in turn, outperforming the baseline by 30 percent in revenue growth), and 27 percent are in entrepreneurs of color. These companies have created more than 8,000 jobs and leveraged $140 million in additional capital, with a 91 percent survival rate. They have seen four and a half times faster revenue growth and have raised three and a half times as many funds as a control group during the same period. Not only are forty-six of these investments successful and

active (with nine exits and five write-offs), but their products and services have served 174,000 low-income students and 149,000 low-income patients, recycled 113 tons of plastic, and offset 24 million tons of CO_2 emissions.

54. Baird, interview, June 2016.

55. Baird's focus on purposeful enterprises also is a fast-growing trend across the country. In spring 2016, Deutsche Bank and Living Cities set out to determine just how abundant these purposeful businesses really were across the country and what problems they were trying to solve. In just ninety days, we found 130 of what we came to term "urban serving businesses"—what many others call social-purpose businesses—active in education, financial services, government services, career services, and health services, either directly or on behalf of government, founded and operating in more than a dozen places. They are increasingly able to generate revenue and attract private capital to fund growth. They have a scalable or replicable business model that can grow within and across geographies. Interesting, they are riding strong tailwinds, benefiting keenly from the widespread adoption of technological innovation, such as big data and smartphones, the democratization of innovation tools, like cloud computing and 3-D printing, and an increased frustration with the status quo and willingness simply to try something new. In short, they are important and viable companies creating jobs and solutions that can and should be operating everywhere.

56. Luu, interview.

57. Kiva Zip is able to provide 0 percent interest, character-based loans of up to $5,000 for small businesses and entrepreneurs who are financially excluded and underserved by crowd-funding the capital online from individuals. See Kiva, "Fund Your Dream, Change Your Life," 2017 (https://borrow.kiva.org/borrow). "Friends and family," or seed capital, is what very early capital is often called. These funds almost always come from a person's savings or from family members. It is the riskiest capital because it often releases before a company even has a proof of concept or product to sell.

58. Angel investors, also called informal investors, invest during early stages of a start-up, often to help propel the business to get off the ground. Angel investors typically invest their own money.

59. Andrew Ross Sorkin, "From Bezos to Walton, Big Investors Back Fund for 'Flyover' Start-ups," *New York Times*, December 4, 2017 (https://www.nytimes.com /2017/12/04/business/dealbook/midwest-start-ups.html?mtrref=techcrunch.com). Investors include the likes of fashion designer Tory Burch, Eric Schmidt of Google's parent Alphabet, Quicken Loans founder Dan Gilbert, Carlyle Group cofounder David Rubenstein, Howard Schultz, and many others.

60. These investment vehicles are simply entities that people can loan money to or invest equity in.

61. One of the more creative efforts is Detroit Homecoming. Since 2014, it has brought more than 300 people with ties to Detroit "home" to reexperience the city and has resulted in investment commitments of more than $260 million in city projects and businesses. For more on Detroit Homecoming, see Christine Ferretti, "Lineup Unveiled for Third Detroit Homecoming," *Detroit News*, August 8, 2016.

62. The OECD defines a high-growth business as "a firm of 10 or more employees that grows either its employees or turnover by an average of more than 20 per cent per year for three consecutive years." See David Audretsch, "Determinants of High-Growth Entrepreneurship," March 28, 2012, University of Indiana, report (https://www.oecd.org/cfe/leed/Audretsch_determinants%20of%20high-growth%20firms.pdf). That can rarely be achieved or sustained in a single market.

63. Tumml's mission is to empower entrepreneurs to solve urban problems. With a hands-on approach, Tumml provides entrepreneurs with the tools to help scale their impact and enhance quality of life in cities everywhere (www.tumml.org). 1776 is a global incubator and seed fund helping start-ups transform industries that impact millions of lives every day—education, energy and sustainability, health, transportation, and cities (www.1776.vc).

64. For a great discussion of entrepreneurial ecosystems, see Phillip E. Auerswald, "Enabling Entrepreneurial Ecosystems," Kauffman Foundation Research Series on City, Metro, and Regional Entrepreneurship, October 2015 (www.kauffman.org/~/media/kauffman_org/research%20reports%20and%20covers/2015/10/enabling_entrepreneurial_ecosystems.pdf).

65. See note 81.

66. An increasing number of grant makers are realizing the obstacles that this next generation of entrepreneurs face and the importance of their success to our overall economy, but these types of activities have not been part of mainstream philanthropy.

CHAPTER 6

1. Derek Douglas, interview with author, May 26, 2016.

2. John Dodge, "Poverty Rates in Many Chicago Neighborhoods Near 60 Percent," CBS Chicago, April 22, 2014 (http://chicago.cbslocal.com/2014/04/22/poverty-rates-in-many-chicago-neighborhoods-near-60-percent/).

3. Douglas, interview.

4. Ibid.

5. Chicago is ranked seventh-largest employer in the city of Chicago, and the only employer in the top-twenty list located solely in Chicago's South Side. See Sabrina Gasulla, "Chicago's Largest Employers by the Numbers," *Crain's Chicago Business*, January 14, 2017 (www.chicagobusiness.com/article/20170114/ISSUE01 /170119906/chicagos-largest-employers-by-the-numbers).

6. Douglas, interview.

7. See University of Chicago Civic Engagement, "UChicago Local," 2017 (http:// civicengagement.uchicago.edu/anchor/economic-impact-and-jobs/uchicago-local/).

8. Douglas, interview.

9. UChicago News, "UChicago to Expand Diversity and Local Employment on Construction Projects," March 15, 2017 (https://news.uchicago.edu/article/2017/03 /15/uchicago-expand-diversity-and-local-employment-construction-projects).

10. Ibid.

11. Nathan M. Jensen, "Evaluating Firm-Specific Location Incentives: An Application to the Kansas PEAK Program," report, Ewing Marion Kauffman Foundation, 2014 (www.kauffman.org/~/media/kauffman_org/research%20reports%20and %20covers/2014/04/evaluating_firm_specific_location_incentives). See also Amy Liu, "Remaking Economic Development: The Markets and Civics of Continuous Growth and Prosperity," report, Brookings, February 2016 (www.brookings .edu/wp-content/uploads/2016/02/BMPP_RemakingEconomicDevelopment _Feb25LoRes-1.pdf).

12. International City/County Management Association, "Incentives for Business Attraction and Retention," June 13, 2012 (http://icma.org/en/Article/102200 /Incentives_for_Business_Attraction_and_Retention).

13. Jed Kolko, "Business Relocation and Homegrown Jobs, 1992–2006," report, Public Policy Institute of California, September 2010 (www.ppic.org/content/pubs /report/R_910JKR.pdf).

14. Timothy J. Bartik, "A New Panel Database on Business Incentives for Economic Development Offered by State and Local Governments in the United States" (http://research.upjohn.org/reports/22). The report, based on a database of twenty-six years of incentives in thirty-three states, affirms what many have long believed, that tax breaks don't do much to convince companies to move and have statistically insignificant impact on growth.

15. Greg Riezi, "The Changing Face of East Baltimore," *Johns Hopkins University Gazette*, January 2013 (http://hub.jhu.edu/gazette/2013/january/east-baltimore -changes-development/).

16. Chris Schildt and Victor Rubin, "Leveraging Anchor Institutions for Economic Inclusion," PolicyLink, 2015, p. 2 (www.policylink.org/sites/default/files/pl_brief_anchor_012315_a.pdf).

17. University of Pennsylvania, "Powering Philadelphia and Pennsylvania: The Economic Impact of the University of Pennsylvania: FY 2015," report, 2016, p. 2 (www.evp.upenn.edu/pdf/Penn_Economic_Impact_Powering_PHL_PA.pdf).

18. Initiative for a Competitive Inner City, "Creating Shared Value: Anchors and the Inner City," June 2011, p. 10 (http://massinc.org/wp-content/uploads/2013/10/Anchor_Paper_Web2.pdf).

19. Steve Dubb, Sarah McKinley, and Ted Howard, "Achieving the Anchor Promise: Improving Outcomes for Low-Income Children, Families, and Communities," report, Annie E. Casey Foundation, August 2013, p. 1 (http://community-wealth.org/sites/clone.community-wealth.org/files/downloads/Achieving%20the%20Anchor%20Promise_composite_FINAL.pdf).

20. Initiative for a Competitive Inner City, "Creating Shared Value: Anchors and the Inner City," p. 2.

21. Michael E. Porter, "Inner-City Economic Development: Learnings from Twenty Years of Research and Practice," *Economic Development Quarterly* 30, no. 2 (2016), p. 107.

22. Initiative for a Competitive Inner City, "Anchor Institutions and Urban Economic Development: From Community Benefit to Shared Value," *Inner City Insights* 1, no. 2 (June 2011), p. 5 (http://community-wealth.org/sites/clone.community-wealth.org/files/downloads/article-icic11%20%281%29.pdf).

23. See Penn Purchasing Services, "Becoming a Diversity Supplier at Penn," 2017 (https://cms.business-services.upenn.edu/purchasing/economic-inclusion/becoming-a-diversity-supplier-at-penn.html).

24. Heather A. Davis, "Penn Recognized for Commitment to Economic Inclusion," *Penn Current*, July 2, 2015 (https://penncurrent.upenn.edu/2015-07-02/latest-news/penn-recognized-commitment-economic-inclusion).

25. University of Pennsylvania, "Powering Philadelphia and Pennsylvania," p. 10.

26. Jackie Dyess, interview with author, July 15, 2016.

27. See World Business Chicago, "CASE: Chicago Anchors for a Strong Economy," 2017 (www.chicagoanchors.com/).

28. Dyess, interview.

29. Bruce Katz and Julie Wagner, "The Rise of Innovation Districts: A New Geography of Innovation in America," Brookings, May 2014, p. 6 (www.brookings.edu /wp-content/uploads/2016/07/InnovationDistricts1.pdf).

30. Diana Budds, "Can You Design Innovation?," Fast Company Design, August 18, 2015 (www.fastcodesign.com/3047888/slicker-city/can-you-design-innovation).

31. Ibid.

32. Brookings scholars Katz and Wagner have studied innovation districts across the country and refer to them as "geographic areas where leading-edge anchor institutions and companies cluster and connect with start-ups, business incubators, and accelerators. They are also physically compact, transit-accessible, and technically wired and offer mixed-use housing, office, and retail." See Anne T. and Robert M. Bass, Initiative on Innovation and Placemaking, "Innovation Districts," Brookings, 2017 (www.brookings.edu/about/programs/metro/innovation-districts).

33. Hortencia Rodriguez and others, "The Development of Boston's Innovation District: A Case Study of Cross-Sector Collaboration and Public Entrepreneurship," report, The Intersector Project, October 2015, p. 8 (http://intersector.com/wp-content /uploads/2015/10/The-Development-of-Bostons-Innovation-District.pdf).

34. See Boston Planning and Development Agency, "Mayor Menino Releases Jobs Report–Innovation District," News and Updates, March 1, 2013 (www.boston plans.org/news-calendar/news-updates/2013/03/01/mayor-menino-releases-results -of-innovation-distri).

35. Jon Chesto, "GE Confirms It's Heading to Boston," *Boston Globe*, January 13, 2016.

36. Melanie D. G. Kaplan, "Inside Fargo, America's Most Undervalued Tech Hub," *Fortune*, December 18, 2015.

37. Ibid.

38. Quentin Hardy, "A Silicon Valley for Drones, in North Dakota," *New York Times*, December 25, 2015.

39. Greg Tehven, interview with author, February 26, 2016.

40. Ibid.

41. Bruce Katz, "How Innovation Districts Can Be Platforms for Economic Growth and Opportunity," Living Cities blog, January 26, 2015 (www.livingcities.org /blog/761-how-innovation-districts-can-be-platforms-for-economic-growth-and -opportunity). The acronym STEM represents the fields of science, technology, engineering, and mathematics.

42. See Jane Talkington, *Innovation Districts: University Examples*, Innovation Districts blog (www.innovationdistricts.blogspot.com).

43. Douglas, interview.

44. Rodriguez and others, "The Development of Boston's Innovation District," p. 22.

PART III

1. People of color who were able to obtain a mortgage often were relegated to owning homes in neighborhoods comprised primarily of people of color. These homes appreciated dramatically more slowly than home values in primarily white neighborhoods and have frustrated the wealth-building hopes for these homeowners and their progeny. See Laura Shin, "The Racial Wealth Gap: Why A Typical White Household Has 16 Times the Wealth of a Black One," Forbes, March 26, 2015 (www.forbes.com/sites/laurashin/2015/03/26/the-racial-wealth -gap-why-a-typical-white-household-has-16-times-the-wealth-of-a-black-one /#576c45411f45).

2. Amy Traub and Catherine Ruetschlin, "The Racial Wealth Gap: Why Policy Matters," Demos, June, 21, 2016.

CHAPTER 7

1. Jon Li, interview with author, January 27, 2017.

2. See Neighborhood Works America, "Lift Programs," 2017 (www.neighborworks .org/Homes-Finances/Homeownership/LIFT-Programs).

3. Li, interview.

4. Ibid.

5. Debbie Gruenstein Bocian, "The State of Lending in America and Its Impact on U.S. Households," Center for Responsible Lending, December 2012, p. 22 (www .responsiblelending.org/sites/default/files/uploads/3-mortgages.pdf).

6. Ibid.

7. Office of Policy Development and Research, "Paths to Homeownership for Low-Income and Minority Households," U.S. Department of Housing and Urban Development, Evidence Matters, Fall 2012 (www.huduser.gov/portal/periodicals /em/fall12/highlight1.html).

8. Keeping Current Matters Crew, "2016: Homeowner's Net Worth Will Be 45x Greater Than a Renter," Keeping Current Matters (blog), October 26, 2015 (www .keepingcurrentmatters.com/2015/10/26/2016-homeowners-net- worth-will- be-45x- greater-than- a-renter/).

9. Thomas Shapiro, quoted in Michael Fletcher, "Study Ties Black-White Wealth Gap to Stubborn Disparities in Real Estate," *Washington Post*, February 26,

2013   (www.washingtonpost.com/business/economy/study-ties-black-white-wealth
-gap-to-stubborn-disparities-in-real-estate/2013/02/26/8b4b3f50-8035-11e2-b99e
-6baf4ebe42df_story.html?utm_term=.123d5045cc90).

10. Rebecca Tippett and others, "Beyond Broke: Why Closing the Racial Wealth
Gap Is a Priority for National Economic Security," Center for Global Policy Solutions, May 2014, p. 4 (http://www.globalpolicysolutions.org/wp-content/uploads
/2014/04/Beyond_Broke_FINAL.pdf).

11. See Thomas M. Shapiro, "Race, Homeownership and Wealth," *Washington
University Journal of Race & Policy*, January 2006.

12. U.S. Department of Commerce, "Quarterly Residential Vacancies and
Homeownership, Third Quarter 2016," U.S. Census Bureau, October 27, 2016 (www
.census.gov/housing/hvs/files/currenthvspress.pdf).

13. Laura Sullivan and others, "The Racial Wealth Gap: Why Policy Matters,"
Institute for Assets and Social Policy and Demos, 2015, p. 2 (www.demos.org/sites
/default/files/publications/RacialWealthGap_1.pdf)

14. U.S. Department of Commerce, "Quarterly Residential Vacancies."

15. Enacted in 1977, this legislation was intended to prevent redlining—the practice of refusing to lend to specific neighborhoods that were deemed too poor and thus
financially risky. The CRA requires FDIC-insured banks to lend on the same terms in
any neighborhood in which they operate. Of course, as the author and wealth manager
Barry Ritholtz points out in his Bloomberg column, "It wasn't Harlem, Philadelphia,
Baltimore, Chicago, Detroit or any other poor, largely minority urban area covered by
the CRA. No, the crisis was worst in Florida, Arizona, Nevada, and California. The
vast majority of the housing collapse took place in the suburbs and exurbs." Barry
Ritholtz, "Lending to Poor People Didn't Cause the Financial Crisis," Bloomberg,
June 22, 2016 (www.bloomberg.com/view/articles/2016-06-22/lending-to- poor-people
-didn-t-cause-the- financial-crisis). An analysis of more than 12 million subprime
mortgages by the *Orange County Register* concluded that nearly $3 of every $4 in subprime loans made between 2004 and 2007 were from lenders not bound by the CRA.
Ronald Campbell, "Most Subprime Lenders Weren't Subject to Federal Lending
Law," Orange County Registrar, November 16, 2008 (www.ocregister.com/2008/11/16
/most-subprime- lenders-werent- subject-to- federal-lending-law/).

16. Elizabeth Laderman and Carolina Reid, "Lending in Low- and Moderate-
Income Neighborhoods in California: The Performance of CRA Lending during
the Subprime Meltdown," Federal Reserve Bank of San Francisco, Working Paper
2008–05 (www.frbsf.org/community-development/files/wp08-051.pdf).

17. Bocian, "The State of Lending in America and Its Impact on U.S. Households."

18. Self-Help Credit Union, "Profile of Martin Eakes, CEO of Self-Help and the Center for Responsible Lending," Vimeo video, 3:34, posted June 12, 2013 (https://vimeo.com/68218063).

19. Mary Reynolds Babock Foundation, "Martin Eakes: Economic Inequality and the Beginning of Self-Help" Vimeo video, 6:14, posted March 24, 2015 (https://vimeo.com/123140416).

20. Janneke Ratcliffe, "Regaining the Dream, Executive Summary," Center for Community Capital, November 2014 (http://communitycapital.unc.edu/files/2014/11/RTD-Case-Studies-Nov-2014.pdf).

21. See note 42 for an explanation of secondary markets.

22. See note 42 for a description of Fannie Mae and Freddie Mac.

23. Mary Reynolds Babock Foundation, "Martin Eakes," 3:33.

24. Since the financial crisis, the credit scores required to get an average loan have been on the rise. Urban Institute has found that if credit score requirements in 2015 were as they were in 2001, more than 1.1 million more loans would have been made in 2015. Laurie Goodman, "In Need of an Update: Credit Scoring in the Mortgage Market," Urban Institute, July 2017.

Heesun Wee, "Some Americans Can't Afford to Buy Homes in Their Hometown," CNBC, February 23, 2016 (www.cnbc.com/2016/02/22/some-americans-cant-afford-to-buy-homes-in-their-hometown.html).

25. Allison Freeman, "The Continuing Importance of Homeownership: Evidence from the Community Advantage Program," *Community Investments* 26, no. 2 (Summer/Fall 2014), p. 8 (www.frbsf.org/community-development/files/ci_vol26no2-Continuing-Importance-of-Homeownership.pdf).

26. UNC Center for Community Capital, "Regaining the Dream: Case Studies in Sustainable Low-Income Mortgage Lending," Policy Brief, November 2014, p. 5 (https://communitycapital.unc.edu/files/2014/11/RTD-Case-Studies-Nov-2014.pdf).

27. Ibid.

28. Freeman, "The Continuing Importance of Homeownership."

29. Self-Help Credit Union, "Profile of Martin Eakes," 0:01.

30. The University of North Carolina, Center on Community Capital, issued a report and case studies on what has been learned to date about extending homeownership to low-income Americans by reviewing the experiences of more

than 22 million low-income homeowners. See UNC Center for Community Capital, "Regaining the Dream."

31. The soft-second loan reduced the overall risk for the financial institution and enabled the homeowner to receive more favorable terms from them. Benefits of the soft second included lower or even interest-free rates for up to ten years and no requirement to purchase mortgage insurance.

32. See Housing and Economic Development, "ONE Mortgage Program," 2017 (www.mass.gov/hed/housing/affordable-own/one- mortgage-program.html).

33. See Massachusetts Housing Partnership, "Program Impact" (www.mhp.net /one-mortgage/program- impact).

34. Ibid.

35. Clark L. Ziegler, Elliot Schmiedl, and Thomas Callahan, "ONE Mortgage: A Model fo Success for Low-Income Homeownership," *Boston College Journal of Law and Social Justice* 37, no. 2 (May 2017), p. 349 (http://lawdigitalcommons.bc .edu/cgi/viewcontent.cgi?article=1118&context=jlsj).

36. Crescent City Community Land Trust, "Shelterforce: The Answer," 2013 (www.ccclt.org/wp-content/uploads/2013/09/Shelterforce_Answers.pdf).

37. Wee, "Some Americans Can't Afford to Buy Homes."

38. Mark Vanderlinden, "Immigrant/ITIN Lending Opportunity Finance Network," presentation, Detroit, Mich., Homewise, November 2015 (http://conference .ofn.org/2015/docs/PPT_MortgageLendingImmigrants.pdf).

39. Office of Policy Development and Research, "Paths to Homeownership."

40. "From House to Home: 2015 Annual Report," Homewise (https://www .homewise.org/2015-annual- report/).

41. NeighborWorks is a network of 240 local-level organizations supported by a congressional appropriation. These local affiliates, like the one in the Twin Cities that helped the Li family, generally do not originate, fund, or broker loans. Instead, they run educational programs to help buyers prepare for the financial responsibilities of homeownership. Along with reducing cost barriers, providing individualized support and financial counseling to first-time borrowers throughout the duration of a loan has proved to help homeowners weather economic ups and downs.

42. Understanding how a secondary market for home loans works is important. Assume a lender makes or originates a $50,000, thirty-year home loan to a new homeowner. If the lender is operating in isolation, then it will not be able to make another $50,000 home loan for thirty years—the lender will need the loan to be paid off so it can get its money back. A secondary market provides the lender with a way to sell the

mortgage, get its $50,000 back long before the thirty years are up, and then use that cash to make another loan. The principle may seem basic, but it is at the core of these solutions: more capital to lend means more homeownership loans can be made. That was the purpose behind Congress's creating Fannie Mae and Freddie Mac, the two institutions that most likely come to mind when the secondary market for home loans is mentioned. Fannie and Freddie were established to make sure that financial institutions would have enough money available to meet the demand from all Americans who wanted to become homeowners. These two enterprises buy mortgages, originated by many different lenders but generally conforming to a set of mainstream underwriting requirements, and then package them into what are called mortgage-backed securities (MBS). Investors are willing to invest in the MBS because Fannie and Freddie, confident in their underwriting requirements, are able to guarantee timely payment of principal and interest on the underlying mortgages. This system provides capital sufficient to fund between 3 million and 4 million homeowners a year.

43. Analysis conducted by Fannie Mae estimates that there are at least 3.25 million potential borrowers who would qualify for this type of product. Fannie Mae's Noelle Melton and Joseph Weisbord, interview with author, November 23, 2017. However, the figure is likely even larger. A 2016 Urban Institute report found that tight credit standards applied between 2009 and 2014 prevented 5.2 million mortgages from being approved to borrowers who otherwise would have met even mainstream underwriting guidelines. Bing Bai, Laurie Goodman, and Jun Zhu, "Tight Credit Standards Prevented 5.2 Million Mortgages between 2009 and 2014," Urban Institute, January 28, 2016 (www.urban.org/urban-wire/tight-credit-standards-prevented-52 -million-mortgages-between-2009-and-2014).

44. Annie Shin, "When the Federal Government Took over Fannie Mae and Freddie Mac," *Washington Post*, August 31, 2017 (https://www.washingtonpost.com /lifestyle/magazine/when-the-federal-government-took-over-fannie-mae-and -freddie-mac/2017/08/28/afe3d2a4-76e5-11e7-8839-ec48ec4cae25_story.html?utm _term=.b74f24db05f8).

45. Freddie Mac developed the Home Possible program and Fannie Mae the Home Ready program to serve this population. The terms of their programs are substantially similar and together would clearly meet demand if it was there from originating banks and potential home buyers. See descriptions of those programs.

46. Office of Policy Development and Research, "The Evidence on Homeownership Education and Counseling," U.S. Department of Housing and Urban Development, Spring 2016 (https://www.huduser.gov/portal/periodicals/em/spring16 /highlight2.html).

47. Author's interview with Wells Fargo's Martin Sundquist, September 5, 2017.

48. Freddie Mac's Danny Gardner, interview with author, January 5, 2018.

49. Melton, Weisbord, and Gardner, interviews.

50. L. Jide Iwarere and John E. Williams, "The Effect of Income, Ethnicity/Race and Institutional Factors on Mortgage Borrower Behavior," *Journal of Real Estate Research, Sacramento* 25, no. 4 (October–December 2003), pp. 509–528 (https://search-proquest-com.databases.library.georgetown.edu/pqrlalumni/docview /200285235/B23118FACB9A4DD2PQ/4?accountid=142883). They attribute this in part to more limited access to information about the home buying and financing process, which have been documented through numerous ethnographic studies.

51. NeighborWorks America, "Lack of Down Payment, Credit Concerns and Student Loan Debt Prevent Many from Achieving Homeownership, Finds Neighbor-Works America Survey," September 25, 2017 (http://www.neighborworks.org/Media -Center/Press-Releases/2017-Archive/Lack-of-down-payment,-credit-concerns-and -student-loan-debt-prevent-many-from-achieving-homeownership).

52. Keeping Matters Current Newsletter, National Association of Realtors, October 9, 2017, reported that 39 percent of renters believe that more than 20 percent down payment is needed to buy.

53. Ibid.

54. Ibid.

55. Ibid.

56. Each state is different but many have down-payment assistance, soft seconds like those provided by ONE Mortgage in Massachusetts, and even low-cost financing.

57. See Detroit Live Downtown, "Incentives," 2017 (www.detroitlivedowntown .org/incentives/) and Greater Circle Living, Cleveland Clinic Employer Assisted Housing Program," brochure, Cleveland Clinic Department of Community Outreach (http://my.clevelandclinic.org/ccf/media/Files/Careers/13417-employer -assisted-housing-brochure.PDF).

PART IV

1. Sixty-four percent of Americans making less than $30,000 a year own a smartphone, the fastest growing segment of the market, up 28 percent in the past two years alone. Pew Research Center, "Mobile Fact Sheet," January 12, 2017 (www.pewinternet .org/fact-sheet/mobile/).

2. Lower-income smartphone owners are especially likely to use their phone during a job search. Compared with smartphone owners from households earning

$75,000 or more per year, those from households earning less than $30,000 annually are nearly twice as likely to use a smartphone to look for information about a job—and more than four times as likely to use their phone to actually submit a job application. Aaron Smith, "U.S. Smartphone Use in 2015," April, 2015 (www.pewinternet.org/2015/04/01/us-smartphone-use-in-2015/).

3. There are huge disparities in broadband penetration in the home based on income, education, and geography. While 53 percent of Americans earning less than $30,000 have the Internet at home, 83 percent of families earning between $50,000 and $75,000 do. Thirty-four percent of high school–educated Americans have broadband at home compared with 80 percent who have some college. About 75 percent of urban and suburban Americans have the Internet but 63 percent of rural dwellers lack access (www.pewinternet.org/fact-sheet/internet-broadband/).

CHAPTER 8

1. Brad Miller, interview with author, June 19, 2017.

2. Data released by Uber mapping ridership in Portland reveal that one in four rides started or ended within a quarter mile of a public transit station. "Uber and Portland Metro's Public Transportation Work Together," *Uber Newsroom*, March 26, 2015 (https://newsroom.uber.com/us-oregon/uber-and-portland-metros-public-transportation-working-together/).

3. Jimena Tavel, "Partnership Will Give UF Students Half-Off Uber Rides," *University of Florida Alligator*, March 21, 2017 (www.alligator.org/news/campus/article_deab0fa6-0ddd-11e7-9a5b-9b65a2ae7465.html).

4. Steven Girardi, "Pinellas Teams Up with Uber, Cab Company in Pilot Program," *Tampa Tribune*, February 22, 2016 (www.tbo.com/pinellas-county/pinellas-teams-up-with-uber-cab-company-in-pilot-program-20160222/).

5. See "Direct Connect," Pinellas Suncoast Transit Authority (www.psta.net/riding-psta/direct-connect/).

6. Miller, interview.

7. "PSTA, Uber Offer Free, Late-Night Rides for Low-Income Residents" (www.psta.net/about-psta/press-releases/2016/psta-uber-offer-free-late-night-rides-for-low-income-residents/).

8. Miller, interview.

9. Adie Tomer and others, "Missed Opportunity: Transit and Jobs in Metropolitan America," Brookings Metropolitan Policy Program, May 2011 (https://www.brookings.edu/wp-content/uploads/2016/06/0512_jobs_transit.pdf).

10. Gregory Acs and Austin Nichols, "Low-Income Workers and Their Employers," Urban Institute, May 23, 2007 (https://www.urban.org/sites/default /files/publication/46656/411532-Low-Income-Workers-and-Their-Employers .PDF)

11. Emily Badger, "The Suburbanization of Poverty," CityLab, May 20, 2013 (www.citylab.com/work/2013/05/suburbanization-poverty/5633/).

12. Elizabeth Kneebone and Natalie Holmes, "The Growing Distance between People and Jobs in Metropolitan America," Brookings Metropolitan Policy Program, March 2015 (www.brookings.edu/wp-content/uploads/2016/07/Srvy_JobsProximity .pdf).

13. Larry Copeland, "The Cost of Owning Your Car? $9,000 a Year," *USA Today*, April 16, 2013 (www.usatoday.com/story/news/nation/2013/04/16/aaa-car-ownership -costs/2070397/).

14. See also Gillian B. White, "Stranded: How America's Failing Public Transportation Increases Inequality," May 16, 2015 (www.theatlantic.com/business /archive/2015/05/stranded-how-americas-failing-public-transportation-increases -inequality/393419/). In a large, continuing study of upward mobility, the longer an average commute in a given county, the worse the chances of lower-income families who lived there moving up the economic ladder.

15. And that is not even factoring in depreciation on the car and the reality that each car repair can easily equal another week of salary and the car ultimately will have to be replaced. "Transportation and Poverty Series (Part 4): The Cost of Car Ownership," Reconnect Rochester, December 2016 (http://reconnectrochester.org /2016/12/transportation-and-poverty-equity-the-cost-car-ownership/).

16. Bureau of Transportation Statistics, "Transportation Statistics Annual Report," U.S. Department of Transportation, 2016 (www.rita.dot.gov/bts/sites/rita.dot .gov.bts/files/publications/transportation_economic_trends).

17. Mijin Cha, "Equity Data Helped NYC Advocates Expand Transit Access through Bus Rapid Transit," *National Equity Atlas*, December 11, 2014 (http:// nationalequityatlas.org/data-in-action/nyc-transpo-atlas).

18. Eric Moskowitz, "Black Commuters Face Longer Trips to Work," *Boston Globe*, November 25, 2012 (www.bostonglobe.com/metro/massachusetts/2012/11/25 /wide-racial-gap-exists-speed-boston-area-commutes/utDAVcJ9B6QUALUi dI9DGL/story.html).

19. Laura Bliss, "In the Twin Cities, Commute Times Vary Dramatically by Race," CityLab, May 14, 2015 (www.citylab.com/commute/2015/05/in-the-twin -cities-commute-times-vary-dramatically-by-race/393275/).

20. "What Is Shared-Use Mobility?," Shared-Use Mobility Center (http://sharedusemobilitycenter.org/what-is-shared-mobility/).

21. Susan Shaheen, "Trends and Future of Shared-Use Mobility," paper presented at Transportation Research Board Annual Meeting, Workshop 138, January 11, 2015 (http://innovativemobility.org/wp-content/uploads/2015/02/Susan-Shaheen-Shared-Use-Mobility-Trends.pdf).

22. Ibid.

23. Greg Lindsey, "Now Arriving: A Connected Mobility Roadmap for Public Transport," New Cities Foundation, 2016, p. 4 (www.newcitiesfoundation.org/wp-content/uploads/2016/10/PDF-Now-Arriving-A-Connected-Mobility-Roadmap-For-Public-Transport-Greg-Lindsay.pdf).

24. Sharon Feigon and Colin Murphy, "Shared Mobility and the Transformation of Public Transit," TCRP Research Report 1882016 (www.trb.org/Main/Blurbs/174653.aspx). Twenty-one percent postponed buying a car, 22 percent decided not to buy a car, and 27 percent had sold a car and had not replaced it.

25. Rosanna Smart and others, "Faster and Cheaper: How Ride-Sourcing Fills a Gap in Low-Income Los Angeles Neighborhoods," BOTEC Analysis Corporation, July 2015, p. 38 (http://botecanalysis.com/wp-content/uploads/2015/07/LATS-Final-Report.pdf). Margo Dawes, "Perspectives on the Ridesourcing Revolution: Surveying Individual Attitudes toward Uber and Lyft to Inform Urban Transportation Policymaking," Massachusetts Institute of Technology, June 2016 (https://dspace.mit.edu/bitstream/handle/1721.1/104994/960048423-MIT.pdf?sequence=1).

26. One estimate suggests that cars in a city are parked up to 95 percent of the time. Feigon and Murphy, "Shared Mobility."

27. Arun Sundararajan and Samuel P. Fraiberger, "Peer-to-Peer Rental Markets in the Sharing Economy," research paper, NYU Stern School of Business, September 10, 2017 (https://papers.ssrn.com/sol3/papers.cfm?abstract_id=2574337).

28. Copeland, "The Cost of Owning Your Car?"

29. Sharon Feigon, interview with author, August 10, 2016.

30. Eric Jaffe, "Carpooling Tries for a Comeback," CityLab, March 17, 2015 (www.citylab.com/transportation/2015/03/carpooling-tries-for-a-comeback/388009/). See also Brian McKenzie, "Who Drives to Work? Commuting by Automobile in the United States, 2013," American Community Survey Reports, Report ACS-32, U.S. Census Bureau, Washington, D.C., 2015 (www.census.gov/hhes/commuting/data/commuting.html). Interestingly, carpool rates are lowest among white commuters; Hispanic and black workers actually continue to carpool to work at rates of 19 percent and 14 percent respectively.

31. Mike Papineau, interview with author, February 9, 2017.

32. Ibid.

33. Clara-Meretan Kiah, "Carpooling App Eases Parking, Decreases FIU's Carbon Footprint," *FIU News*, December 2016 (https://news.fiu.edu/2016/12/carpooling -app-eases-parking-decreases-fius-carbon-footprint/107289).

34. Ellen Huet, "Can These New Start-ups Convince Americans to Carpool?," *Bloomberg BusinessWeek*, February 16, 2016 (www.bloomberg.com/news/articles /2016-02-16/can-these-new-startups-convince-americans-to-carpool).

35. Papineau, interview with author, March 29, 2017.

36. Fehr Peers, "Microtransit" (www.fehrandpeers.com/microtransit/).

37. See "The Rise of the Microtransit Movement," SmartCircle (www.smart -circle.org/blog/microtransit/). SmartCircle has documented the evolution of microtransit, defining it as both a "downsizing" of public transport, like a fourteen person van in Kansas City versus a large bus and an "upscaling" in private individual transport. "Downsizing" refers to on-demand public transport initiatives such as Bridj, a Boston start-up facilitating shared van rides for commuters that make reservations ahead of it. A well-known example of the second type—"upscaling"—might be Uber, which is using private vehicles as a platform for on-demand transportation (and facilitating carpooling at the same time). Together, these two types are referred to as microtransit and can be seen as a new form of modality, between private individual and collective public transportation.

38. Joshua Brustein, "Uber and Lyft Want to Replace Public Buses," Bloomberg, August 15, 2016 (www.bloomberg.com/news/articles/2016-08-15/uber-and-lyft-want -to-replace-public-buses).

39. Hope King, "New Jersey Town Is Subsidizing Uber Rides," CNNMoney, October 3, 2016 (http://money.cnn.com/2016/10/03/technology/uber-subsidized -commutes-summit-new-jersey/).

40. Shared-Use Mobility Center, "Shared Mobility and the Transformation of Public Transit," research analysis prepared for American Public Transportation Association, March 2016 (http://sharedusemobilitycenter.org/wp-content/uploads/2016 /04/Final_TOPT_DigitalPagesNL.pdf).

41. Miller, interview.

42. Alex Gibson, "Eliminating Public Transit's First-Mile/Last-Mile Problem," TransLoc, January 26, 2016 (http://transloc.com/eliminating-public-transits-first -milelast-mile-problem/).

43. Greg Lindsay, "Now Arriving: A Connected Mobility Roadmap for Public Transit," New Cities Foundation, 2016, p. 1 (www.newcitiesfoundation.org/wp

-content/uploads/2016/10/PDF-Now-Arriving-A-Connected-Mobility-Roadmap
-For-Public-Transport-Greg-Lindsay.pdf).

44. Ibid., p. 2.

45. Funded with $1.6 million from California's cap-and-trade revenues, the service will locate 100 vehicles and 100 charging stations in disadvantaged communities around the city, including the Westlake District, Picc-Union, South Los Angeles, and Koreatown. If the city reaches its goal of recruiting 7,000 users, the system will ultimately be self-sustaining. See Park Lee, "LA is Bringing 100 Electric Carsharing Vehicles to its Poorest Neighborhoods," Curbed, December 21, 2016 (http://la.curbed .com/2016/12/21/14046080/electric-carsharing-los-angeles-bluecalifornia).

46. The study was conducted by the National Resource Defense Council on behalf of Mile High Connects, a partnership of private, philanthropic, and nonprofit organizations committed to equitable access to economic opportunity. Logan Sand, Samantha Beckerman, and Catherine Cox Blair, "First and Last Mile Connections," National Resource Defense Council, January 2016 (www.nrdc.org/sites/default /files/shared-mobility-cs.pdf).

47. Ibid.

CHAPTER 9

1. Bento J. Lobo, "The Realized Value of Fiber Infrastructure in Hamilton County, Tennessee," University of Tennessee at Chattanooga, June 18, 2015, p. 8 (http://ftpcontent2.worldnow.com/wrcb/pdf/091515EPBFiberStudy.pdf).

2. To be clear, $219 million of the Electric Power Board's total $330 million cost was funded, in part, by a federal stimulus grant and private bonds. This amount has been paid back to the community through stimulation of nearly $1 billion into the local economy. See Edward Wyatt, "Fast Internet Is Chattanooga's New Locomotive," *New York Times*, February 3, 2014, and Lobo, "The Realized Value of Fiber Infrastructure," p. 8.

3. See "Comcast Sues EPB in Hamilton County on Eve of Bond Issue," *Chattanoogan*, April 22, 2008.

4. Dave Flessner, "EPB to Offer Discounted Internet for Low-Income Households," *Chattanooga Times Free Press*, April 28, 2015 (www.timesfreepress.com/news /business/aroundregion/story/2015/apr/28/epb-offer-discounted-internet-low -income-hous/301146/).

5. Peter Moskowitz, "Chattanooga Was a Typical Postindustrial City," *The Nation*, June 3, 2016 (www.thenation.com/article/chattanooga-was-a-typical-post -industrial-city-then-it-began-offering-municipal-broadband/).

6. Slav Kandyba, "Chattanooga Looks to Rebrand as 'Gig City,'" *National Monitor*, December 29, 2014 (http://natmonitor.com/2014/12/29/chattanooga-looks-to-rebrand-as-gig-city/).

7. Brady Dale, "11 Things Cities Should Know about the FCC's Broadband Vote," Next City, February 27, 2015 (https://nextcity.org/daily/entry/fcc-municipal-broadband-vote-affect-cities).

8. Dave Flessner, "EPB Fiber Optics Gives Chattanooga a Boost," *Chattanooga Times Free Press*, September 16, 2015 (www.timesfreepress.com/news/business/aroundregion/story/2015/sep/16/epb-fiber-optics-gives-city-boost/325362/).

9. Moskowitz, "Chattanooga Was a Typical Postindustrial City."

10. Harold DePriest, interview with author, March 14, 2016.

11. Ibid.

12. Ibid.

13. Ibid.

14. Mark Dutz, Jonathan Orszag, and Robert Willig, "The Substantial Consumer Benefits of Broadband Connectivity for U.S. Households," Internet Innovation Alliance, July 2009, p. 7 (https://internetinnovation.org/files/special-reports/CONSUMER_BENEFITS_OF_BROADBAND.pdf).

15. The Executive Office of the President, "Community-Based Broadband Solutions: The Benefits of Competition and Choice for Community Development and High-Speed Internet Access," January 2015, p. 6 (https://muninetworks.org/sites/www.muninetworks.org/files/White-House-community-based-broadband-report-by-executive-office-of-the-president_1.pdf).

16. Ibid.

17. Barack Obama, Remarks by the President on Promoting Community Broadband, Cedar Falls, Iowa, January 14, 2015, White House Briefing Room (www.whitehouse.gov/the-press-office/2015/01/14/remarks-president-promoting-community-broadband).

18. Internet access was associated with a 12 percent increase in the probability of voting in the 2000 election. Caroline J. Tolbert and Ramona S. McNeal, "Unraveling the Effects of the Internet on Political Participation?" *Political Research Quarterly* 56, no. 2 (June 2003) (www.jstor.org/stable/3219896?seq=1#page_scan_tab_contents).

19. John B. Horrigan and Maeve Duggan, "Home Broadband 2015," Pew Research Center, December 21, 2015 (www.pewinternet.org/2015/12/21/home-broadband-2015/).

20. Ibid.

21. John B. Horrigan, "The Numbers behind the Broadband 'Homework Gap,'" Pew Research Center, April 20, 2015 (www.pewresearch.org/fact-tank/2015/04/20/the-numbers-behind-the-broadband-homework-gap/).

22. Remarks of Commissioner Jessica Rosenworcel, Texas Computer Education Association, Austin, February 4, 2015 (https://apps.fcc.gov/edocs_public/attachmatch/DOC-331901A1.pdf).

23. Horrigan, "The Numbers behind the Broadband 'Homework Gap.'"

24. Anthony P. Carnevale, Tamara Jayasundera, and Dmitri Repnikov, "Understanding Online Job Ads Data," technical report, Georgetown University Center on Education and the Workforce, April 2014, p. 11 (https://cew.georgetown.edu/wp-content/uploads/2014/11/OCLM.Tech_.Web_.pdf).

25. Council of Economic Advisers, "The Digital Divide and Economic Benefits of Broadband Access," issue brief, March 2016, p. 7 (www.whitehouse.gov/sites/default/files/page/files/20160308_broadband_cea_issue_brief.pdf).

26. Tom Geoghegan, "Why Is Broadband More Expensive in the U.S.?" *BBC News*, October 28, 2013 (www.bbc.com/news/magazine-24528383).

27. Council of Economic Advisers, "Mapping the Digital Divide," issue brief, July 2015, p. 2 (https://obamawhitehouse.archives.gov/sites/default/files/wh_digital_divide_issue_brief.pdf).

28. Pew Research Center, "Mobile Fact Sheet," January 12, 2017 (www.pewinternet.org/fact-sheet/mobile/). See also Emma Bowman, "Pew: 'Smartphone-Dependents' Often Have No Backup Plan for Web Access," National Public Radio, April 1, 2015 (www.npr.org/sections/alltechconsidered/2015/04/01/396587714/pew-smartphone-dependents-often-have-no-backup-plan-for-web-access).

29. Horrigan, "The Numbers behind the Broadband 'Homework Gap.'"

30. Horrigan and Duggan, "Home Broadband 2015."

31. Moskowitz, "Chattanooga Was a Typical Postindustrial City."

32. John Murawski, "Wilson Asks FCC to Override N.C. Law It Says Shields Time Warner, Comcast," *News and Observer*, August 27, 2014 (www.newsobserver.com/news/technology/article10042214.html).

33. Christopher Mitchell and Todd O'Boyle, "Wilson Gives Greenlight to Fast Internet," Broadband Communities, January–February 2013, p. 51 (www.bbpmag.com/2013mags/jan-feb/BBC_Jan13_Greenlight.pdf). For a review of competitor's price rates, see Murawski, "Wilson Asks FCC to Override N.C. Law," Wilson, North Carolina *News and Observer*, August 27, 2014 (www.newsobserver.com/news/technology/article10042214.html).

34. Moskowitz, "Chattanooga Was a Typical Postindustrial City."

35. Susan Crawford, "Why You Should Live in Ammon, Idaho," Backchannel, January 14, 2015 (https://backchannel.com/why-you-should-live-in-ammon-idaho -5a37dbeb1e29#.4lnpau4sk).

36. Scott Carlson and Christopher Mitchell, "RS Fiber: Fertile Fields for New Rural Internet Cooperative," Institute for Local Self-Reliance and Next Century Cities, April 2016, p. 7 (https://ilsr.org/wp-content/uploads/downloads/2016/04/rs-fiber -report-2016.pdf).

37. Ibid., p. 9.

38. Ibid., p. 12.

39. Ibid., p. 11.

40. Ibid.

41. Andrew Tellijohn, "Ideas in Action: Collaborative Effort Brings Fiber-Optic Broadband to Rural Region," *Minnesota Cities Magazine*, September–October 2016 (www.lmc.org/page/1/IdeasInActionSeptOct2016.jsp).

42. Scott Carlson and Christopher Mitchell, "RS Fiber: A New Rural Internet Cooperative," *Broadband Communities Magazine*, Institute for Local Self-Reliance, August/September 2016.

43. Comcast has begun offering a fiber service that costs between $159 and $300 a month, not including installation costs. See Kia Kokalitcheva, "Comcast's Google Fiber Killer Will Be Very Expensive," *Fortune*, July 13, 2015.

44. Sarah Kessler, "Google Fiberhoods: Better Than Tupperware Parties," Fast Company, August 1, 2012 (www.fastcompany.com/1844287/google-fiberhoods-better -tupperware-parties).

45. See Google Fiber, "Where Is Fiber?," 2017 (https://fiber.google.com /about/).

46. Google has slowed its expansion of Google Fiber for a number of business reasons covered widely in the popular press. See Daisuke Wakabayashi, "Google Curbs Expansion of Fiber Optic Network, Cutting Jobs," *New York Times*, October 26, 2016. But, as Susan Crawford writes, its work to date has had great value in unleashing demand for fiber, stimulating competition in the markets it has entered, and highlighting the need for high-speed Internet access as a public good. See Susan Crawford, "Google Fiber Was Doomed from the Start," Backchannel, March 14, 2016 (https://backchannel.com/google-fiber-was-doomed-from-the-start -a5cdfacdd7f2?mc_cid=d76683f62f&mc_eid=853116fcd0#.3a1sb0346).

47. See Google Fiber, "Fast, Free Internet for 100 Austin Community Organizations," Google Fiber, official blog, December 13, 2013 (https://fiber.googleblog .com/2013/12/fast-free-internet-for-100-austin.html).

48. See Google Fiber, "Unlocking the Connection for Austin's Public Housing Residents," Google Fiber, official blog, November, 20, 2014 (https://fiber.googleblog .com/2014/11/unlocking-connection-for-austin.html).

49. Ibid.

50. Ibid.

51. Harold D. Wallace Jr., "Power from the People: Rural Electrification Brought More Than Lights," National Museum of American History, blog, February 12, 2016 (http://americanhistory.si.edu/blog/rural-electrification).

52. See Community Networks, "Community Network Map," Institute for Local Self-Reliance, updated May 2017 (https://muninetworks.org/communitymap).

53. See the discussion of state restrictions on local efforts to provide high-speed Internet in the next section below. But even in many of those twenty-one states, the legislative restrictions, requiring waiting periods or referendums, can be overcome through patience and persistence. There are 251 municipally owned electric and gas companies in thirty-eight states. See "251 Publicly Owned Electric and Gas Utilities," Utility Connection, 2017 (www.utilityconnection.com/page2e.asp).

54. See "Water and Wastewater Utility Home Pages: Listings by State," Utility Connection, 2017 (www.utilityconnection.com/page4s.html).

55. DePriest believes that public utilities like EPB are well positioned to provide these services because they are experienced in buying the technical expertise that they need—in this case, to design and build out the network—and they have loyal customers and customer-centric back-office operations, like credit, collections, and billing, that are often the Achilles' heel of other providers. DePriest, interview.

56. Ibid.

57. Jason Koebler, "The 21 Laws States Use to Crush Broadband Competition," Motherboard, January 14, 2015 (https://motherboard.vice.com/en_us/article/the-21 -laws-states-use-to-crush-broadband-competition). See also Community Broadband Networks, "Community Connectivity Toolkit," Community Networks, 2017 (https:// muninetworks.org/content/community-connectivity-toolkit).

58. Koebler, "The 21 Laws States Use."

59. Daniel Fisher, "FCC Loses Bid to Preempt Municipal Broadband Laws in Tennessee, N.C.," *Forbes*, August 10, 2016.

PART V

1. As early as 1620, before even landing, the travelers on the Mayflower entered into the Mayflower Compact, which gave equal voice to the men in the body politic, regardless of class or standing. The very first town hall in the United States was

established not long after that, in 1633, in Dorchester, Massachusetts. Per the town's records, every Monday at the sound of an 8 a.m. bell, townspeople held a meeting to settle and establish "such orders as may tend to the generall good as aforesayd." The practice soon spread throughout New England as an effective means for citizens to decide on important issues of the day. The informal, majority-rules forum became a foundation of early American democracy. Of course, the settlers' commitment to an egalitarian society never was intended to extend to the Native Americans already on the shores and African Americans brought here and sold as slaves starting as early as 1619. So many of today's racial and ethnic disparities can be traced back to the actions and culture created by those interactions and reflect what Nobel laureate Gunnar Myrdal called the ongoing "struggle for America's soul" or the conflict between the ideals that white Americans proclaimed and their betrayal in daily life.

2. Alexis de Tocqueville, *Democracy in America*, 1885, chap. 4 (www.gutenberg .org/files/816/816-h/816-h.htm#link2H_4_0002).

3. Robert D. Putnam, *Bowling Alone: The Collapse and Revival of American Community* (New York: Simon and Schuster, 2000), p. 16.

4. Jacob Hacker and Paul Pierson, *American Amnesia: How the War on Government Led Us to Forget What Made America Prosper* (New York: Simon and Schuster, 2016), p. 164.

5. Putnam, *Bowling Alone*, p. 42.

6. Gerhard Peters and John T. Woolley, *Voter Turnout in Presidential Elections: 1828–2012*, American Presidency Project (www.presidency.ucsb.edu/data /turnout.php) (presidential election turnout since 1968); United States Election Project (https://docs.google.com/spreadsheets/d/1or-N33CpOZYQ1UfZo0h8y GPSyz0Db-xjmZOXg3VJi-Q/edit#gid=1670431880) (gubernatorial turnout, on average, since 1980); and Voter Turnout Plummeting in Local Elections," October 2014 (http://www.governing.com/topics/politics/gov-voter-turnout-municipal -elections.html).

7. Hacker and Pierson, *American Amnesia*, p. 57.

8. Myrdal, quoted in Arthur M. Schlesinger Jr., *The Disuniting of America: Reflections on a Multicultural Society* (New York: Norton & Co., 1998), p. 33.

9. de Tocqueville, *Democracy in America*.

10. Myrdal's book, *An American Dilemma: The Negro Problem and Modern Democracy* (New York: Harper & Row, 1944), has been widely quoted over the years, including as support for the Supreme Court's decision in *Brown v. Board of Education*.

11. Myrdal, quoted in Schlesinger, *The Disuniting of America*.

12. Ibid.

CHAPTER 10

1. See Spiritual Travels, "Thomas Merton's Mystical Vision in Louisville," 2017 (www.spiritualtravels.info/articles-2/north-america/kentucky-a-thomas-merton-tour /thomas-mertons-mystical-vision-in-louisville/).

2. Mayor Greg Fischer, interview with author, April 2017.

3. Ibid. See Charter for Compassion, "Louisville, a Model Compassionate City," 2017 (www.charterforcompassion.org/louisville-a-model-compassionate-city).

4. Theresa Reno-Weber, conversation with author, January 25, 2017. Reno-Weber served in this role from 2012 until 2016, when she was named the president and CEO of the Louisville Metro United Way.

5. See Louisville, Kentucky, "Louie Stat," 2017 (http://louiestat.louisvilleky.gov/).

6. The topics rotate, switching from human resources to public health to sustainability. Hope Reese, "How One City Government Harnesses Data to Improve Efficiency, Save Money, and Protect the Environment," *Tech Republic*, October 5, 2016 (www.techrepublic.com/article/how-one-city-government-harnesses-data-to -improve-efficiency-save-money-and-save-the-environment).

7. Theresa Reno-Weber, personal interview.

8. Ashley Lopez and Jacob Ryan, "Inside Louisville's Decades-Long Problem with Housing Segregation," WFPL (Louisville), January 29, 2016 (http://wfpl.org/a -look-at-a-decades-old-segregation-problem-in-louisville/).

9. See LousivilleKy, "Racial Equity Here," Center for Health Equity, 2017 (https://louisvilleky.gov/government/center-health-equity/racial-equity-here).

10. Ted Smith, interview with author, January 22, 2017.

11. Ibid.

12. Ibid.

13. Author's email exchange with Katie Dailinger, June 9, 2017.

14. Hacker and Pierson, *American Amnesia*, p. 57.

15. Jason Shueh, "New Orleans Cuts Murder Rate Using Data Analytics," Government Technology, October 22, 2014 (www.govtech.com/data/New-Orleans-Cuts -Murder-Rate-Using-Data-Analytics.html).

16. Ibid.

17. Ibid.

18. See Bloomberg Philanthropies, "Innovation Teams," 2017 (www.bloomberg .org/program/government-innovation/innovation-teams/#innovation-delivery -teams-nola).

19. Mayor's Innovation Delivery Team, "The Case for Innovation: Neighborhood Economic Vitality," Annual Report, Memphis, Tenn., 2014, p. 9 (http://

innovatememphis.com/wp-content/uploads/2014/01/MIDT-NEV-ANNUAL
-REPORT.pdf).

20. See Bloomberg Philanthropies, "Innovation Teams."

21. Living Cities, "Living Cities and Bloomberg Philanthropies Partner to Accelerate Civic Innovation," PR Newswire, April 27, 2015 (www.prnewswire.com /news-releases/living-cities-and-bloomberg-philanthropies-partner-to-accelerate -civic-innovation-300071959.html).

22. There are iTeams in twenty cities across the globe, offices of new urban mechanics in three U.S. cities, and chief innovation officers (or similar titles) in thirty-five places. See Bloomberg Philanthropies, "Innovation Teams."

23. Quoted in Stephanie Castellano, "Making 'Lean' Work for Government," Association for Talent Development, January 8, 2016 (www.td.org/Publications /Blogs/GovLearning-Blog/2016/01/Making-Lean-Work-for-Government).

24. See Denver, Mile-High City Mayor's Office Programs and Initiatives, "Peak Performance," 2017 (www.denvergov.org/content/denvergov/en/mayors-office/pro grams-initiatives/peak-performance.html).

25. See Denver Peak Academy, "Achieving Peak Performance," 2014 (www.cml .org/Issues/Government/Municipal/2014-06-17-Preconference-Session-Achieving -Peak-Performance/).

26. Project on Municipal Innovation Team, "Improving Performance by Invest- ing in People," Data-Smart City Solutions, December 2, 2014 (http://datasmart.ash .harvard.edu/news/article/improving-performance-by-investing-in-people-589).

27. What Works Cities, "How Denver Has Saved over $15 Million by Investing in Staff," blog post, Bloomberg Philanthropies, 2017 (https://whatworkscities.bloom berg.org/denverpeakacademypodcast/).

28. David Edinger, personal communication with author, June 14, 2016.

29. Denver Peak Academy, "Congratulations to Our All Outside Black Belt Co- hort!!," blog post, 2017 (https://denpeakacademy.com/2015/08/28/congratulations-to -our-all-outside-black-belt-cohort/); Grayce Liu, "GM's Message 11.7.14," Neighbor- hood Councils Empower L.A.," November 7, 2014 (http://empowerla.org/gms-message -11-7-14/).

30. Steve Adler, interview with author, May 2016.

31. R. J. Berry, interview with author, May 2016.

32. Adler, interview.

33. See Center for Social Inclusion, "Our Programs: Government Alliance on Race and Equity," 2017 (www.centerforsocialinclusion.org/ideas/government).

34. See Local and Regional Government Alliance on Race and Equity, "Member," 2017 (www.racialequityalliance.org/members/).

35. What Works Cities is run by Results for America, funded by Bloomberg Philanthropies, and is helping 100 mid-size cities to use evidence and data to improve services, inform local decision-making, and engage residents. See Baltimore City Health Department, "Baltimore City Experiences Record Low Infant Mortality Rate in 2015," Baltimore City Health Department, October 5, 2016 (http://health .baltimorecity.gov/news/press-releases/2016-10-05-baltimore-city-experiences -record-low-infant-mortality-rate-2015).

36. See Pay for Success, "What Is Pay for Success?," Nonprofit Finance Fund, 2017 (www.payforsuccess.org/learn/basics/).

37. In 2014 Massachusetts launched a PFS project to reduce recidivism by youth. The nonprofit partner—Roca—received investments from financial partner Third-Sector Capital Partners, to keep formerly incarcerated youth out of jail. Massachusetts will pay back the investors who include Living Cities the principal, and possibly profit, if Roca's work is successful, or possibly nothing if the work fails. Massachusetts benefits because it saves more money than the principal by keeping youth out of jail through reduced court costs and policing. "The break-even rate for the Massachusetts PFS is a 40 percent recidivism reduction, the level at which the program savings and payouts will both equal $22 million. If Roca achieves a 70 percent reduction in recidivism, the payout will be capped at $27 million, and the state will save an additional $18 million over the contract period." Pay for Success, "Massachusetts Juvenile Justice Initiative," Nonprofit Finance Fund, 2017 (www.payforsuccess.org/project/massachusetts-juvenile-justice-pfs-initiative). For more information about projects in Utah and Colorado, see Pay for Success, "Utah High-Quality Preschool Program," Nonprofit Finance Fund, 2017 (www.payforsuccess .org/project/utah-high-quality-preschool-program), and Pay for Success, "Denver Housing to Health Initiative," Nonprofit Finance Fund, 2017 (www.payforsuccess .org/project/denver-housing-health-initiative).

38. Erika C. Poethig and others, "Introducing the Pay for Success Initiative at the Urban Institute," Urban Wire, March 16, 2015 (www.urban.org/urban-wire /introducing-pay-success-initiative-urban-institute).

39. Ibid.

40. The amount of innovation and experimentation that has been taking place in local governments over the past decade has been dizzying. From these "hundred flowers" that have bloomed, a framework to help elected leaders build the necessary

mechanics to govern today has emerged. Last year, *Governing* magazine, the nation's leading media platform for state and local government leaders, and my organization, Living Cities, launched that framework, what we call Equipt to Innovate. Equipt to Innovate encourages a city to focus on seven elements: being dynamically planned (for example, what gets planned, gets done), broadly partnered (for example, public and private asthma partners in Louisville), resident involved (for example, SeeClick-Fix in chapter 11), race informed (for example, Racial Equity Here), smartly resourced (for example, Pay for Success), employee engaged (for example, Peak Academy), and data driven (for example, What Works Cities). To get an idea of how well cities are actually equipping themselves to innovate, we have begun surveying mayors, city managers, and chief innovation officers in each of the nation's 250 most populous cities, asking them to rate their performance on ten specific outcomes for each of the seven elements. In 2017 *Governing* began reporting on the survey's results and identifying which cities are top performers. This work also will allow us to identify areas in which cities are having more difficulty—areas to focus on. Mark Funkhouser, "The Innovation Equation," *Governing*, September 4, 2016 (www.governing.com/equipt /The-Innovation-Equation.html).

41. What Works Cities, "How Denver Has Saved over \$15 Million by Investing in Staff."

42. See Roca, "Pay for Success," 2017 (http://rocainc.org/work/pay-for-success/).

43. See chapter 11.

44. GovTech Fund is the first venture capital fund dedicated to government technology start-ups. A description and history of the fund can be found on its website (http://govtechfund.com/).

CHAPTER 11

1. Reflective Democracy Campaign, "Who Leads Us?," Women Donors Network, 2015 (www.womendonors.org/what-we-do/strategic-initiatives/reflective-democracy/).

2. See Urban Habitat, "Boards and Commissions Leadership Institute," 2014 (www.urbanhabitat.org/leadership/bcli).

3. Discussions with Twin Cities Institute alumni highlight some of the program's most important benefits. David Martinez, who was appointed to the Ramsey County Workforce Investment Board, emphasizes how critical it is to "get people comfortable to serve." David Martinez, interview with author, April 2016. Similarly, Jamez Staples, who sits on the powerful Metropolitan Council's Transportation Advisory Board, talks about learning from institute alumni who "help you start to see yourself in a position when you hadn't previously seen anyone who looked like you in

those positions." Jamez Staples, interview with author, April 2016. A surprising number of fellows referred to knowing how to stand up for yourself and your beliefs using *Robert's Rules of Order* while in a commission meeting as one of the most empowering experiences that they had ever had. Martinez and Staples and other BCLI graduates, conversations with author, Spring 2016.

4. Ellen Wu, interview with author, May 2016,

5. Terri Thao, interview with author, March 2016.

6. See Nexus Community Partners, "Boards and Commissions Leadership Institute: Alumni," 2017 (http://nexuscp.org/our-work/boards-and-commissions-leadership-institute/alumni/).

7. Code for America has worked to deliver services like GetCalFresh, to make it faster and more accessible for people to apply for food assistance, and Clear My Record, to give people a second chance at jobs and housing by clearing past convictions. Jen Pahlka, interview with author, April 2017.

8. Ibid.

9. Jake Solomon, interview with author, June 2016.

10. Pahlka, interview.

11. Solomon, interview.

12. Ibid.

13. Ibid. Tim O'Reilly also said this himself, "What's Really At Stake in Better Interfaces to Government," Code for America blog, November 8, 2013 (https://www.codeforamerica.org/blog/2013/11/08/whats-really-at-stake-in-better-interfaces-to-government/).

14. Solomon, interview.

15. Jen Pahlka, interview.

16. Alexander Shermansong, interview with author, July 2016.

17. See Civic Consulting Alliance, "History," 2017 (www.ccachicago.org/about/history/).

18. Aaron Hurst, "How Pro Bono Business Can Help Hurting City Halls," *Huffington Post*, March 3, 2011; Toni Preckwinkle, "Good Government through the Looking Glass," *Huffington Post*, July 19, 2011.

19. Shermansong, interview.

20. Ibid.

21. Committee Encouraging Corporate Philanthropy, "The New Competitive Advantage: Giving in Numbers Brief 2016" (http://cecp.co/home/resources/giving-in-numbers/).

22. Shermansong, interview.

23. For Peak Academy, see chapter 10.

24. To review all projects, see Civic Consulting Alliance, "Impact: All Projects," 2017 (www.ccachicago.org/impact/all-projects/).

25. Shermansong, interview.

26. Ben Berkowitz, interview.

27. See SeeClickFix, "About Us," 2017 (https://en.seeclickfix.com/about).

28. Berkowitz, interview with author, March 2016.

29. City of Detroit, "In Its First Six Months, Improve Detroit Smartphone App Has Helped Residents Get More Than 10,000 Problems in City Fixed," City of Detroit, press release, October 9, 2015 (www.detroitmi.gov/News/ArticleID/492/In-its -first-six-months-Improve-Detroit-smartphone-app-has-helped-residents-get-more -than-10-000-problems-in-city-fixed).

30. Ibid.

31. Berkowitz, interview.

32. Ibid.

33. Ibid.

34. Tom Grubisich, "PublicStuff Gets Answers for Local Citizens, Even in Chinese," *Street Fight*, March 28, 2013 (http://streetfightmag.com/2013/03/28/publicstuff -gets-answers-for-local-citizens-even-in-chinese/).

35. Ben Rattray, interview with author, July 2016.

36. See Change.org, "How an Online Petition Works," 2017 (www.change.org /en-IN/guides/how-an-online-petition-works).

37. Ben Rattray, "150 Million People Fundraising for Change," Change.org, June 30, 2016 (www.change.org/l/us/150-million-people-fundraising-for-change).

38. Ibid.

39. Rattray, interview.

40. Ibid.

41. Ibid.

42. Abby Goldberg, "Governor Quinn: Don't Let Big Plastic Bully Me!" Change .org, 2017 (www.change.org/p/governor-quinn-don-t-let-big-plastic-bully-me).

43. Ibid.

44. Erin Meyer, "Governor Gives Grayslake Girl Good News on Plastic Bag Ban: Teen Had Sought Veto of Industry-Backed Bill," *Chicago Tribune*, August 27, 2012.

45. Andrew Tu, "Let Spencer Collins Keep His Little Free Library," Change.org, 2017 (www.change.org/p/city-of-leawood-kansas-let-spencer-collins-keep-his-little -free-library).

CHAPTER 12

1. *Cleveland Tomorrow: The Encyclopedia of Cleveland History*, Case Western University, Cleveland, Ohio (http://ech.case.edu/cgi/article.pl?id=CT5).

2. Yolanda Kodrzycki and Ana Patricia Muñoz, "Lessons from Resurgent Cities," Federal Reserve Bank of Boston, 2010 (www.bostonfed.org/publications/annual -reports/2009/lessons-from-resurgent-cities.aspx).

3. Ibid.

4. Eric S. Rosengren, "Can Economic Opportunity Flourish When Communities Do Not?," Federal Reserve Bank of Boston, October 18, 2014 (www.bostonfed .org/news/speeches/rosengren/2014/101814/101814text.pdf).

5. Kodrzycki and Muñoz, "Lessons from Resurgent Cities," p. 14.

6. Ibid.

7. Rip Rapson, interview with author, November 2016.

8. United States Census Bureau, "Quick Facts, Lawrence, Massachusetts" (www .census.gov/quickfacts/table/PST045216/2534550,25).

9. Working Cities Challenge, "Overview of Lawrence, Massachusetts" (www .bostonfed.org/workingcities/massachusetts/round1/cities/lawrence.htm).

10. Shiloh Turner and others, "Understanding the Value of Backbone Organizations in Collective Impact," part 2, *Stanford Social Innovation Review*, July 18, 2012 (https://ssir.org/articles/entry/understanding_the_value_of_backbone_organi zations_in_collective_impact_2).

EPILOGUE

1. See Board of Governors of the Federal Reserve System, "Report on the Economic Well-Being of U.S. Households in 2016," May 2017 (www.federalreserve .gov/publications/files/2016-report-economic-well-being-us-households-201705 .pdf).

2. William H. Frey, *Diversity Explosion: How New Racial Demographics Are Remaking America* (Brookings, 2014), p. 32.

3. Many companies already have recognized the business value of adopting an explicit focus on advancing racial equity. Angela Glover Blackwell and others, *The Competitive Advantage of Racial Equity*, October, 2017 (http://www.policylink.org /sites/default/files/The%20Competitive%20Advantage%20of%20Racial%20Equity -final.pdf).

4. Timothy Renick, interview with author, April 21, 2017.

5. These are just three examples of long-standing, effective funder/investor collaboratives that have attacked complex problems. Living Cities (www.livingcities

.org) is focused on closing the racial income and wealth gaps. The Energy Foundation (www.ef.org) is working to build a strong, clean energy economy. The Convergence Partnership (www.convergencepartnership.org) is fostering healthier and more equitable environments for all children and families.

6. But similar social enterprises are contributing to the implementation of the other solutions, highlighted throughout the book. Especially in early-college high school (chapter 1), college completion (chapter 2), cradle-to-career system change (chapter 4), and technology-rich shared-mobility options (chapter 8).

7. The consulting firm, PWC, issues quarterly reports that track venture capital investments by sector and category and reports on year over year trends. See "US Moneytree Report," PWC (www.pwc.com/us/en/technology/moneytree.html).

8. The Robert Wood Johnson's Pioneer Fund is described in greater detail on its website. See Robert Wood Johnson Foundation, "Submit a Pioneering Ideas Brief Proposal," (www.rwjf.org/en/how-we-work/submit-a-proposal.html).

INDEX